Organization Theory
and Postmodern Thought

Organization Theory
and **Postmodern Thought**

edited by **Stephen Linstead**

SAGE Publications
London · Thousand Oaks · New Delhi

SAGE Publications Ltd
6 Bonhill Street
London EC2A 4PU

SAGE Publications Inc
2455 Teller Road
Thousand Oaks, California 91320

SAGE Publications India Pvt Ltd
32 M-Block Market
Greater Kailash – I
New Delhi 110 048

British Library Cataloguing in Publication data

A catalogue record for this book is
available from the British Library

ISBN 0 7619 5310 8
ISBN 0 7619 5311 6 (pbk)

Library of Congress catalog card number available

Typeset by Annette Richards
Printed and bound in Great Britain by Athenaeum Press, Gateshead

Contents

Notes on Contributors

Pippa Carter was formerly a Senior Lecturer in the Business School at the University of Hull. She continues to research rhizomically in the field of organisation theory, with particular regard to the ontological and epistemological conditions of organisation, the function of management and the nature of work. Especially, she is interested in the potential contribution to these concerns of Poststructuralism and of the Modernist/Postmodernist debate. She is co-author of *Rethinking Organisational Behaviour* (FT/Prentice Hall, 2000).

Heather Höpfl is Professor of Management at the University of Essex and was previously Professor of Organisational Psychology and Head of the School of Operations Analysis and HRM at Newcastle Business School, University of Northumbria, UK. She has worked in a number of different jobs and fields. On completing her first degree she went to work in Operations Research for an engineering company in Bristol. She then became a school teacher, a tour manager for a touring theatre company and a researcher working on a research project with ICL and Logica. She completed her PhD at Lancaster on "The Subjective Experience of Time" at Lancaster University in 1982. She is co-editor of *Culture and Organization* and publishes widely. Recent books include *Casting the Other: Maintaining Gender Inequalities in the Workplace* edited with Barbara Czarniawska (Routledge 2002) and *Interpreting the Maternal Organization*, edited with Monika Kostera (Routledge 2002).

Norman Jackson has recently taken early retirement from the University of Newcastle Upon Tyne in order to spend more time on research. His research interests are centred on a generally Poststructuralist approach to organisation theory. He sees organisation(s) as, primarily, instruments of social control, comprehensible only through the analysis of power. His publications have explored, *inter alia*, aesthetics, corporate governance, epistemology, etc., and he is co-author of *Rethinking Organisational Behaviour (FT/Prentice Hall, 2000)*. He is particularly convinced by the Foucaldian notion of *labour as dressage*.

Campbell Jones is Lecturer in Critical Theory and Business Ethics at the University of Leicester and co-editor of the journal *ephemera: critical dialogues on organization* (www.ephemeraweb.org). The chapter that appears in this collection is part of a broader project that involves engaging deconstruction, and in particular the work of Jacques Derrida, in order to think the limits of various critical vocabularies for the analysis of organization. In addition to deconstruction and organization, he has written on automobility, business ethics, entrepreneurship, violence, women actors and vampires.

David Knights is Head of the School of Management and Professor of Organisational Analysis at Keele University. David's research interests include Organisational and Discourse Analysis, Epistemology, Innovation and Strategy, Education, and IT. His most recent books both jointly authored are: *Management Lives: Power and Identity in Work Organization,* Sage, 1999; and *Organization and Innovation: Gurus Schemes and American Dreams,* Milton Keynes: Open University Press, 2003. He is joint editor of *Gender, Work, and Organisation.*

Hugo Letiche is the ISCE Professor of 'Meaning in Organisation' at the University for Humanistics Utrecht Netherlands where he is Director of the DBA/PhD programme in the 'Humanisation of Organisation' and of the MA in 'Humanisation of Organisation & Intervention'. He teaches at the Rotterdam School of Management and has previously taught at the Nutsseminarium University of Amsterdam, Lancaster University, Keele University and the Erasmus University. Current research centres on (i) coherence and complexity and (ii) dialogue, complexity and healthcare. Recent articles have been on 'phenomenological complexity theory' in the *Journal of Organizational Change Management* and *Emergence,* postmodern culture and organisation in *Consumption Markets and Culture, Management Learning,* and *Culture & Organization*; and gender in *Gender Work & Organisation* and the *Finnish Journal of Business Economics.* His research interests originated in phenomenological cultural studies and psychology and evolved via the postmodernism debate in organisational studies to now focus on organisational aesthetics and ethnography as well as complexity theory

Stephen Linstead is Professor of Organizational Analysis, Director of Research and Head of the Work, Management and Organization subject group at Durham Business School, University of Durham. His current research interests centre on the contributions which ideas and practices from the humanities can contribute to the theory and practice of organizing, including philosophy, aesthetics and fictional writing. He also continues to research on gender, power and organizational change and draws his methodological inspiration from social anthropology. He co-edits the journal *Culture and Organization* and is fascinated by kitsch. He has recently co-edited special sections or issues of the journals *Organization, Culture and Organization* and the *Journal of the British Society for Phenomenology* on the work of Henri Bergson, the latter two with the philosopher John Mullarkey. Recent books include *Text/Work* (Routledge 2002) and *Management and Organization : A Critical Text* (with Liz Fulop and Simon Lilley – Palgrave Macmillan 2003).

Assunta Viteritti is assistant professor at the *Department Innovation and Society* (DIeS) of the University "La Sapienza" in Rome, Italy. Her research focuses on the construction of identity in complex organizations and currently she is involved in researching the field of educational processes in institutional reform in Italy.

1
Introduction: Opening Up Paths to a Passionate Postmodernism

Stephen Linstead

We didn't start the fire
It was always burning since the world's been turning
We didn't start the fire
No we didn't light it
But we tried to fight it

There is no shortage of books or journal papers attempting to summarize, or to a lesser extent empirically to explicate, the significance of the work of what is essentially a small number of recent French philosophers for the social sciences. To a lesser extent this is true by now of the field of organization studies. So why should another text be necessary? Indeed, are we already 'past postmodernism' and onto the next theoretical innovation, faddish or otherwise (Calás and Smircich, 1999)? Was postmodernism indeed always and only a 'fatal distraction' from the proper critical business of organization studies and indeed, an immoral and unethical one at that (Thompson, 1993; Feldman, 1996, 1997, 1998)?

The contributors to this book do not think so. They agreed to participate in this project because they shared a sense that many of the existing treatments attempt to summarise and encapsulate 'postmodernism' for the uninitiated – often from secondary sources themselves – and as a consequence, intentionally or otherwise, *discourage* readers from seeking out the original texts. Postmodernism can be considered, consequently, to have been 'done' and the daunting problem of getting to grips with the complex, difficult and nuanced arguments of the original writers – who after all were mostly and primarily philosophers rather than sociologists or applied social thinkers – disappears. These texts therefore close down their topic in the very act of drawing attention to it and lend support to a growing body of comment which absorbs itself with what are regarded as the effects of postmodern thought – from deconstruction to neo-Foucaldian HRM – with little or no recourse to the original sources of these interpretations. Whilst we might agree that the author may not have the last word on any text of their own making, they ironically may offer the resources for a greater multiplicity and richness of interpretation than their derivatives, most of which are inevitably guilty of some sort of simplification or reductionism. The contributors to this book find this approach is not uncommon and is puzzling: it admits a commitment to positions rather than ideas, to agonistic and often antagonistic debate rather than enquiry, to outcomes rather than processes, and indeed to speaking rather than listening.

So this book has one major objective – to 'open up' the thinking of each of the selected authors or group of authors for its readers, in a way that will encourage them to explore the original works for themselves. Often, when we recall our first encounter with an author whose work has been not just influential but inspirational to us, we can bring to mind a particular piece and the particular setting in which we first read that piece, a moment or event when such insight struck us that we felt so excited and alive to its possibilities that we wanted to rush out and tell someone. This often comes with a sense of liberation and a consequent urge to trace and retrace the process that had led the 'author' to the place in which we found them; get to know the sources they discussed in the way that they came to know them – and find our own means of coming to terms with them. That is surely the *passion* of reading, indeed of scholarship, which lightens its otherwise arduous detail-work.

The contributors to this book were charged with conveying something of the sense of excitement they felt when reading the author they had been asked to address, and to encourage and invite the reader to explore further whilst flagging what the contributor thought were the most important aspects of this work for the theory of organizations and organizing. What remains to be done in this introduction then, is to frame the current context of this reception by identifying some – and only some – of the intellectual lineage of postmodernism. Several texts have already attempted this quite successfully and we won't go over the same ground here. But postmodernism is often accused of having no sense of history, an accusation which is quite absurd. Postmodern writers such as Foucault just think history differently. They question accounts of history as we know it and often appear not to feel obligated to present systematic and detailed accounts of historical facts and records. Rather they recognize the way that history lives in and exerts pressure on its recreation in the present. As both Derrida and Foucault have intimated, the intellectual history of the twentieth century could be expressed in terms of the variety of responses – both French and German – to the work of Hegel, a theme very much and very consciously alive in their work, and which is characterized by a reluctance to accept Hegel's idea of the end of History either as actuality or possibility. Postmodernism's lack of a sense of its own genealogy might be inferred from the fact that some major influences, such as Bataille on Baudrillard and Bergson on Derrida, though tangible and important in particular works are not always directly cited by these authors even when they are most present. They can therefore be overlooked even by those critics who read the original works but are perhaps not more widely-read in Continental philosophy. The range of possible influences is of course vast – in coming to an understanding of the rich genealogy of the postmodern scene, uncovering and interpreting a hidden influence is part of the excitement of the discovery of the possibilities of the text's 'interior', and much of its pleasure. But first, we perhaps need to address the question of why 'postmodernism'? Why and how do we use the term in this book?

Defining Postmodernism

A common distinction among sociologists in the 1980s, which has now become popular in organization theory, was the distinction between 'postmodernism' and 'post-structuralism' (for example, Hancock, 1999). Post-structuralists in this formulation concentrate on the work of language and discourse and would accordingly include Derrida and Foucault, whilst postmodernists might be further distinguished into those with a hyphen (post-modernists), who analyse the contemporary social conditions of an epoch, and those without a hyphen (postmodernists), who concentrate on the theoretical milieu which has developed to sustain these conditions as a response, or a variety of response, to modernism. This latter group would include Baudrillard, probably as an exemplar of the first tendency and Lyotard, perhaps as an example of the latter (Hassard, 1993: Ch.6; Parker, 1992). Interestingly, much of this taxonomic activity has taken place with relatively little reference to French structuralism (as distinct from the Parsonian variety more familiar to Western sociology) of whose history poststructuralism can be seen to be part, as François Dossc (1997a, 1997b) argues. The distinctions made often pick up on shifting disagreements and differences between the protagonists – Derrida and Baudrillard, Derrida and Foucault, Baudrillard and Lyotard, Deleuze and Foucault for example – on specific issues which are real enough but which occlude significant family resemblances. On the other hand, there has been more than enough broad-brush familial generalization to obscure significant differences as well. So whichever terminological convention we choose to follow, it needs to be used with care and with reference to specific issues with regard to its appropriateness.

That said, the distinction between poststructuralism and postmodernism is, though tempting, often rather too easily made and in this book we cautiously treat the second term to be inclusive of the first. The reason for this is partly pragmatic and partly theoretical. Pragmatically, almost all of the key players have disowned, at some point or another, either label and even the terms which they themselves have coined – because these labels and terms were never intended to be as restrictive as subsequent interpreters have held them to be. So whilst Derrida laments the term deconstruction and claims not to be a deconstructionist, Lyotard by the same coin regrets introducing the term postmodern to debates on social knowledge; Foucault rejects structuralism, poststructuralism and postmodernism even claiming at one point to be happy to be a (sort of) positivist (Foucault, 1972: 125). Even Baudrillard disowns the term postmodernism. But when they do this, they are not simply playing intellectual games to tantalize us. They mean and deserve to be taken seriously because of their suspicion of language and labelling and its deadening effects which reduce the multiplicity, paradox of and struggle with ideas to a series of homogeneous 'positions'. We should not therefore be surprised that the strict distinctions between post-structuralism and postmodernism have also proved difficult to sustain in terms of a concentration on either text or social context, because the work of individuals has moved around, as one might expect, to consider a wider variety of themes and issues. Foucault's work, which can by some be seen as moving through stages, is perhaps better regarded as an interweaving of themes which emerge to emphasis, fade away and re-emerge in a different guise later, without compulsion to avoid contradiction of the way in which they were treated earlier. The politics which was, for some interpreters at least, always implicit in Derrida's work has become much more explicit since the 1990s. Poststructuralism has become more inextricably bound up with postmodernism in recent years and maintaining the strict distinction is no longer helpful. Indeed, one of the animating desires of this book is to move beyond 'ismism' to access ideas, but 'isms' may still serve as ladders which we eventually cast away. Nevertheless, where we think a separation of terms remains helpful we have employed it, as this is not so much a statement of doctrine as praxis.

Theoretically to explain this stance we can turn to Lyotard's much misunderstood statement that the postmodern is that which comes *before* the modern. That is not to say that it is the nascent modern, because it also pre-exists the premodern. It is in a sense primordial, but its existence is constant rather than superseded or epochal. It simultaneously pre-exists the modern and yet is knowable only *through* and *after* the modern – with the modern seen as a moment, or point of leverage, in thought. The postmodern, following this line, is that which ultimately escapes all the regimes of order and signification with which we try to 'capture' and represent it. Pure experience, event, chaos, flow or whatever else is said to inhabit it, are ambivalent, ambiguous, paradoxical and problematic for purposeful human existence and we therefore develop ways and means of managing meaning and responding to the perplexities of nature and, perhaps, God. Premodern approaches, tending to be based on superstition, myth, magic, religion and limited conceptual structures are one response. Modern approaches based on rationality, logic, order, scientific objectivity, calculation and measurement are a different but related approach. French structuralism, especially in the hands of Lévi-Strauss, demonstrated the 'savage' mind to be no less complex or conceptual than the 'modern' mind, equally capable of devising intricate formal symbolic structures, but operating according to different rules and sets of relations. These sets of relations were essentially arbitrary and poststructuralism concentrated its attentions on exposing the arbitrary dimensions of the signification systems on which assumptions of knowledge and fact about the world were predicated whether modern or premodern. Because no representation could ever be fully adequate to capture all dimensions of reality, all systems of representation had to be self-referential and determined by relations of difference within the system as well as any assumed correspondence with the 'nature' of things. Even at their most elaborate, such systems depend on reductions, aporia, hidden oppositions and binaries and other inevitable representational inadequacies. Post-structural approaches reveal these inadequacies and force us to question the effects and consequences of these assumptions without, as structuralism did, offering any 'better' or more authentic patterns from which to build. Poststructuralism therefore reveals more clearly the flux inherent in the raw material from which modern knowledge is constructed, and whose movement and play still adhere within the systems of modernity. In other words, it reveals the *postmodern* of Lyotard *within* – not beneath, behind or beyond – the structures of modernity. Because the tendency of both poststructuralism and postmodernism is towards engagement with the postmodern *in this sense*, we can claim that it makes sense for us to employ a loose or soft terminology in this book in which we regard the postmodern as encompassing the poststructural.

If as we have said postmodernism arises from a kind of thinking beyond modernism, then we might expect the roots of postmodernism to lie alongside the roots of modernism and be related to early attempts to think beyond those foundations. We could therefore go back at least to the pre-Socratics, the Solipsists, the Skeptics and find some relevant ideas, just as Derrida grounds much of his critique of Western philosophy in his readings of Ancient Greek thought and Foucault turns his attention to them in relation to embodiment and subjectivity. As the modern takes shape so alongside it does the postmodern – as an alternate, a simulation, a perversion, a faulty version, an improper variant, an irregular or just plain wrong interpretation (Carroll, 1987). The postmodern could therefore be thought of as the *para-modern*. When we turn such an understanding towards theory we find that the postmodern is *paratheory*. It questions the status and limitations of theory, including critical theory; it questions the rules by which theory is constructed and operates and the consequences of transgression; it questions the relation between the theoretical and the empirical; it considers theory as a form of representation, or writing; it pursues its ends not through homology, the elevation of similarities in a logic of unity, but through heterology – a disconnected logic of the fragment. Organization theory is almost a tautology in these terms: organization is writing; writing is theory; theory is organization. A paratheoretical approach looks for the fissures in this cosy state of affairs, the failures, the immanences, the bursts of energy, the collapses, the silences and the refusal of the unsaid and the non-known to become the said or the known. Looking *through* the techniques – rhetorical, theoretical, scientific, philosophical – through which modernity has organized its sense of self, of history and of purpose, those phenomena which refuse to be so organized, like laughter, death and ecstasy offer an alternative resource for a heterologous view to be taken, a heterodoxy to emerge through paratheoretical strategies. This alternate – a constantly shifting alternate rather than an alterna*tive* – is what the thinkers discussed in this book attempt to open up.

The postmodern understood in this way is powerful but elusive, a formless form of desire, an energy rather than a structure. Postmodernism as a result may seem like a family composed entirely of black sheep. But where treatments of postmodernism and poststructuralism have concentrated on the construction of schemes and systems of difference which have tended to produce, or at least occasion, considerable academic bickering and frequently impenetrable arguments, the contributors to this book would argue that the sense of and appreciation of this energy, this *passion*, this electric sense of possibility, has been lost. They have all attempted to share their own passion for the postmodern in their chapters and to reveal some of the enticing and infectious passion within the works of their chosen authors as an invitation to the reader to step inside, to get to know them better. It is then not such an easy task to attempt a brief summary of their arguments in this introduction, but I hope I can do it without robbing their words of too much of that elusive crackle that can be so easily summarised into quiescence.

Introduction to the chapters

In the following chapter, David Knights considers the work that has probably had more influence on organization studies up to this point than that of any other postmodern thinker. He takes an unorthodox approach to the work of Michel Foucault arguing that there has already been a growing literature that seeks to link organization analysis and Foucault by drawing on his unique insights in the study of work and organization writing – that is, Foucault *into* organization theory. But feeling that this might just continue the tendency to add yet another perspectival position to the battery of incommensurable paradigms that already populate the field leads him to argue for a radical break with modernist theory, rather than 'a fudge that seeks to reconcile modernist demands for generality within the context of localised circumstances of concrete organising'. Foucault, he argues, would have approved of both the heretics and the moulding of his own work to suit some other purpose, as he continually provoked others to bend his work to their interest as he had himself done with Nietzsche and others, following his commitment to taking thought beyond itself or thinking what appears to be unthinkable.

Foucault's work was broadly about how human life *organizes itself* and is *organized*. Whatever is the focus for an organizing activity, power, knowledge and subjectivity are involved. Knights begins by displaying the classificatory results of having trawled through the work of Foucault to indicate how it is principally about power/knowledge, subjectivity, and truth/ethics, going on to show how these conceptions and interests are also the central features of organizational analysis, in the process sacrificing some 'sacred cows'. In particular, Knights wants to expose and debate the humanistic assumptions of organization theory from the anti-humanist position associated with Foucault, but noting that even for Foucault this position was not entirely clear cut and human rights were very important. Epistemology, gender/sexuality, and social inequality are the focal points of the following discussion as Knights discusses their relative absence from organization theory and the question of autonomy and subjectivity which runs through them. Writing organization into Foucault, he argues, makes the imposition of certain subjectivities and suppression of others increasingly impossible to sustain. The discourse of postmodern organization then is a fruitful vehicle for a *refusal* to accept the rules and representations of the past despite the fact that they give comfort, security and stability.

Campbell Jones, much in the manner of Derrida himself, questions whether some of the labels and even accusations which have been applied to or levelled at his work are in fact fully justified. Is deconstruction appropriately regarded as a method? Is Derrida a relativist? Is deconstruction negative or critical? As Derrida argues for a rethinking of relations, Jones carefully examines whether some of the terms often used in connection with Derrida's work as interchangeable, such as indeterminacy and undecidability, are in fact so and whether a crucial distinction or distinctions have been missed in some of the commentaries on Derrida and attempts to apply his work to organization studies.

Jones is sceptical of the appellation postmodern to Derrida, as he is of the label relativist in any radical sense – both cases where critics frequently pursue the reduction of the complexity and ambivalence of his ideas to the point of absurdity, as Derrida has frequently been forced to point out himself. Deconstruction, for example, does not equate simply to critique as opposition; on the other hand, neither is it affirmative in any simple sense. 'Skeptical' or 'affirmative' as optional postmodern styles (Rosenau, 1992) are simply too crude. Derrida refuses to settle on the poles of any binary oppositions and remains, often subtly, in motion between them but in a relation of intimacy rather than distance. Although Derrida leaves no programme for us to follow, he doesn't subside into the resignation of passive nihilism but opens the space for us to find a position 'from which we *must* decide what to do, without resort to excuses or formulae'. Derrida's work contains a persistent and radical experience of *possibility*, based on an opening or openness to the possibilities of an alternative future in which deconstruction entails *actively* transformative readings which open the way to a *radically* transformative politics and ethics. These offer two possibilities for organization studies. The first would be a broader application of strategies of deconstructive reading to a range of 'empirical' texts from organizational life and a range of 'theoretical' texts about organization in areas where it has been largely ignored, including the deconstructive reading of critical analyses of organization. The second would entail a different way of understanding deconstruction, which would involve not just applying the model of deconstruction that has been used in organization studies to date, but subjecting that model to a careful and rigorous deconstructive reading. This would not attack or indict the way that deconstruction has been used in organization studies but would work in the space that has been opened by the many valuable efforts to introduce deconstruction whilst remaining dissatisfied and keeping an open eye to the possibility of other future efforts to set deconstruction to work in the field.

Hugo Letiche, assisted by Juup Essers and following Lyotard's own injunction, believes that the task of his chapter, to do justice to Lyotard, is impossible as it is central to Lyotard's thought that one cannot in any such text do *justice* to someone's ideas. So the task is paradoxical: if one tries to do justice to Lyotard, one has to argue against what he has said. Throughout his work, Lyotard has distrusted the power of narrative, that is, of descriptive text, of statements of how things 'are' or of accounts of happenings. The products of organizational research – texts which seem to be narratives about companies, practices, organizations and businesses – are really disguised tracts about norms and values, attempts to tell us what we should do and/or treatises on the beautiful. Lyotard asserts that normative, prescriptive and aesthetic texts are often disguised as narratives in order to palm them off onto unsuspecting readers. Lyotard's work is about the injustices of reading, in that one cannot read without being manipulated and abused. Different language games, or regimes of phrases, remain at heart incommensurable – subject to a '*différend*' inhabited by misunderstanding. Although such different regimes of phrases can perhaps be 'bridged' on the surface, the 'bridges' are problematic. As Letiche emphasizes, the intellectual (i.e. political and managerial) 'moves', needed to get from the one cognitive position (as an example, a descriptive narrative of social circumstances), to another (to illustrate, a prescriptive statement of policy and plans), remain brittle and vulnerable. Accordingly, Letiche argues, Lyotard's work confronts organizational studies with its inability to resolve the questions it posed (and given the continued interest in paradigm analysis, continues to pose) itself in the incommensurability debate. The only solutions seem to be either to try and prop up modernism through some form of meta-paradigm (Pfeffer, 1993) or multiplicity (Hassard and Kelemen, 2002), or to try to create meaning grounded in specific nameable contexts. The incommensurability debate has mainly been conducted on the level of high Modernism, asking what general principle(s) define(s) an acceptable form of epistemological rigour as well as permit one to take local circumstances and concrete organizing into account. As Letiche points out, from a Lyotardian perspective such a position is self-contradictory. Informed by Lyotard, we can begin to appreciate how radical the epistemological break has to be if we hope to create a 'postmodern' organizational studies aware of itself and acting in mutual reciprocity with its field of research.

Heather Höpfl offers a subtle and sensitive reading of the treatment of authority and the maternal in the work of Julia Kristeva. This is particularly apposite when considering the manipulative and appropriative styles of culture change in organizations of the last two decades. Here she argues, the violence of the phallogocentric male authority has been reinforced by the appropriation and manipulation of the feminine in the pursuit of an even more complete and hence even more authoritative, complete, male self. However, what is achieved here, she argues, is the construction of a travesty of all that is feminine: a grotesque parody of the feminine parading its lack. Women are either seen as at the boundary, marking the margins of the male self, or oddly central, perhaps to some other arena. They are either 'angelic or the locus of death, the means of salvation by enabling authorship or symbolised as an archetype of betrayal', the very condition of male authority. If organizations, as phallogocentric trajectories, are lacking the Mother, and maternal qualities, then the construction and elevation of feminine attributes to some counterfeit mother (either male or female) will not resolve the difficulties. Kristeva here has been critical of women's desire for *phallic power* which sees the pursuit of what men possess as being the result of distortions of the mother-daughter relationship, and thus futile and misplaced. The daughter becomes a son in order to fight for her inheritance but at a great cost for women.

In translating Kristeva's work into an organizational context Höpfl argues that it is perhaps best to consider her contribution to praxis, to the micro activities of day-to-day practice and interaction with others. Her work is intimately concerned with borders and their demarcation, exile and homelessness, strangeness, estrangement, the boundary of the body and sociality and love, and it concerns ethics and motherhood. For Kristeva motherhood is the model of love which governs psychoanalytical practice: the psychoanalytic cure for the patient can only be found in transference and, for Kristeva, this means love. This then is her ethical position: her *herethics* based on a praxis of love. This is a radically different way of being from that conventionally associated with organizational behaviour and offers a gentle but powerful challenge to malestream organization theory.

Pippa Carter and Norman Jackson set out to argue that Deleuze and Guattari could be seen as the first postmodern organization theorists. They argue that Deleuze and Guattari's writing represents radically different thinking about the nature and function of organization in contemporary society and accordingly a challenge to all the principles and tenets of conventional Organization Theory. In their place, and redefining the subject, Deleuze and Guattari offer a complex, but rigorous, new agenda for social and organizational relations.

Deleuze and Guattari offer more than the abandonment of rationality for relativism, for in pursuing a radical way forward towards praxis they seek a utility lacking in relativism alone – one which will allow organization outside capitalism. Whilst the grasp of the capitalist machine might seem to be all embracing, Deleuze and Guattari see at least two broad lines of escape, or lines of flight. However much control of the signifier is sought, it can never be absolute – meaning escapes. Desire is an immanent force which 'resides' in us all and is the reservoir of potentiality and becoming – desire escapes. Their work is premised upon a conception of the social and the individual as immanent, to the extent that it is not meaningful to treat them as separate, or to talk of them in distinct terms – the word 'individual' rarely occurs in their texts. Thus it can be argued that, while advocating a radical transformation, this does not imply a non-organized society but that we can think rationales for organizing other than the capitalist machine.

For Deleuze and Guattari, organizations do not have to be the way they are and other purposes could inform our mode of organization. We could have a radical reassessment of what organizational outputs are necessary for social survival, betterment, independent of the implications of this for a capitalist system of values. What is needed is for us to develop a capacity for thinking and action which is active and affirmative, rather than reactive, passive and negative. Because of the immanent relation with the social, this would inevitably become distributed throughout society, offering alternative ways of thinking about organization based upon the infinity of possibilities and potentialities. Deleuze and Guattari advocate a politics of multiplicity and creativity, unfettered by any dominant discourse. Change must be judged and evaluated according to the extent to which desire, multiplicity and creativity are emancipated, to which the outcome is social relations which exist for the betterment of us all, rather than just for the favoured few characterized by collective values and in which everything is political.

Deleuze and Guattari characterize their work as 'minor'. Minor philosophies, literatures, and so on, are those which resist appropriation and signification, being rhizomic. Although it is possible to make connections with the work of other writers, Carter and Jackson argue that Deleuze and Guattari's work is not really like that of anyone else and has qualities and characteristics which actively resist translation into a language already appropriated by capitalism. It is *not* possible, they argue, taking Knights' position on Foucault further, to make a conventional organization theory out of Deleuze and Guattari's analysis of organizations. Their work cannot be assimilated into conventional organization theory to add explanatory power. Majoritarian thought may be the norm, but it inevitably serves interests other than its own, so to think difference – *to produce new thinking on organization(s)* – a minor approach is necessary. This, they argue, is what Deleuze and Guattari offer.

Hugo Letiche, in a second contribution, explores Jean Baudrillard's constant attempts to escape the existent. Where Sartre's thought is grounded existentially and Lyotard's epistemologically, Baudrillard abandons metaphysics for *pataphysics*, making it up as he goes along, exaggerating whatever is in his focus to a point beyond excess when it collapses back into its Other. Though he is not by any means a theorist of the Other, which perhaps distances him from other postmodern writers, otherness adheres to his theorizing as he formulates imaginary solutions that go beyond existing repertoires of response. This is because for Baudrillard the consumer society has destroyed all 'reality'; there can only be imagined solutions, there being no reality left upon which one can base any other solutions. Pataphysics is therefore socially enforced creativity, rather than an expression of individual sovereignty, which inverts the philosophy of excess of Bataille.

Despite his obsession with image and imagination, Letiche argues that Baudrillard is a materialist, but it is a materialism grounded in the man-made, virtual world. His raw material is produced by state-of-the-art capitalist companies; his economy is based on information and communication technologies; it is a knowledge economy. He reflects pataphysically not on matter, but on *products*. In so doing, he tries to discern the logic of materialist change and then accelerate it towards its object. As Letiche argues, 'his intention is to be more performative than the most performative; more dynamic than the most dynamic; more powerful than the strongest power' and thus to escape the logic of the material by outdoing it. Baudrillard's frantic vision of the consumer society is not hyper-consumerism, but *catastrophic* consumerism – pushing consumption until it *implodes*.

Baudrillard's relevance to organization studies is of course major in his consumption work, but in relation to postmodernism is paradoxical. This is because Baudrillard accepts postmodern assumptions, for example in relation to organization as process (subject) rather than organization as structure (object), but draws the opposite conclusions. If modern capitalism has dissolved into a society of simulation of service industries and information economies then the only dynamic option left is to out-simulate simulation – by accepting the primacy of the object, the organization itself in all its simulation. He means to take organization literally. For Baudrillard, attempts to resuscitate the decentred subject or reinsert agency into organization theory are mistaken – the only possibilities are to be more organized than the organized and embrace 'the absurdity of ecstatic control and the insane overdetermination of all actions' or follow his own highly individualist strategy of preserving the ego behind an ephemeral and situationalist text. As Letiche argues, although Baudrillard chooses a problematic path, his claim that by going further in the direction of objectification than objectification would itself normally go, to be more organized than organization, its hysterical energy can be channelled in order to create an absurd text that deconstructs – tears apart and renders totally paradoxical – the dominant logic, and becomes a form of both critique and resistance, repays attention even if only because of the ideas turned up on the catastrophic journey.

Assunta Viteritti introduces the work of three very different Italian interpreters of the postmodern debate, whose work is important though less frequently cited than their French counterparts. Gianni Vattimo would be regarded as the official representative of the philosophical strand of Italian postmodern thought, and grounds his work in Heidegger's hermeneutical philosophy and in Nietzsche's nihilism. He argues for the possibility of thinking in terms of a *weak* rationality, where any ontological and unifying claim is abandoned in favour of a *viable* reason which accepts its immersion, its *being thrown in the world*. Reason, then, renounces the ambition of exhaustive explanation and knowledge, becoming an immanent component of human experience. However, such weak thinking entails neither giving up, nor abrogating, meaningfulness for human agency. It is rather an attempt to re-instigate a possibility for a new, weak beginning.

Umberto Eco draws on poststructural linguistics, where the traditional, privileged domains of linguistic inquiry have undergone a dramatic change. Eco enters the transformation of semiology, as it moves away from the logic of correspondence, conveyed by the idea of the dictionary, to embrace the images of the encyclopaedia and the labyrinth, where the direction and construction of discourse are provided through subjects' interaction. Language then resembles, more and more, what Deleuze and Guattari define as a rhizome, a *locus* for production of interpretation, which, according to Eco, is not unrestricted but can be constrained by the sense attributed to it, differently, by agents.

Viteritti argues that Rella's theoretical work, developed as literary criticism, *traverses* modernity: a modernity living on its frontier. Rella investigates those *figures* capable of evoking, thinking and living the transformation of modernity. In his view many declensions of modernity are possible and the postmodern option is the search for possibilities, an exploration for still other paths within the same modernity. Rella, a scholar of Marx and Benjamin, looks for the routes that lead to revivifying some of the jaded figures of the modern, whose vitality is far from exhausted.

A review of the ideas proposed by Vattimo, Eco and Rella, leads Viteritti to consider the organization as a space, neither pre-definable nor predictable by models of *strong* rationality. Drawing from Vattimo, organizational processes are inspired by a *weak rationality* and organizational actors – who are firstly social actors – find themselves immersed in processes of availing themselves of, and synthesizing, meanings traceable to each participant's hermeneutical tradition, or history of interpretive experience. For Eco, organizations are *partial encyclopaedias*, a location of *unlimited semiosis*, contextually organized through the practices of actors who reduce the indeterminate and infinite series of possibilities. The organization is a field where actors continuously make meaning-references, meaning in reference to other meanings, where rationality is only a temporary, mobile and unaccomplished outcome: an *open text* in which interpretations co-operate to produce, contextually, non-definite and non-predictable models of rationality. For Rella the organization would be the space where rationalization is *de facto* impossible and anyway impracticable, because the strong light of rationalization always produces its own shadows – that can be, for example, the outcomes in terms of power imbalances induced by the strong rationalization of planning. We therefore have to consider the complexity of social life, and thus organizational life also, as a *threshold* where the actors who are carriers both of myths and reason move; polyglot and nomadic actors who speak more than one language. Accordingly, an organization is a territory continuously in construction by the *becoming* of the heterogeneity of components in action.

Moving nomadically within a landscape whose figures melt and change; speaking with several voices none of whom is to be trusted; resisting by refusing to oppose; stretching the modern beyond its own boundaries to the point of catastrophic implosion; becoming ethical through a praxis of love; acting not from first principles but from mutual reciprocity; refusing the rules of the past as a limit on the future; recursive deconstruction as opening up the possibilities for just organization; thinking beyond present forms to organize beyond current socio-political and economic relations, beyond capitalisms and their alternatives. These are some of the dimensions of the passions, shared by the writers introduced in these pages, we have chosen to call postmodern. They offer enduring challenges to thinking about organization and organizations, and if we have been successful in our efforts, these introductions to the richness of their ideas will not only be enjoyable in themselves but will also encourage the reader to get to know them better.

References

Calás, M.B. and Smircich, L. (1999) 'Past Postmodernism? Reflections and tentative directions', *Academy of Management Review*, 24 (4): 649–71.
Carroll, D. (1987) *Paraesthetics – Foucault, Lyotard, Derrida*. London: Routledge.
Dosse, F. (1997a) *History of Structuralism. Vol. 1 – The Rising Sign*. Minneapolis: University of Minnesota Press.
Dosse, F. (1997b) *History of Structuralism. Vol. 2 – The Sign Sets*. Minneapolis: University of Minnesota Press.
Feldman, S.P. (1996) 'The ethics of shifting ties: management theory and the breakdown of culture in modernity', *Journal of Management Studies*, 33 (3): 283–99.

Feldman, S.P. (1997) 'The revolt against cultural authority: power/knowledge as an assumption in organization theory', *Human Relations*, 50 (8): 937–55.

Feldman, S.P. (1998) 'Playing with the pieces: deconstruction and the loss of moral culture', *Journal of Management Studies*, 35 (1): 59–79.

Foucault, M. (1972) *The Archaeology of Knowledge*. New York: Pantheon.

Hancock, P. (1999) 'Baudrillard and the metaphysics of motivation: a reappraisal of corporate culturalism in the light of the work and ideas of Jean Baudrillard', *Journal of Management Studies*, 36 (2): 155–75.

Hassard, J. (1993) *Sociology and Organization Theory: Positivism, Paradigms and Postmodernity*, Cambridge: Cambridge University Press.

Hassard, J. and Kelemen, M. (2002) 'Production and consumption in organizational knowledge: the case of the paradigms debate', *Organization*, 9 (2): 331–55.

Parker, M. (1992) 'Postmodern Organizations or Postmodern Organization Theory?', *Organization Studies*, 13 (1): 1–17.

Pfeffer, J. (1993) 'Barriers to the advance of organization science: paradigm development as a dependent variable', *Academy of Management Review*, 18 (4): 599–620.

Rosenau, P.M. (1992) *Postmodernism and the Social Sciences: Insights, Inroads and Intrusions*. Princeton, NJ: Princeton University Press.

Thompson, P. (1993) 'Postmodernism: fatal distraction', in J. Hassard and M. Parker, (eds) *Postmodernism and Organization*. London: Sage. pp. 183–203.

2
Michel Foucault

David Knights

The successes of history belong to those who are capable of seizing the rules, to replace those who had used them, to disguise themselves so as to pervert them, invert their meaning and redirect them against those who had initially imposed them. (Foucault, 1977: 147)

Introduction: writing organizational analysis into Foucault

There has been a growing literature that seeks to link organization analysis and Foucault by drawing on his unique insights in the study of work and organization (e.g. Miller, 1987; Knights and Willmott, 1989; Rose, 1989; Knights and Morgan, 1991; Knights, 1992; Sewell and Wilkinson, 1992; Barker, 1993; Knights, 1997; Knights and McCabe, 1997; McKinlay and Starkey, 1998). The writing of this chapter began by seeking to build on this tradition and, more particularly, was concerned to consolidate our understanding of the distinctive contribution of Michel Foucault's social analysis and its significance for organization studies. An immediate question raised itself, however, as to whether there is not a problem in wanting to write Foucault into organization theory.

On reflection it became clear to me that this could simply result in another perspective in organization theory to add to and compete with an already over-crowded field. Indeed, it may already be too late as may be seen from the proliferation of Foucaldian approaches to organization analysis. But when discussing the debate on the incommensurability of paradigms in organization studies, Letiche (Chapter 7 in this volume) argues: 'the debate exhausted itself with no-one convincing anyone else of much of anything'. Perspectival positions cannot avoid the problem of relativism where it is impossible to judge one against the other except in terms of presuppositions and prejudices. Following Lyotard, Letiche suggests that a 'postmodern' organization studies demands a radical epistemological break with modernism and not a fudge that seeks to reconcile modernist demands for generality within the context of localized circumstances of concrete organizing.

If we take this view seriously, maybe it is necessary to avoid appropriating bits of Foucault for purposes of re-energizing organization theory and do the reverse – write organization theory into Foucault. While this may be seen as heretical within mainstream organization theory, presumably Foucault would have approved of both the heretics and the moulding of his own work to suit some other purpose. He continually provoked others to bend his work to their interest as he had himself done with Nietzsche and others. More importantly, however, this project also attempts to follow Foucault's commitment to taking thought beyond itself or thinking what appears to be unthinkable.

Foucault was concerned throughout his intellectual career with the epistemological rules of the formation of disciplines, the disciplining of populations and subjects through power-knowledge relations and the self-formation of the ethical subject. However, it does not constitute too great a violation to perceive his work as having been broadly about how human life *organizes itself* and is *organized*. Similarly, once we reject the absurd notion of perceiving the subject matter of organization theory exclusively as the bounded entity that commonly attracts the label organization, the two forms of study can be seen as having parallel, if not identical, concerns. In this sense, organization analysis[1] focuses on the principles and processes of *organizing* wherever it occurs. Foucault, by contrast, was concerned with the organization of knowledge, power and subjectivity. But whatever is the focus for an organizing activity, power, knowledge and subjectivity are involved. It makes little difference to these three concepts whether the organizing activity is concerned directly with the idea (i.e. conception/design) or its implementation and, thereby, its realization in practice. From the organization of production through distribution to consumption, knowledge is mobilized and modified, subjectivity is secured and sustained, power is exercised in more or less effective ways, and ethical discourses formed and reformed. Of course, equally, knowledge can be displaced or destroyed, subjectivity ridiculed or resisted, power undermined or undone and moral relations exhausted or emasculated. While these concepts may not be exhaustive of the content of organizing, other aspects can readily be accommodated within their remit.

Epistemologically, however, there is an even stronger basis for writing organizational analysis into Foucault rather than the other way around. This relates to the distinctiveness of Foucault's epistemological approach to the humanities. In his early work, Foucault (1973) argued that the humanities occupied the space that lies between the representations of the positive human sciences and the subjectivity that makes them possible (see Table 1.1)

Representations of:	Through:	Objectifications of:	Truth effects in norms of:
1. Life	biology	the body and its functions	health
2. Language	linguistics	speech and communication	well being
3. Labour	economics	production and exchange	wealth

Table 1.1: The positive human sciences

The stimulant for his interest in the rules that '*govern* statements, and the way in which they *govern* each other so as to constitute a set of propositions which are scientifically acceptable' (Foucault, 1980: 112), was a concern to

understand radical and sudden transformations of scientific knowledge. He had
seen this radical transformation in the growth of psychiatry and the construction
of madness (Foucault, 1977a). While he had already identified the circulation of
the effects of power among scientific statements as important, he had not yet
fully recognized these discursive regimes in terms of relations of power or
struggles, strategies and tactics (Foucault, 1980: 114). Growing dissatisfied with
some of the central elements of this archaeology of knowledge within which
this insight regarding the space that the humanities should occupy was buried,
Foucault (1980, 1984) turned away from an examination of the 'rules of
formation' and 'regimes of truth' through which scientific knowledge
progresses. Because of this, he abandoned the focus on an archaeology of
'epistemes of truth' in favour of genealogical analyses of power and knowledge
that exhibit the conditions that make it possible for power to have particular
truth effects.

   This chapter begins by displaying the classificatory results of having trawled
through the work of Foucault to indicate how it is principally about
power/knowledge, subjectivity, and truth/ethics, after which it is then necessary
to show how these conceptions and interests are also the central features of
organizational analysis. At the same time, writing organizational analysis into
Foucault may mean sacrificing some 'sacred cows'. For example, whereas
organization theory tends to reflect and reinforce humanistic values, Foucault
has professed an anti-humanist position. This is not so clear cut as it might
appear, however, since whilst claiming to be anti-humanist, Foucault also
argues that human rights are all that we have in our armoury when resisting the
powers that subjugate us.

   This chapter seeks to contribute to a debate on humanism partly because of
this conflict with organization theory but also for reasons of its relationship to
some weaknesses in both discourses. These need to be confronted if this
enterprise of writing organization analysis into Foucault is to be effective.
Variable as and between the two discourses, these weaknesses revolve around
epistemology, gender/sexuality and social inequality, and are the focus for the
remainder of the chapter. Foucault, for example, displays a limitation in
disregarding issues of gender and focusing attention primarily on
power/knowledge rather than social inequality. Organizational analysis, for its
part, has given very little attention to the subject matter of epistemology and
sex/gender issues (see for example Burrell, 1984; Cooper and Burrell, 1988;
Burrell and Hearn, 1989; Calás and Smircich, 1992; Knights, 1992, 1997). We
now turn to our first section, which seeks to summarize the whole of Foucault's
work in a classificatory schema. While necessarily violating its subject matter,
as do all classifications, this I consider an acceptable heuristic, as long as the
temptation of reifying its construction is resisted.

'Pinning Foucault down'

One way of organizing the diverse, difficult and dramatic character of
Foucault's work is to break it up into historically discontinuous periods. The

most common of these periodizations is provided by distinguishing between the archaeological and the genealogical phases (Dreyfus and Rabinow, 1982; Burrell, 1984; Knights, 1992) and, more recently, to add in the final ethical phase (McNay, 1992). While it is difficult to discuss Foucault's writings as a whole without distinguishing these different phases, I do not want simply to repeat what others have already skilfully achieved. Accordingly, the following table takes the periodization a stage further by creating what might be seen as a classification of Foucault's work. It is recognized that classifying is a form of labelling and thereby an exercise of power and, indeed, often an act of violation.[2] For the sake of the classification, it is necessary to push and prod analyses or discourses into categories that strain to fit them and then are found to be overlapping or inconsistent with other categories in the scheme. This recognition did not stop Foucault from engaging in classification when, for example, he sought to distinguish the point in the seventeenth century at which classical or pre-modern society became modern. Consequently, the following is a reflection as well as a violation of Foucault.

Power/Knowledge Regimes

Society	Pre-modern	Modern	Postmodern
History	Processes of individualization		
Power	Sovereign	Disciplinary	Governmental
Exercised through	Spectacles of torture	Hierarchy/normalization/ examination	Responsibility
Knowledge	Exclusive	Partially distributed	Inclusive
Effects	Fear of punishment	Divisive	Identification
Self	Struggles for dignity	Struggles for autonomy	Struggles for identity
Identity	Subjugated	Normalized	Aestheticized
Resistance	Limited	Extensive	Occurs in space between multiple identities
Subjectivity	Totalized	Individualized	Subjectivized
Ethics	Absolute	Publicly regulated	Localized
'Truth'	Function of God/Nature	Effect of power/consent	Tied to identity

Table 1.2: The Foucaldian edifice

This analysis is not to be seen as a conventional approach to the examination of history since Foucault does not see these developments in evolutionary terms. They are not, therefore, the equivalent of the historicist stages from feudalism through capitalism to socialism in Marx's historical materialism. In that sense, pre-modern, modern and postmodern characterizations should not be seen as displacing one another in a linear sequence although clearly, each is dependent on its predecessor as the conditions of its own possibility. These characterizations, of course, are an effect of 'problems' of the present not the past. Here we can see why Foucault (1977) described his distinctive form of analysis as a 'history of the present'. It is not 'grand narrative' or totalizing theory so much as strategic analysis that acknowledges its own 'immersion within an existing, mobile field of knowledge' (Dean, 1994: 23). The analysis cannot then be distinct from, or immune to, the problematic features of the contemporary, fragmentary and conflicting situations that it seeks to study.

Having said this, however, Foucault (1980, 1982) does see modern regimes of power/knowledge as increasingly having the effect of transforming individuals into subjects that are turned in on themselves, self-regarding and, thereby, individualized. In large part, this was because the social sciences were providing ever more sophisticated and elaborate understandings of the human subject and modern regimes sought to utilize this knowledge to encourage self-discipline. This represented an 'economy of power' since the resources necessary for its exercise were distributed among the population and of little or no cost to governmental institutions. While recognizing that processes of individualization were 'progressive' from a governmental point of view, Foucault (1982) saw them as far from such with respect to individuals. He continually advocated that we resist the process of individualization by *refusing to be what we have become*. It is perhaps for this reason that he turned to an ethics and aesthetics of the self in his later work. Caring for the self and making one's life into a work of art (Foucault, 1985, 1986) is simultaneously an acceptance of the individualized resources and a form of resistance to the kind of subjectivity that the regime imposes. In showing how the subjectivized discourses that we today see as constituting our identities can be traced to Ancient Greek or Roman society, the linear 'progressive' character implicit in the notion of a creeping individualization is countered. For we can see how aspects of each power regime can be seen to coexist in a complex mêlée of conflicting and contradictory discourses both in the present and in the distant past when they had yet to be invented, so to speak.

Although generally understood to have changed from an archaeological, through a genealogical to an ethical/aesthetical phase, Foucault's method should not be periodized any more than his history. Even though Foucault began to recognize different points of focus as he reflected on his own work, each phase is present to some degree in the different stages of his work. While it is necessary to examine the distinctions between the three major focal points of his work – knowledge, power and subjectivity – as well as to recognize how he gave pre-eminence to one or the other at different points, it is important to keep in mind the relationships between them.

These relationships have tended to be ignored by those drawing on Foucault, especially in the field of organization studies. The greatest neglect here has been the first, and perhaps most difficult, archaeological period and to a lesser extent the third ethics phase. But in leaving out the earlier and later phases and their subject matter, the organizational literature (e.g. Barker, 1993; Sewell and Wilkinson, 1992; Webster and Robins, 1993) lacks a historical perspective or, to be more precise, there is the absence of a genealogical analysis. Neither the literature nor the authors are transformed by the experience of drawing on

Foucault. Instead, in the appropriation it is Foucault who is transformed to an impoverished deterministic version of his former self.

To understand disciplinary power and surveillance, it is necessary to see how it partly developed out of resistance to the use of torture or more coercive forms of punishment under sovereign regimes (Knights and McCabe, 2000a). It is also important to recognize how institutions characterized by panopticon-like surveillance mechanisms anticipate regimes of governmentality, where individuals are transformed into subjects who secure their identities, and sense of meaning and reality from the discourses the regime invokes (Knights, 1992; Knights and Murray, 1994). In prisons, for example, the inmates' belief that they are being watched invokes self-restraint whether or not such surveillance is actually practised. It is because the knowledge about surveillance is only partially distributed that it works so effectively as a discipline. For clearly, if the knowledge of surveillance were exclusive as under sovereign regimes or inclusive as under governmental regimes, it would not have the effect of disciplining subjects. But the divisiveness of disciplinary knowledge where subjects are separated off from one another as the 'good' from the 'bad', the normal from the abnormal, the criminal from the law abiding or the sick from the healthy (Foucault, 1982) also generates resistance. Subjects struggle for autonomy and a sense of a self free from the stigmatizing labels that are produced to mark them out or discriminate against them (McWhorter, 1999).

Because of the closer relationship between the middle period interest in discipline and the organization of work, this and often even more narrowly the one book – *Discipline and Punish* – has been over-represented in organization studies. This, I feel, is largely the product of a selective appropriation of Foucault for organization theory. It is partly why I am seeking to reverse the whole exercise so as to write organization theory into Foucault. The different concepts or ideas that Foucault developed were continually revised throughout his life, and their relationship therefore needs to be treated with some care. With a limited degree of license, for example, it can be argued that in relation to notions of the self, contemporary preoccupations have moved from a concern with dignity and autonomy to one of identity. Again this does not mean that autonomy displaces dignity only to be itself displaced by identity in a kind of historical evolution.[3] Each of these aspects of self coincides; it is simply that the emphasis on one or other aspect changes in the direction suggested. As a consequence, resistance in postmodern organizations will tend to be more focused on issues connected with threats to one or other identity than with preserving dignity or autonomy.

Conventionally resistance is seen as an opposition to, or rejection of, the discursive practices that are seen to be the target of that resistance. Even authors that focus heavily on identity would appear to follow this line of reasoning. For example, Castells (1997: 9–10) argues that there are three forms of identity:

1. *Legitimizing identity* where dominant institutions extend and rationalize their domination through identity (see also Sennett, 1986). This is the basis of civil society.

2. *Resistance identity* where the dominated challenge dominant identities on the basis of different principles (identity politics). This is the basis of communes or communities.
3. *Project identity* where the building of a new identity redefines and seeks to transform dominant institutions. This produces subjects in Touraine's (1995: 11) sense of 'individuals against communities and individuals against markets'.

In order to link these conceptions of identity with Foucault's (1982) work, we could argue that legitimizing identity is similar to the notion of subjection where individuals are tied to themselves and others through a self-disciplined subjectivity. Resistance identity may be seen as a form of rebellion against domination and project identity appears more akin to revolution against exploitation or institutional domination. But, it may be argued, identity management no longer occurs predominantly along the two dimensions of rebellion and revolution; that is, of seeking an alternative community or of a project designed to overthrow the system (Castells, 1997: 9–10). Only when identity management relates largely to resisting any threat to autonomy or 'dignity in conditions of its continual erosion' (Sennett and Cobb, 1977), does it tend to be either rebellious or revolutionary. Work and organization have been important sites for such rebellion or revolution, although in recent times resistance has often manifested itself simply in the concern to *escape* from work (Palm, 1970; Knights and Collinson, 1987; Collinson, 1992).

However, when the focus is predominantly about protecting one or a series of identities as a way of making a statement about the world, often it takes the form not of an escape from, so much as an escape into, work (Sturdy, 1992). Such 'constructive' forms of resistance occur at all levels of the organization and frequently involve the criticism of management by employees or other managers. Resistance is then encapsulated in a projection onto significant others of a failure to behave competently or to deliver what is promised. Within Castells' (1997) typology, such resistance lies between what he terms the legitimizing of identity (expectations of conformity) and resistance in the form of the construction of alternative identities or rebellion. While it invariably involves a claim to be closer than others to the organization and its proclaimed objectives, it is clearly a psychological means of elevating the self over others. It is resistance without risk since not only can it always be legitimized as in support of the values shared by members of a common project, it also helps to reproduce the comforting and protective cloak of the collective activity and the security of identity that it sustains.

An alternative interpretation of project identity would be to see it as having parallels to the existentialist response to contingency, where the separation of self from the contingent, overflowing excess of 'other' renders individuals anxious, insecure and in danger of falling into a meaningless void. Projects for the self are a way of transforming an amorphous and oppressive indeterminate and meaningless potential into an object of commitment and a source for a meaningful and secure identity. It is, of course, possible to transcend the meaningless void rather than escape it through project intentionality. But this would require a discarding of the ontology of subject–object separation that reflects and reproduces individualized conceptions of identity. This could then result in a 'social identity' that is not simply or primarily a source for security, as is the case with the three forms of identity discussed by Castells (1997). *Social identity* is not dependent for its construction, sustenance or transformation on any one single institution, discursive practice or social movement but polymorphous with respect to its own self-reflexive reproduction. It is probably a necessary condition of the struggle 'against the submission of subjectivity' (Foucault, 1982: 213). In terms of postmodern ideas, social identity is multiple, flexible, fragmented and transformational. Having said that, social identity cannot be seen to exist anywhere in pure form as if uncontaminated by the anxieties and insecurities that emanate from the desire to control individualized identities.

Power and subjectivity in organizational analysis

Table 1.2 above helps us to see the whole of Foucault's work in a much-condensed form and below Table 1.3 develops this to show how organizational analysis can readily be inserted into the Foucaldian edifice without creating too much distortion. For there is little difficulty in understanding the history of management and organization as involving the three issues that have absorbed Foucault throughout his work – power, knowledge and subjectivity. In relating these to management and organization, it is clear that control, productivity and motivation are their managerial equivalents and that the major historical perspectives can be examined in relation to them, as follows:

Theory	Focus or Perspective		
Foucault	Power	Knowledge/truth	Subjectivity/ethics
Managerial	Control	Productivity	Motivation
Technical	Classical (e.g. Fayol)	Scientific Management (Taylor)	Group Theory (e.g. Sayles)
Social	Classical (e.g. Barnard)	Population Ecology (e.g. Hannan and Freeman)	Human Relations (e.g. Mayo)
Institutional	Bureaucracy (Weber)	Market competition (e.g. Williamson)	Internal market (e.g. Quality Management)
Integrated	Global Corporatism	Knowledge Management	Job insecurity

Table 1.3: History of management and organizational analysis

An integrated perspective in organization theory

There is not space here to discuss each of the perspectives outlined in Table 1.3, and indeed such a discussion would be quite tedious since most of the theories will be familiar to the reader. The main purpose of the diagram is to demonstrate the overlap between the three concepts that have preoccupied Foucault and the concerns of management and organization theory. However, the last, integrated, perspective is less familiar so there is some rationale in discussing this as a way of illustrating the intelligibility of the links being drawn. An example of an integrated development empirically, in the form of multi-divisionalization, and in the literature in the form of transaction-cost analysis (Williamson, 1994), is the transition from bureaucracy to market. This can be seen as an institutional strategy for integrating control, productivity and motivation. Multi-divisionalization involves a restructuring of the very large (often global or multi-national) corporation into a series of smaller business units. This internal construction of separate businesses subjected to the vagaries of the market is to prevent them from hiding behind the oligopolistic conditions of their bureaucratic parent. Operating as a profit-centre in its own right, each unit is seen to benefit from the discipline of the market even to the extent of acting as a supplier or buyer to its own sister units within the overall corporation. Largely because of the domination of an economics or institutional framework, there is a paucity of empirical research in this field attempting to make the links suggested here. However, it may be argued that the multi-divisional corporation is a precursor of global corporate control, where employees live constantly under the threat that production can always be moved to a low cost, low conflict labour market anywhere in the world. It is also the case that such organizations become knowledge-intensive and adept in team working as a means of sustaining the levels of productivity and motivation necessary to remain part of the corporation and not be sold off to the best bidder. Knowledge management in the context of market pressure is an effective way of ensuring control at a distance whilst team working facilitates self-discipline and employee motivation at the sharp end of the production process.

But Foucault's view that wherever there is power there is also resistance suggests that the earlier model needs to be superimposed on the analysis of organization and management. To take the last category of the global corporation as a typical development of the integrated approach to management, we can perhaps examine the concept of resistance. Is the multi-divisional organization capable of displacing any potential resistance? Organizational researchers have always found examples of resistance to control, productivity and motivation but, within the literature, this is conventionally theorized in terms of the conflicting material or economic interests of management and the workforce. Without undervaluing such research, the model produced here suggests an additional and complementary analysis, where it is argued that resistance occurs also because of a defence or expression of identity.

Whilst this is speculative, it may be expected that within the global corporation asset specificity (i.e. restrictions in the mobility and flexibility of fixed capital including specialist skills) would limit the degree to which control could be the principal strategy for managing employees. However, employees may work more productively and efficiently than might otherwise be the case if there were not the potential threat[4] of switching production to low cost/low conflict economies. Yet even in the absence of such threats in non-global corporations, we have found that employees work productively and efficiently partly because their identity is tied up in so doing (Knights and McCabe, 1997, 1999). As suggested earlier, employees may resist management not because of an escape from, so much as an escape into, work and/or the corporation.

From a Marxist perspective, resistance is invariably seen as a reflection of a conflict of material interests where management is simply the symbolic representation of wage exploitation. But employee accusations of management incompetence cannot always or necessarily be viewed in this manner. As was intimated earlier, often employees resist because managers are seen as incompetent in providing the material and symbolic support necessary for production to operate efficiently. For efficient production can be seen as providing both material and symbolic security for employees.

Organizations (especially those of global proportions) are increasingly managing through productivity and motivation rather than control and, therefore, knowledge management and team working are pre-eminent. Where team working is effective, the collaborative spirit on the shop or office floor provides mutual social support for employees to resist managers who constrain employees from doing their jobs to the best of their abilities. When knowledge management is a key to productivity and employees see their security linked in some way to performance, they become highly critical if managers get it wrong or their knowledge is inadequate. This occurs quite frequently where there is a failure to draw on the practical knowledge that employees employ routinely, a problem that is difficult for managers to overcome, particularly when this knowledge is tacit rather than explicit.

It is for this reason that resistance sometimes takes the form of what postmodernists describe as ironic and playful distancing from work activities. This may have parallels with the kind of mental distancing described by Palm (1970) and Sennett and Cobb (1977) to account for subordinates seeking to protect their dignity against its erosion within relations of power and inequality. But it has perhaps more connection with the role distancing described by Goffman (1961), where the display of distance is intended to demonstrate superiority as when older children ride on a carousel. For in perceiving managers to be struggling and failing in strategies of 'knowledge management', employees can genuinely feel superior. Accordingly, jokes, laughter and ridicule at the expense of management can help sustain their identity (Collinson, 1992). However, where the effects of 'bad' management affect production to the point of threatening job security, employee humour and irony can quickly turn into direct criticism of, and resistance to, managers' practices. Again we have numerous examples of this in organizations that have not acquired global status but it is speculative as to whether larger and more powerful corporations could contain, deflect or even eradicate such resistance. For the reasons given, I very much doubt this possibility.

Confronting some problems

In this final section, I am concerned to focus on some lacunae or difficulties in the work both of Foucault and organization studies. The first problem is the humanism to which organization studies on the whole subscribes, but Foucault rejects. This leads on to a discussion of epistemology, which organization studies has neglected, with limited exceptions (e.g. Burrell and Morgan, 1979; McIntyre, 1981; Knights, 1995, 1997; Hatch, 1997). Foucault, on the other hand, focused very heavily on epistemology in his early work only to marginalize it later in favour of studies of discursive practices and power–knowledge relations. It is a central argument of this chapter that, while ostensibly dismissive of his early explorations, Foucault remained faithful to the epistemological location of his own work. Finally, I provide a brief discussion of problems of gender and sexual inequality, which again proves to be an ambivalent issue within Foucault's work but of marginal concern to mainstream, and to some extent even of critical, organization studies. With each of these problems, space allows me only to scratch the surface of what would be necessary to do justice to their importance.

Humanism[5]

Discipline and Punish concentrates largely on one aspect of Foucault's thesis on the impact of the humanities and humanistic thinking on human subjects. It focuses particularly on the way that individuals are marked out, categorized or classified through the use of case files and documentary evidence, which has the effect of rendering them individualized, often docile but definitely manageable. This individualization process, however, occurs also through the imposition of autonomy within humanistic regimes. Although not explicitly articulated, humanism promotes a human-centred world where individuals are seen as autonomous subjects, as well as the agents and objects of knowledge (Foucault, 1980).

Humanism also carries with it an ethical imperative, which separates individuals off from one another, forces them back on their own resources, and insists that they be responsible for themselves (Foucault, 1982: 212). This is at the heart of 'free'-market economics, the Protestant work ethic and the American Dream's individual desire for financial success. It was especially highlighted during the New Right era of Anglo-American politics but continues to eschew any form of dependency, rendering it tantamount to being pre- or sub-human; only children and the physically or mentally ill can be legitimately dependent. The individualizing discourse that results compels individuals to seek out the truth of their own identity through, for example, the confession, psychoanalysis or therapy (Foucault, 1979).

In the organizational studies literature, both defenders (e.g. Sewell and Wilkinson, 1992; Barker, 1993; Steingard and Fitzgibbons, 1993) and critics (e.g. Thompson and Ackroyd, 1995; Ezzy, 1997) of Foucault take his conception of power to be totalizing. Disregarding the subtleties of Foucault's analysis, the defenders believe that subjects are mere passive reflections of power/knowledge discourses. In the organizational studies literature, this deterministic account of Foucault has begun to claim orthodoxy[6] so much so that the critics of Foucault use it against him. This reading of Foucault then leads theorists either to support or criticize a notion of management as omniscient/omnipotent. Whilst sympathetic to the critic's rejection of a view of management as omnipotent or omniscient, their criticism is only applicable to some deterministic uses of Foucault, not to Foucault himself.

Both these supporters and critics miss altogether the form of power/knowledge that Foucault identifies as having the most virulent and all-embracing impact on humankind. This is the discourse of humanism, which since the nineteenth century, has effectively redesigned human subjectivity. Foucault's anti-humanism led him to believe that the most subtle form of discipline was indeed the demand that humanism places on us all to be individually self-referential, a target of others' judgements and responsible for our own subjective well-being. Although Foucault (1980) was always aware that power will be resisted, he was more troubled by humanism because it lay at the very root of our knowledge of life (i.e. body and soul), labour (i.e. production and consumption) and language (i.e. speech and communication) in the modern era. The individualizing effect of humanism works on three levels. First it operates *philosophically* to impose upon individuals a sense of their own autonomy. Second, it is *political* in keeping case records on individuals for purposes of administering and managing them. Third it functions *ethically* to turn individuals into subjects who feel responsible for themselves and their subjective well being. These effects may be seen as so exhaustive as to virtually preclude any possibility of resistance and this would appear to fuel Foucault's anti-humanism.[7]

This is the basis for his argument that we have to resist what we have become 'through the refusal of this kind of individuality which has been imposed on us for several centuries' (Foucault, 1982: 216). His opposition to psychotherapy was precisely because he saw it as a reflection of humanistic discipline, which plays the trick of making us obsessed with discovering our 'true' selves, as if there were an essential origin of identity that we could discover. As he puts it, 'the target nowadays is not to discover what we are, but to refuse what we are' (ibid.). In resisting the humanistic self of autonomy and individualism, Foucault (1986) sought to construct a new ethical and aesthetic conception of subjectivity where individuals were to treat the self like a work of art, a life project that was not so far from the 'managed self' of humanism. This reflects and reproduces the ambivalence and ambiguity surrounding the notion of human rights and the Enlightenment (Foucault, 1984).

Elsewhere (Knights, 2000) I have argued that while a defence of autonomy is problematic in that it reflects and reinforces a discourse of individualism, it is dangerous to be against autonomy *per se*, for some semblance of autonomy is necessary in order to criticize precisely those discursive practices of autonomy that are individualistic in their effects. So just as Foucault (1984) was ambivalent in his relationship to Enlightenment reason, we might be best advised neither to be absolutely for nor against autonomy.

Foucault's critique of humanism was based on his view that it could be seen as the greatest confinement and simplest method of incarceration since, under its auspices, 'self-formation is reduced to self-subjugation' (Bernauer, 1993: 9).

However, his ambivalence derived from an equal conviction that the Enlightenment, which to a considerable degree had served to translate humanistic values into institutional practice, was our only hope since it had 'aspirations for a permanent critique of the present age' (Bernauer, 1993: 8).

Epistemology

Foucault concentrated on epistemological issues in what is known as his archaeological period where he was concerned with identifying or uncovering common features underlying a wide range of diverse and discontinuous sets of discourses. In his most famous archaeological text, *The Order of Things: An Archaeology of the Human Sciences*, Foucault (1973) focused on the historical, social and philosophical rules and regularities (or the 'unconscious of knowledge'). These rules, Foucault argues, underlie the formation of the human sciences but ordinarily elude the conscious awareness of the scientist. In particular, he was concerned with showing how a set of classical disciplines, apparently as distinct and discrete as grammar, political economy and natural history, shared a set of rules and procedures for rendering statements true. Foucault's emphasis was on the transition to modernism, or 'when man [sic] constituted himself in Western culture as that which must be conceived of and that which is to be known' and, thereby, became 'the object of science' (1973: 345). This was when the classical disciplines closest to human life were transformed as theorists began to generate representations of a linguistic, economic and biological nature drawn from objectified observations of speaking, producing and living subjects, respectively. As 'an event in the order of knowledge' (ibid.), this transformation involved human beings becoming the objects as well as the subjects or agents of knowledge. It is an event that underlies the 'perpetual controversy between the sciences of man and the sciences proper – the first laying an invincible claim to be the foundation of the second' (ibid.), while having some difficulty with regard to their own foundation and justification.

This difficulty is even greater for the management and organizational sciences, which emulate the rules and procedures of positive knowledge (e.g. biology, economics and linguistics). Although biology, for example, may have been subjected to political manipulation (e.g. the Lysenko affair), management knowledge is never independent of the power that managers and their corporations exercise. But as Rabinow (1986: 10) made clear, Foucault 'never intended to isolate discourse from the social practices that surround it'; those who examine these newer disciplines, therefore, must also draw on insights deriving from a genealogical analysis.

In his archaeological period, Foucault investigated the rules and procedures that make it possible for writers within a number of discrete and disparate disciplines to make statements that claimed the status of truth. In his genealogical investigations, by contrast, analogous discourses and institutions were shown to engage a multiplicity of unconnected strategies and tactics in exercising their power over subjects. Foucault explored the various conditions that rendered it possible for these 'technologies of power' to emerge historically. Genealogy contrasts sharply with conventional history, which in emulating the methods of the positive sciences focuses on the historical event as developing sequentially through time and space and subject to a 'discoverable' set of causal determinants which preceded it. The assumption underlying such an analysis is the Enlightenment, and particularly the Hegelian idea that history unfolds in a unilinear and 'progressive' manner and that its course is strongly influenced by particular individuals (the 'great man' thesis).

Foucault countered these views first by suggesting that institutions and the discourses surrounding them often emerge out of a series of accidents and arbitrary or superficial localized events. So, for example, Foucault (1979: 191) traced the 'birth of the sciences of man' not to major philosophical breakthroughs in the great academies but to such 'lowly' events as the development of files and records constituting 'the individual as a describable, analysable object' (Foucault, 1979: 190) within institutions of correction, mental asylums, hospitals and schools. Foucault's second counter to conventional history was to remove all trace of the human subject from the centre of his analysis: he argued that social practices and their discursive formations are independent of those who speak for them (Foucault, 1973, 1979a). By this, Foucault did not mean to imply that the intentions of subjects are non-existent but merely that their outcomes in aggregated sets of social practices are wholly independent of what was intended (see Dreyfus and Rabinow, 1982).

The discourses of psychiatry, medicine and the human sciences and the institutional practices (e.g. internment, hospitalization, imprisonment) in which they are embedded may be seen as methods for dividing up populations between 'the mad and the sane, the sick and the healthy, the criminals and the "good boys"' (Foucault, 1982: 208). In short, these disciplines and institutions exercise power through the 'normalizing' procedures of exclusion and surveillance whereby 'deviants' (e.g. the sick, paupers, criminals) are physically separated and the 'incompetent' marginalized through hierarchical distinction.[8]

By examining those discourses claiming the status of science, Foucault clearly focused on the conditions of subjectivity that made it possible, for example, to generate representations of a linguistic, economic and biological nature, and thus objectify speaking, producing and living subjects, respectively. If, as I have been suggesting, we write organization theory into Foucault, our studies will also occupy the space that lies between the representations of the positive sciences of biology, economics and linguistics and the subjectivity that makes those representations possible. Biology provides increasingly more secure representations, culminating in accounts of the genetic and molecular structure of the body. Economics represents exchange in terms of complex supply-demand market structures in which competition and efficiency are seen to be in a relationship of mutual dependency and reinforcement. Linguistics represents the language we speak in terms of semiotic structures in which metaphor and metonymy or semantic and syntactical relations are explored. None of these disciplines ever speak about the subjectivity that is the condition of their possibility – it is simply taken for granted.

Each of these examples of positive knowledge supplies its representations of structures at least at one remove from the subjectivities of the humans that make them possible. Some might want to argue that the remaining social sciences fill in some of the gaps left by these positive knowledges and others may suggest that we can simply study the subjectivities themselves. Psychology tends towards the latter but converts subjectivity into another set of positive representations that refuses to see a precarious space between externalities and the subject, both of which have become elements of a 'pure' representational world – subjects and bodies, and language as well as exchange. Filling in the gaps is another common strategy and results in a proliferation of positive discourses that seek an exhaustive inclusion of everything that can be represented. Management and organization studies and a large range of sub-disciplines such as human resources, information systems, marketing operations and strategy tend to take this form.

Two problems can be seen as arising from this proliferation of positive knowledge that specializes on smaller and smaller parts of 'reality'. First is the problem of representing ever-diminishing divisions of the world and analysing them as if they were discrete independent entities with little or no connection to one another. Understanding would appear to become inversely related to the multiplicity of narrow yet discrete representations.[9] Second is the problem of what to do with the representations once they have been constructed since it is not clear that a change in the object of enquiry guarantees a distinctive scientific mode of analysis. These sub-disciplines readily become inferior offspring of the discipline closest to their focus – economics, mathematics, psychology or sociology. Foucault is distinctive in that whilst he perhaps thought he had abandoned his earlier interest in epistemology in his later writings, he adhered to an approach of studying a whole series of events from within the space that lies in between positive representations and the subjectivity that makes them possible. This is what makes his work so distinctive and attractive to a vast range of discourses from philosophy to literary criticism and from politics to organization studies. It is another reason for wanting to write organizational analysis into Foucault and not the other way around. For as I have already intimated, Foucault can be appropriated *without his radical way of thinking affecting the appropriator*. Appropriating Foucault for organizational analysis is guaranteed to miss the distinctive appeal of his radical departure from dominant epistemological paradigms. This takes us to the subject of sexuality where, it could be argued, Foucault has been most radical and sometimes 'outrageous' in transgressing normalization.

Gender, sexuality and inequality

It could be argued that it is only when existing subjectivities are reflected upon and/or rejected that discourse begins to recognize itself to be in the radical space between representations and their conditions of possibility. Feminism and perhaps discourses on masculinity are two such areas and thereby of specific value in seeking to write organization theory into Foucault. While there are several supporters of Foucault in these areas, there is also a backlash that is questioning the relevance of Foucault for the project of gender and sexual equality. This is a large and continuing debate and I therefore only scratch the surface, but I would argue that here as in organization theory, in order to benefit from Foucault's insights, there has to be a radical break with the epistemological and political past.

I suggest that the central questions revolve around whether and/or how Foucault's anti-humanist discourse can contribute to radical transformations around the issue of gender, sexuality and other inequalities. Those antagonistic to Foucault argue that the decentring or fragmentation of the subject leaves feminism and other radical movements (e.g. gay liberation, minority ethnic groups, the disabled) in a dilemma since traditionally these movements have sought to emancipate their target groups. If being a woman, an ethnic or disabled minority is not a unified or homogenous experience shared by members of the category, then the basis for emancipation becomes elusive if not illusory. In the following discussion, I will concentrate on gender and sexuality but the arguments would be perfectly applicable to other minority groups and radical movements.

Not only is the target of feminism – female emancipation – rendered obsolete but also the active agent of its realization can no longer be seen as unproblematic. Worse still as McNay (1992: 1) points out, the suspension of 'concepts such as truth, freedom and rationality' undermine the very idea of 'emancipatory political projects which necessarily rest on certain "metaphysical" assumptions about what constitutes oppression and freedom'. Benhabib (1992), for example, cannot accept those postmodern ideas that deny a space for an active subject as the agent and recipient of feminist demands for emancipation. For, she argues, this would undermine the reason for, and the content of, a feminist politics. We can endorse her aim of introducing a 'gendered' perspective upon modernist narratives that are often oblivious of such dimensions. However, Benhabib's defence of a feminist politics is in danger of sliding into the essentialism that many feminists have been at pains to dismiss from their discourse. This is because she seeks to universalize the liberal/humanist ideal of the autonomy-striving subject for purposes of preserving what she considers to be the necessary conditions of emancipation. What she seems to ignore is how the belief in an autonomous subject whether in the form of the individual, nation state, race, class or sex has fuelled and fashioned the history of systems of domination against which feminism and other radical movements have sought to struggle. Benhabib (1992) attempts to replace the death of the Subject, History and Metaphysics that are perpetrated by postmodernism by what she terms weaker versions but, in many ways, this simply leads her back to a humanistic defence of the autonomous self (Knights, 1997, 2000). She cannot then avoid the problems of essentialism and dualism that she has been so concerned to eradicate from feminist discourse (Knights, 1992, 2000).

As I have already argued, rejecting autonomy outright is probably as dangerous as defending it to the (or against its) death. But another way of looking at this might be to ask whether the Enlightenment truly delivered on the autonomous self or whether its discourse effectively diverted us from critically examining its own claims. One aspect of autonomy, as handed down to us by the Enlightenment, is its disembodied and cerebral character – a force that readily leaves us ill-equipped to examine the target of much disciplinary and governmental power. For, as Foucault has repeatedly claimed, it is the body that is targeted by modern regimes of power. Moreover, the prevalence of cognition in liberal humanistic discourses of autonomy desensitizes us to any alternative, thereby failing to alert us to how we have been disciplined through our bodies. 'Power in the institutions that developed through the nineteenth century tended to act not so much on the mind and its representations as on the body and its gestures, not so much on reasoning as on doing' (McWhorter, 1999: 72). Yet humanistic critics of Foucault still want his defenders to provide a purely cognitive and rational justification for abandoning humanism. This is the kind of double bind that expects anti-humanists to provide justification for their position precisely from within the universal rationality of the very humanism they critique. As Foucault (1984: 42) has argued, this is blackmail because it refuses to allow us to use humanism, the Enlightenment or autonomy against itself. It also renders humanism 'inaccessible to critique, since the only critique it would accept would be one carried out under the terms it imposes and controls' (McWhorter, 1999: 71). The blackmail forces us out of the space between representations of, for example, gender, sexuality or race and the conditions of subjectivity that make such subjugating representations possible. This leaves us incapable of standing outside, reflecting and perhaps refusing the subjectivities that these representations force upon us. Writing organization, and perhaps other, studies into Foucault will make this imposition of certain subjectivities increasingly impossible to sustain. The discourse of postmodern organization is possibly a fruitful vehicle for this refusal to accept the rules and representations of the past, even though we know them to give comfort, security and stability.

Notes

1 This switch from theory to analysis is not accidental – it is part of a systematic attempt to move the study of organizations away from the positivistic tendency to see its enterprise as a historically progressive contribution to theory production that is tested through empirical analysis. The change of nomenclature reflects a move towards the integration of thinking about, observing, and representing what we study as a continuous challenge that has no stable and inviolable set of principles or findings upon which to draw for security.

2 However, in one sense, I am simply following Foucault's (1980, 1982) own tendency to re-define at each stage of his development what he had been up to all along.

3 This is paralleled in Foucault's (1982: 213) argument that 'nowadays, the struggle against the forms of subjection – against the submission of subjectivity – is becoming more and more important, even though the struggles against forms of domination and exploitation have not disappeared'.

4   The analogy with the panopticon discussed earlier can be drawn here for it is not the exercise of power so much as the threat of its exercise that brings about self-discipline.
5   This sub-section draws on Knights and McCabe (2000).
6   Some critics argue that that surveillance and control enabled by an electronic panopticon is much greater than Sewell and Wilkinson suggest (Webster and Robbins, 1993).
7   It is partly because humanism appears as the greatest confinement that Foucault (1973, 1977a) launches along the path of establishing an anti-humanist alternative to the history of knowledge. This demonstrates how history proceeds not 'progressively', as a continuity emanating from a sovereign human consciousness, but as a result of discursive formations, displacements, discontinuities and transformations.
8   These last few paragraphs have drawn heavily on Knights (1992).
9   It is this largely that leads to rhetorical demands for interdisciplinary studies (Knights and Willmott, 1997).

References

Barker, J.R. (1993) 'Tightening the iron cage: concertive control in self-managing teams', *Administrative Science Quarterly*, 38: 408–37.

Benhabib, S. (1992) *Situating the Subject*. London: Sage.

Bernauer, J.W. (1992) *Michel Foucault's Force of Flight: Toward an Ethics for Thought*. London: Prometheus Books.

Burrell, G. (1984) 'Sex and organizational analysis', *Organization Studies*, 5 (2): 97–118.

Burrell, G. and Hearn, J. (eds) (1989) *The Sexuality of Organization*. London: Sage.

Burrell, G. and Morgan, G. (1979) *Sociological Paradigms and Organizational Analysis*. London: Heinemann.

Calás, M. and Smircich, L. (1992) 'Rewriting gender into organization theorising: directions from feminist perspectives', in M. Reed and M. Hughes (eds), *Rethinking Organization: New Directions in Organization Theory and Analysis*. London: Sage.

Castells, M. (1997) *The Power of Identity – The Information Age: Economy, Society and Culture*, Vol. 2. Oxford: Blackwell.

Collinson, D. (1992) *Managing the Shopfloor: Subjectivity, Masculinity and Workplace Culture*. Berlin: de Gruyter.

Cooper, R. and Burrell, G. (1988) 'Modernism, postmodernism and organizational analysis: an introduction', *Organization Studies*, 9 (3): 91–112.

Dean, M. (1994) *Critical and Effective Histories: Foucault's Methods and Historical Sociology*. London: Routledge.

Dreyfus, H.L. and Rabinow, P. (eds) (1982) *Michel Foucault: Beyond Structuralism and Hermeneutics I*. Brighton: Harvester Press.

Ezzy, D. (1997) 'Subjectivity and the labour process: conceptualising "good work"', *Sociology*, 31 (3) August: 427–44.

Foucault, M. (1973) *The Order of Things: An Archaeology of the Human Sciences*. New York: Vintage Books.

Foucault, M. (1977) 'Nietzsche, genealogy, history', in D. B. Bouchard (ed.), *Language, Counter-memory, Practice*. Oxford: Basil Blackwell.

Foucault, M. (1977a) *Madness and Civilisation*. London: Tavistock.

Foucault, M. (1979) *The History of Sexuality Vol.1: An Introduction*. Harmondsworth: Penguin.

Foucault, M. (1979a) *Discipline and Punish*. Harmondsworth: Penguin.

Foucault, M. (1980) 'Truth and power', in *Power/Knowledge: Selected Interviews and Other Writings 1972–7*, ed. and trans. M. Gordon. London: Tavistock. pp. 109–33. Reprinted in P. Rabinow (ed.) (1984) *The Foucault Reader*. Harmondsworth: Penguin. pp. 51–75.

Foucault, M. (1982) 'The subject and power' in H. L. Dreyfus and P. Rabinow, *Beyond Structuralism and Hermeneutics*. Brighton, Sussex: Harvester Press.

Foucault, M. (1984) 'What is enlightenment?', in P. Rabinow (ed.), *The Foucault Reader*. Harmondsworth: Penguin. pp. 32–50.

Foucault, M. (1985) *The Uses of Pleasure*. New York: Pantheon.

Foucault, M. (1986) *The Care of the Self*. New York: Pantheon.

Goffman, E. (1961) *Role Distance*. New York: Bobbs Merrill.

Hatch, M. J. (1997) *Organization Theory*. Oxford: Oxford University Press.

Knights, D. (1992) 'Changing spaces: the disruptive power of epistemological location for the management and organizational sciences', *Academy of Management Review*, 17 (3), July: 514–36.

Knights, D. (1995) 'Refocusing the case study: the politics of research and researching politics in IT management', *Technology Studies*, 2 (2): 230–84, published April 1996.

Knights, D. (1997) 'Organization theory in the age of deconstruction: dualism, gender and postmodernism revisited', *Organization Studies*, 18 (1), January/February: 1–19.

Knights, D. (2000) 'Autonomy-retentiveness! Problems and prospects for a post-humanist feminism', *Journal of Management Inquiry*, 9 (2): 173–86.

Knights, D. and Collinson, D. (1987) 'Disciplining the Shopfloor: a comparison of the disciplinary effects of managerial psychology and financial accounting', *Accounting, Organizations and Society*, 12 (5): 457–77.

Knights, D. and McCabe, D. (1997) '"How would you measure something like that?" Quality in a retail bank', *Journal of Management Studies*, 34 (3), May: 371–88.

Knights, D. and McCabe, D. (1999) '"There are no limits to authority"? TQM and organizational power relations', *Organization Studies*, 20 (2): 197–224.

Knights, D. and McCabe, D. (2000a) '"Ain't misbehavin?": opportunities for resistance under new forms of "quality" management', *Sociology*, 34 (3): 421–36.

Knights, D. and McCabe, D. (forthcoming) 'Foucault', in R. Batt (ed.), 'Critical perspectives on teams: a debate on alternatives to conventional interpretations', *Organization*.

Knights, D. and Morgan, G. (1991) 'Corporate strategy, organizations and subjectivity: a critique', *Organization Studies*, 12 (2): 251–73.

Knights, D. and Murray, F. (1994) *Managers Divided: Organisational Politics and Information Technology Management*. London: Wiley.

Knights, D. and Willmott, H. C. (1989) 'Power and subjectivity at work: from degradation to subjugation in social relations', *Sociology*, 23 (4): 535–58.

Knights, D. and Willmott, H. (1997) 'The hype and hope of inter-disciplinary management studies', *British Journal of Management*, 8 (1): 9–22.

McIntyre, A. (1981) *After Virtue: A Study in Moral Theory*. London: Duckworth.

McKinlay, A. and Starkey, K. (eds) (1998) *Foucault, Management and Organization Theory*. London: Sage.

McNay, L . (1992) *Foucault and Feminism*. Cambridge: Polity.

McWhorter, L. (1999) *Bodies and Pleasures: Foucault and the Politics of Sexual Normalization*. Bloomington and Indianapolis: Indiana University Press.

Miller, P. (1987) *Domination and Power*. London: Routledge Kegan Paul.

Palm, G. (1970) *The Flight from Work*. Cambridge: Cambridge University Press.

Rabinow, P. (ed.) (1986) *The Foucault Reader*. Harmondsworth: Penguin.

Rose, N. (1989) *Governing the Soul: the Shaping of the Private Self*. London: Routledge.

Sennett, R. (1986) *Authority*. London: Secker and Warburg.

Sennett, R. and Cobb, J. (1977) *The Hidden Injuries of Class*. Cambridge: Cambridge University Press.

Sewell, G. and Wilkinson, B. (1992) 'Someone to watch over me: surveillance, discipline and the just-in-time labour process', Sociology, 26 (2), May: 271–91.

Steingard, D.S. and Fitzgibbons, D.E. (1993) 'A postmodern deconstruction of Total Quality Management (TQM)', Journal of Organizational Change Management, 6 (5), 27–42.

Sturdy, A. (1992) 'Clerical consent: "shifting work" in the insurance office', in A. Sturdy, D. Knights and H. Willmott (eds), Skill and Consent. London: Routledge.

Thompson, P. and Ackroyd, S. (1995) 'All quiet on the workplace front?: A critique of recent trends in British Industrial Sociology', *Sociology*, 29 (4): 615–33.

Touraine, A. (1995) 'De la globalizacion al policentrismo', *El Pais*, July 24.

Webster, F. and Robins, K. (1993) '"I'll be watching you": comment on Sewell and Wilkinson', *Sociology*, 27 (2): 243–52.

Williamson, O. E. (1987) *The Economic Institutions of Capitalism Firms, Markets, Relational Contracting*. New York: Free Press.

3

Jacques Derrida

Campbell Jones

Introduction: possibilities of deconstruction

There can be no question here of offering a comprehensive summary of, or commentary on, Derrida's work or of the way that it has been taken up in organization studies. Even if this was our goal, we would immediately be confronted by the simple mechanics of size – Derrida's work includes more than forty books, as well as innumerable essays, lectures and interviews. These works cover a wide range of topics, from phenomenology to literature, psychoanalysis, art, architecture, politics and ethics, and stretch across the Western philosophical, literary and social scientific traditions. Even when couched in terms of a 'deconstruction of the history of Western metaphysics', this is an enormous project, and the size of Derrida's *oeuvre* reflects the enormity of that project.

We confront a similar obstacle when we consider the various ways that Derrida's work has been taken up in organization studies. Derrida was first evoked in organization studies in the early 1980s, with early mentions by Cooper (1984) and Turner (1983) in relation to structure and structuring processes followed by more detailed treatments by Frug (1984), who drew on concepts from Derrida to critique some of the stories that legitimate bureaucracy in legal discourse, and Gowler and Legge (1984a, 1984b) beginning to deconstruct evaluation research in personnel management. Soon after, Hoskin and Macve (1986) drew on Derrida in their framing of accounting as a form of writing, and Cooper (1986, 1990) outlined a deconstruction of the boundaries of organization and of the relation between organization and disorganization.

Through the 1990s interest in Derrida expanded rapidly, with a number of authors following Derrida in the 'deconstruction' of various aspects of organization. For some this involved deconstructing the 'classic texts' of organization studies. Mumby and Putnam (1992) exposed the devaluation of physical labour and femininity in the concept of bounded rationality outlined in Herbert Simon's *Administrative Behavior* (1945), and Kilduff (1993) identified certain unexamined classical residues in March and Simon's critique of classical organization theory in *Organization* (1958). Other writers offered deconstructive readings of specific texts in order to offer alternative readings of accounting (Arrington and Francis, 1989), organizational leadership (Calás and Smircich, 1991), decision making (Chia, 1994, 1996: 193–215), information systems (Beath and Orlikowski, 1994) and organizational behaviour (Summers et al., 1997).

Others followed Derrida in expanding the concept of 'text' beyond the conventional borders of the book, and began to deconstruct foundational concepts across broader textual domains. Hence, various authors began to deconstruct the grounds of organizational culture (Linstead and Grafton-Small, 1992), organizational ethnography (Linstead, 1993a, 1993b), charismatic leadership (Calás, 1993), Total Quality Management (Steingard and Fitzgibbbons, 1993; Xu, 1999), marketing (Fischer and Bristor, 1994), globalization (Steingard and Fitzgibbbons, 1995), transaction cost economics (Noorderhaven, 1995), Human Resource Management (Legge, 1995: 307ff., 1996), Business Process Re-engineering (Boje et al., 1997) and business ethics (Letiche, 1998; Willmott, 1998).

Whilst many writers worked with published texts in organization studies, others used concepts from Derrida in relation to examples of language occurring in organizations. Martin (1990), Mumby and Stohl (1991) and Gergen (1992: 219–20) proposed deconstructive readings of stories from everyday organizational settings, questioning and unsettling the assumptions upon which these stories rest. Boje exposed the contradictory nature of official texts produced at and by Disney enterprises (Boje, 1995) and Nike (Boje, 1998). Most recently we have seen deconstructions of a maternity leave policy (Peterson and Albrecht, 1999), a report by a manager in the UK National Health Service (Learmonth, 1999) and an autobiographical account of organizational life (Rhodes, 2000). In all of these works organizational 'texts' are opened up to possibilities of interpretation that go well beyond traditional ethnographic studies of organizational life.

Derrida's work has also had a considerable impact on debates about 'postmodernism' in organization studies. A number of commentators have introduced and recommended Derrida as offering a postmodern approach, to the point that it often appears that deconstruction is the postmodern method *par excellence* (see for example, Cooper and Burrell, 1988; Cooper, 1989; Parker, 1992; Hassard, 1993, 1994; Hassard and Parker, 1993; Chia, 1996; Alvesson and Deetz, 1996/1999; Kilduff and Mehra, 1997; Calás and Smircich, 1997, 1999). Derrida is often placed alongside other French thinkers of his generation, usually Foucault, Deleuze and Guattari, Baudrillard, Lyotard and Kristeva, as in this volume, and on the basis of this association is taken to share certain postmodern sensibilities. Derrida's work has been influential upon, at the same time as it was influenced by, these authors, and an understanding of Derrida is important for understanding the many diverse tendencies that are referred to by the term 'postmodernism'. At the same time, however, it would be foolish to associate Derrida simply or directly with postmodernism. Such an association would be problematic both because of the significant disagreements between Derrida and most of those labelled 'postmodernists' and also because of his explicit rejection of much that goes under the name of 'postmodernism'.[1]

In this chapter I will not attempt to comment comprehensively on all of these complex debates and developments. Rather, I will try to offer some entry points – at the same time as intervening in these debates – by marking some of the limits to the way that Derrida has been received in organization studies to date. I begin by setting the scene with a discussion of the emergence of the term 'deconstruction' in Derrida's work and then look at some of the adventures of deconstruction in organization studies. I consider three possibilities: (1) the possibility that deconstruction might be a 'method'; (2) the possibility that deconstruction might be negative or some form of 'critique'; and (3) the possibility that deconstruction might result in relativism or the 'indeterminacy of meaning'. The chapter concludes by outlining some of the developments in Derrida's most recent work, and discusses some of the possibilities that might be opened up by these developments.

What is deconstruction?

Although it was almost totally unknown fifty years ago, the word deconstruction is now widely used in everyday speech. It is a particularly popular term in academic circles, where it is used to describe almost any kind of critical analysis, in the sense that one might begin a class: 'and so today we will deconstruct X...'. It is commonly thrown into dinner-party conversation and liberal journalism, and its appeal has been used to market films (Woody Allen's *Deconstructing Harry*, 1997) and music (Meredith Brooks' CD *Deconstruction*, 1999, as well as the recording label 'DeConstruction Records'). Apparently television chef Jamie Oliver ('the Naked Chef') is a master of the 'deconstruction' of food. But deconstruction also refers to the quite specific practice of reading, interpreting and writing about texts, associated with the work of French philosopher Jacques Derrida, and it is this use that we will privilege here.

Derrida was born in Algeria in 1930. Coming to France shortly after the Second World War he studied philosophy in Paris at the Ecole Normale Supérieure. Upon graduating he taught at the Sorbonne and the Ecole Normale Supérieure, and at the time of writing is Director of Studies at the Ecole des Haute Etudes en Science Sociales in Paris and Professor of Humanities at the University of California at Irvine.[2] Between 1953 and 1954 Derrida wrote his Master's thesis on 'the problem of genesis' in the work of phenomenologist Edmund Husserl, which was followed by a number of essays on Husserl (Derrida, 1990b, 1962/1978, 1967/1973, 1967/1978: 229–51/154–68). In this early writing Derrida subjected Husserl's work to the kind of close and probing scrutiny which would later become recognized as typical of 'deconstruction', and asked questions which are now recognizably deconstructive, such as asking if, despite 'the rigor and subtlety of Husserl's analysis' it might 'nonetheless conceal a metaphysical presumption' (1967/1973: 2–3/4). In 1990, when his Master's thesis was published almost forty years after it was written, Derrida noted the continuity of themes from this early work on Husserl to his later work. He drew attention to the persistence of the concept of 'contamination', and the early argument that many of the oppositions and exclusions on which phenomenology rests – 'transcendental/"mundane", eidetic/empirical, intentional/non-intentional, active/passive, present/non-present, timely/untimely [ponctuel/non ponctuel], originary/derived, pure/impure' are subject to contamination at their point of origin (Derrida, 1990b: vii). These themes which appear in this early work foreshadow the development of what later came to be known as deconstruction.

In the 1960s Derrida published a series of essays on a range of authors and in 1967 the almost simultaneous publication of three books, *Speech and Phenomena*, *Writing and Difference* and *Of Grammatology* marked his definitive entry into French intellectual life. In the essays collected in the second half of *Writing and Difference*, and in particular in the first part of *Of Grammatology* we find probably the most systematic outline by Derrida of deconstruction as a coherent and unified 'theoretical matrix' (1967/1976: 7/lxxxix). Although he is suspicious of laying out a system or a method, he explains these developments in a later interview:

> [F]rom about 1963 to 1968, I tried to work out – in particular in the three works published in 1967 – what was in no way meant to be a system but rather a sort of strategic device, opening onto its own abyss, an unclosed, unenclosable [*non clôturable*], not wholly formalizable ensemble of rules for reading, interpretation and writing. (1980/1983: 446/40)

In these works of the late sixties, and in particular in *Of Grammatology* we first find Derrida talking of deconstruction. Derrida later hesitates to define deconstruction, and goes so far as to argue that 'All sentences of the type "deconstruction is X" or "deconstruction is not X", *a priori*, miss the point, which is to say that they are at the least false' (1983/1985: 392/7, emphasis in original). But at this early stage (and occasionally at some later stages) he offers some quite systematic outlines of what could easily be read as a 'programme' of deconstruction. In an interview at this time he offers the following formulation:

> To 'deconstruct' philosophy, thus, would be to think – in the most faithful, interior way – the structured genealogy of philosophy's concepts, but at the same time to determine – from a certain exterior that is unqualifiable or unnameable by philosophy – what this history has been able to dissimulate or forbid. (1972/1981b: 15/6)

Derrida is quite clear about why he chose the word 'deconstruction', or, as he prefers to say, how the word 'imposed itself' on him (1992/1995b: 225/211, 1983/1985: 388/1). 'Deconstruction' was a rare word, although it could be found in the dictionary *Littré*, and Derrida suggests a number of reasons for its suitability. It fitted with what Derrida was trying to do partly because 'it plays on several registers, for example linguistic or grammatical, but also mechanical or technical' (1992/1995b: 225/211). More importantly it bore resonance of debates about structuralism which were popular at that time, and in part was attractive because of the way that it was considered 'at the same time to be a structuralist and anti-structuralist gesture' (1992/1995b: 225/212).

The term deconstruction also made explicit reference to Heidegger's proposals about 'the task of a destructuring of the history of ontology' and of a 'destructuring of the traditional content of ancient ontology' (Heidegger, 1927/1962/1977: 27, 30/41, 44/63, 66).[3] This is a significant connection for Derrida, who makes constant reference to Heideggerian themes and texts throughout his work. Derrida describes the way that the word 'deconstruction' operated as 'a kind of active translation that displaces somewhat the word Heidegger uses: "Destruktion", the destructuring [*destruction*] of ontology, which also does not mean the annulment, the annihilation of ontology, but an analysis of the structure of traditional ontology' (1992/1995b: 226/212).

Derrida's writings of the sixties were soon to expand into an enormous *oeuvre* which set to work ideas emerging from his reading of Husserl and from the Heideggerian project of destructuring or deconstructing the grounds of the Western metaphysical tradition. A significant and influential intellectual movement emerged under the name of deconstruction, with Derrida as its central point. Here I will attempt to trace some of the movements of deconstruction, paying particular attention to the way that deconstruction emerged in organization studies and considering what deconstruction became in the process. Deconstruction, particularly in organization studies, has often been seen both by apologists and detractors as a method, as being negative towards its object, and involving some form of often paralysing relativism. We will therefore discuss each of these 'possibilities' in turn.

Deconstruction as method

Almost as soon as Derrida began publishing, and particularly following the translation of his work into English in the 1970s, commentators began to treat deconstruction as a 'method' which might be applied to a range of objects. Deconstruction took off first of all in departments of literary criticism, notably in the United States after the conference at Johns Hopkins University in 1966 at which Derrida announced his presence as a major world intellectual figure with his critique of structuralism, where in the hands of literary critics such as Geoffrey Hartman, J. Hillis Miller and Paul de Man, centred at Yale University, deconstruction became enormously popular, becoming *the* method for analysing or at least for describing the analysis of literature (see, for example, Bloom et al., 1979; *Genre*, 1984). Through the 1980s the philosophers joined the game – a little late, the 'tortoise to our hare' quips Bennington (1994: 11) – and deconstruction emerged both as a style of philosophy and a set of rules for reading philosophical texts (see, for example, Gasché, 1986; Norris, 1982, 1987).

A key point in the introduction for Derrida into organization studies came with the publication of an article on Derrida by Robert Cooper (1989) in the third of an influential series of papers on 'modernism, postmodernism and organizational analysis' (see also Cooper and Burrell, 1988; Burrell, 1988, 1994). Cooper argued for the importance of Derrida in the context of increasing interest in language and symbolism in the social sciences and organization studies, and suggested that 'Derrida's work holds much promise for the further development of the "symbolic turn" in organization theory' (1989: 480). As part of his efforts to establish the contribution of Derrida to organization studies Cooper offered what has become one of the most influential outlines of deconstruction.

On Cooper's account 'the text – any discourse, whether political, social, philosophical, etc. – is the field of operation of deconstruction. Derrida's object in deconstruction is to reveal the ambivalences, or, more accurately, the self-contradictions and double binds, that lie latent in any text' (1989: 481–2). For Cooper the target of deconstruction is *logocentrism*, which he defines as 'a structure with a fixed centre or point of origin that also censors (i.e. to "centre" is also to "censor") the self-errant tendencies in the text' (1989: 482). Logocentrism operates in the way that texts come to be structured around binary oppositions, through privileging one side of the binary over the other. Cooper identifies oppositions such as structure/process and organization/ disorganization, and more broadly 'good–evil, truth–error, man–woman, nature–culture, mind–matter, life–death, where the second term in each pair is regarded as the perverted, corrupt and therefore undesirable version of the first' (1986/1990: 313/180, see also 1989: 483). Logocentrism tries to create a pure and safe conceptual world, in which the second of these terms does not influence, impact or infect the former. Thus Cooper draws an analogy between logocentrism and what Norbert Elias (1978) has called 'the civilizing process', the process of 'cleaning up' and 'taming' (Cooper, 1989: 482), which creates – at the expense of the 'unclean' and the 'wild' – a pure and clear view of society.

Cooper frames deconstruction as a tool for identifying and questioning logocentric binaries. As a way of problematizing logocentrism, and also in order 'to prevent the possibility of logocentric incorporation, deconstruction employs a double movement of *overturning* and (what I shall call) *metaphorization*' (Cooper, 1989: 483, emphases in original). In his outline of deconstruction as a two phase movement, Cooper draws on Derrida's comments in 'The double session' (Derrida, 1972/1981a: 200–317/173–285) and explicitly on an interview in 1971 in which Derrida outlines deconstruction in terms of a 'double gesture' (1972/1981b: 56ff./41ff.). Derrida's explanation of this double gesture is worth citing at length:

> On the one hand, we traverse a phase of *overturning*. I insist strongly and constantly on the necessity of this phase of overturning, which some have perhaps too quickly tried to discredit. To do justice to this necessity is to recognise that in a classic philosophical opposition we are not dealing with the peaceful coexistence of a *vis-à-vis*, but rather with a violent hierarchy. One of the two terms governs the other (axiologically, logically, etc.), or has the upper hand. To deconstruct the opposition is, first of all, at a given moment, to overturn the hierarchy. To overlook this phase of overturning is to forget the conflictual and subordinating structure of the opposition. Therefore one might proceed too quickly to a *neutralization* that *in practice* would leave the previous field untouched, leaving one no hold on the previous opposition, thereby preventing any means of *intervening* in the field effectively ... on the other hand ... it is also necessary to mark the interval between inversion, which brings low what is high, and the irruptive emergence of a new 'concept', a concept that can no longer,

and never could be, included in the previous regime. (Derrida, 1972/1981b: 56–7/41–2, emphases in original)

Cooper (1986/1990) illustrates this double movement of deconstruction in his discussion of the opposition organization/disorganization. The point of his analysis is not simply to reverse or invert this binary, but to expose the way in which order and organization have been privileged in the social sciences, and particularly in organization studies, and to show that organization is not originary or natural but must be actively produced. So Cooper's deconstruction does not simply overturn the opposition organization/disorganization, but rather shows that disorganization is not a mere 'supplement' but is *constitutive* of organization, and that organization 'can only be "organized" or "systematized" through an external force that is wholly foreign to it' (1986/1990: 316/182). With the displacement or 'metaphorization' of the opposition organization/ disorganization comes the possibility of a conception of organization significantly different from that which has dominated the social sciences and organization studies.

Cooper does not extend his outline of deconstruction beyond sketching this two phase movement and offering examples of how deconstruction might work. In this he seems to follow Derrida's cautions about the dangers of reducing deconstruction to a method by boiling it down to a simple set of rules. Others taking up deconstruction in organization studies have, however, been tempted to find in deconstruction a set of methodological principles or rules. Calás, for example, identifies the four steps which 'all deconstructive analyses follow' (1993: 310), Boje outlines a 'seven-step deconstruction process' (Boje, 1998: 462; 2001: 21; Boje and Dennehy, 1993: 340), and Martin offers a summary of the nine 'analytic strategies used in deconstruction'. In Martin's summary deconstruction involves:

1. Dismantling a dichotomy, exposing it as false distinction
2. Examining silences – what is not said
3. Attending to disruptions and contradictions, places where the text fails to make sense
4. Focusing on the element that is most alien to a text or a context, as means of deciphering implicit taboos – the limits to what is conceivable or permissible
5. Interpreting metaphors as a rich source of multiple meanings
6. Analysing 'double-entendres' that may point to an unconscious subtext, often sexual in content
7. Separating group-specific and more general sources of bias by 'reconstructing' the text with iterative substitution of phrases
8. Exploring, with careful 'reconstructions', the unexpected ramifications and inherent limitations of minor policy changes
9. Using the limitations exposed by 'reconstruction' to explain the persistence of the status quo and the need for more ambitious change programmes. (Martin, 1990: 355)[4]

This type of summary could be useful, at least for the purposes of introducing readers to the broad contours of a certain form of deconstructive reading. Indeed, I have cited it here in its entirety because of the way that it offers an introductory orientation to deconstruction. It offers the kind of outline of 'method' expected in most areas of the contemporary social sciences, providing a simple set of steps which could then be mechanically applied by the social scientist. But at the same time as outlines such as this may be valuable, there are a number of dangers with formalizing deconstruction in this way. There is a danger of reducing deconstruction to the status of being *only* a method and failing to take into account the epistemological, ontological, political and ethical aspects of deconstruction, in addition to Derrida's distinctive mode of engagement with texts. There is also a danger that reading might be seen as an application which takes place from a position imagined to be 'outside' the text being read, from a position of safe exteriority, if not objectivity. Further, there is a danger that deconstruction would come to be seen as a method which might be 'applied' in the same way to all texts, rather than recognizing the need to move, adjust and change in relation to the text in question.[5]

Perhaps the presentation of deconstruction as a method might be thought of as a *pharmakon*, the word which Plato uses to describe writing and which, as Derrida (1972/1981a: 69–197/61–171) exposes, means both poison *and* cure. Derrida often exposes the way that things can be *both* this and that, when we usually only see the alternatives as either/or. So it might be useful to describe deconstruction as a method for the purposes of gaining a general orientation, but as should become clear, there is considerably more to deconstruction than a set of rules for the reading of texts. If we admit to this complexity then we might encounter one of the kinds of situation upon which Derrida invites us to reflect – where we cannot say either/or, or decide for or against whether we should describe deconstruction as a method or not. We have an encounter with an undecidable situation, where the description of deconstruction as method is necessary but impossible. Hence we might say that we *cannot not* describe deconstruction as a method, at the same time as we grapple with the dangers of doing so.

Negativity or affirmation? Deconstruction as/and critique

In addition to being understood as a method, deconstruction is often taken to be negative or oppositional to its object. Many see Derrida's efforts to overturn and displace metaphysical or logocentric assumptions to be a purely negative operation, and deconstruction is therefore seen to be a form of critique, if not as an extreme contemporary version of nihilism. In organization studies, while some authors caution against treating deconstruction as critique, and make efforts to distinguish deconstruction from destruction (Calás and Smircich, 1991: 569; Noorderhaven, 1995: 618; Legge, 1996: 1002), deconstruction has generally been treated as an oppositional or critical strategy. Many use the terms deconstruction and critique interchangeably, in such a way that an author will switch between talking of their work as deconstruction and as critique. To choose one from many possible examples, in the opening lines of his paper 'The concept of decision: a deconstructive analysis', Chia writes 'In this paper, I attempt a *critical* study of the concept of decision' (Chia, 1994: 781, emphasis added; for other particularly clear examples see Chia, 1996: 177; Feldman, 1998: 59; Hassard, 1993: 11, 1994: 312; Mumby and Stohl, 1991: 318).

Even when deconstruction is not presented as critique it is still generally presented as an oppositional strategy. For example, Cooper and Burrell speak of deconstruction as 'reversing the process of construction' (1988: 99), and for Hassard deconstruction involves 'inverting the notion of construction' (1993: 10, 1994: 311). Arrington and Francis hold that deconstruction reflects the view that modernism is 'an untenable philosophical position' (1989: 1), and for Martin 'Deconstruction peels away the layers of ideological obscuration', and 'dismantles a dichotomy by showing it to be a false distinction' (1990: 340, 342). Linstead and Grafton-Small argue that following Derrida the idea of the integrated subject 'is no longer tenable' and that the assumption of an immediate link between speech and phenomena is 'exploded' by Derrida's work (1992: 343, 342).

A reading of deconstruction as oppositional, negative and critical seems to be quite at odds with Derrida's efforts to present deconstruction as affirmative. Derrida has continually insisted that deconstruction is not a negative operation, that it does not imply nihilism and that it needs to be clearly distinguished from critique. This insistence on the affirmative character of deconstruction has perhaps become stronger over time, and is stated clearly in a number of his later interviews (see, for example, 1992/1995b: 60, 78, 89, 224, 226, 368/54, 73, 83, 211, 212, 357). But it is also apparent in his early work when he argues that logocentrism is not a sickness or a pathology, and in relation to metaphysical concepts when he writes that 'there is no question of "rejecting" these notions; they are necessary and, at least at present, for us, nothing is conceivable without them' (1967/1976: 25/13). For Derrida, deconstruction 'is not negative, even though it has often been interpreted as such despite all sorts of warnings. For me, it always accompanies an affirmative exigency, I would even say that it never proceeds without love' (1992/1995b: 88–9/83). These themes of love and affirmation are emphasized elsewhere:

> I love very much everything that I deconstruct in my own manner; the texts I want to read from the deconstructive point of view are texts I love, with that impulse of identification which is indispensable for reading ... my relation to these texts is characterised by loving jealousy and not at all by nihilistic fury (one can't read anything in the latter condition). (Derrida, 1982/1985: 119/87)

Such comments are consistent with the Heideggerian project of the destructuring of the history of ontology which, as Heidegger stressed, 'does not wish to bury the past in nullity, it has a *positive* intent' and 'should stake out the positive possibilities of the tradition, and that always means to fix its boundaries' (Heidegger, 1927/1962/1977: 31/44/67, 66, emphasis in original). This also reflects the use of the term deconstruction in the place of 'destruction' which, as Derrida explains 'too obviously implied an annihilation or a negative reduction' (1983/1985: 388/2). Derrida's deconstructive readings are sympathetic and move far too closely to the texts he comments on to be considered oppositional or critical in the sense of taking a stand, or making a decision 'for' or 'against' the text. As Spivak puts it, the goal of deconstruction is not the usual critical distance but rather critical intimacy (1999: 425).[6]

Reframing deconstruction as affirmative holds the potential for rethinking the way that deconstruction has been and might be used in organization studies. While most of the users of deconstruction in organization studies are opposed to the texts they read and seek to rubbish or dispose of these texts, we could see deconstruction in quite a different, more affirmative, light. This is not to recommend conservatism or to discourage critique, but to recognize that deconstruction is motivated by a certain spirit of friendship, by what Derrida calls 'what I would like to love' (1992/1995b: 54/49). The texts which Derrida subjects to deconstruction are texts which are not rejected outright, whilst at the same time they are not accepted uncritically.

Deconstruction and critique

If deconstruction is not negative or oppositional and is not critique in the usual sense, then what happens, for Derrida, to traditional forms of critique? A popular image in contemporary social and organization theory is that traditional forms of critique have recently been surpassed, outmoded and rendered redundant by the emergence of approaches such as deconstruction (or by deconstruction in combination with Foucault's genealogies or Lyotard's paralogy and comments about metanarratives). In organization studies this view and its contestation have played out in a debate between deconstruction and traditional forms of critique. Almost regardless of which side one takes in this debate, or if one equivocates, the battle lines between deconstruction and traditional forms of critique seem to be clearly drawn (see for example Alvesson and Deetz, 1996/1999; Cooper and Burrell, 1988; Parker, 1992, 1995; Reed, 1997; Thompson, 1993).

These tendencies can be seen as part of a particular way of representing and positioning deconstruction in organization studies. Alvesson and Deetz, for example, position deconstruction against approaches which reinforce the *status quo* (which they call 'normative' and 'interpretive' approaches) but also argue that deconstruction needs to be positioned *against* traditional forms of critique, and in particular against the Critical Theory of the Frankfurt School (see Alvesson and Deetz, 1996/1999: 196/190; 2000: 24; also Deetz, 1996: 198). They position deconstruction as a 'dialogical' discourse alongside a 'postmodern' orientation which rejects the consensualist stance of normative and interpretive research, but needs to be clearly distinguished in opposition to traditional versions of critique.

This kind of positioning is useful in that it clearly indicates that deconstruction, at least as it is practised by Derrida, is not an uncritical or conservative force which reproduces or leaves texts unchallenged. But at the same time it rests on a seriously problematic distinction between deconstruction and critical theory. This distinction, and in particular this relation of opposition, has been clearly rejected by Derrida. At the same time as distinguishing deconstruction from critique, Derrida insists that deconstruction is not opposed to traditional forms of critique. Deconstruction may question the simplicity of, and difficulties with, certain forms of critique, but at the same time Derrida *also* insists that 'analysis can lead one, in a specific, concrete situation, to advance "classical" discourses or actions … in a simple, clear, univocal form, in the style I would call neo-classical' (1992/1995b: 64/58). For Derrida, 'Frontal and simple critiques are always necessary; they are the law of rigor in a moral or political emergency … the classical inversion or reversal … is also unavoidable in the strategy of political struggles: for example, against capitalist, colonialist, sexist violence' (1992/1995b: 87, 89/82, 84; see also 63–5/58–9).[7]

The point is not to convert this into a relationship of privilege for either, but to recognize both the necessity for traditional forms of critique *and* the need to mark their limits, to engage (affirmatively) in their deconstruction. For Derrida this is a 'divided duty', which involves 'cultivating the virtue of such *critique, of the critical idea, of the critical tradition*, but also submitting it, beyond critique and questioning, to a deconstructive genealogy that thinks and exceeds it without compromising it' (1991/1992b: 76/77, emphasis in original). Such comments present serious problems with the form that the distinction between deconstruction and critique has assumed in organization studies. They threaten to problematize the assumptions of those positioned on both sides of this opposition, by forcing us to rethink the relation between Derrida and the critical tradition. If deconstruction is engaged in a persistent dialogue with the critical tradition then the relation of opposition between deconstruction and critique which is so common in organization studies might be destabilized.

But it is not enough to simply 'overturn' or abolish the opposition between deconstruction and critical theory. We might instead move to displace or reframe this opposition. Such a reframing might suggest a closer relation between deconstruction and critique in which deconstruction worked as an ally, even if ally at a distance, to critique. Or perhaps better, we might see *both* a more distant relation (insofar as deconstruction could be taken to be affirmative and not 'critical') *and* a closer relation (insofar as deconstruction works with, or alongside, the critical tradition).

The consequences of such a reading which pays closer attention to the way that deconstruction has been used by Derrida, bear significant consequences for these debates in organization studies. Such a reading also raises serious questions about the range of texts which have been subjected to deconstructive reading. The texts which have been deconstructed in organization studies have generally fallen within the 'mainstream' of organization studies, and a critical impulse has operated against them. But in the same way that Derrida has made efforts to deconstruct the Western critical tradition, we might also turn a deconstructive eye to the critical tradition in organization studies. This would involve deconstructive engagements with classic authors such as Marx and Weber and those working in their traditions. It would also engage with feminist and anti-racist discourses, and the currently popular and emerging Foucaldian and Critical Realist interpretations of organization.[8] These engagements with critical studies of organization would bear in mind that deconstruction of these texts would not be to oppose or to confront them, but to mark their limits and expose their difficulties in the hope that they might be extended and radicalized.

Relativism: the 'indeterminacy of meaning'

As well as being taken for a method and for being negative, it is widely assumed that deconstruction ultimately implies some form of textual relativism. By opening up questions of interpretation and showing how certain texts can be read differently from how they were in the past, some are left with the impression that Derrida assumes that *all* texts can be read in *any* way that one likes. Such cases are regularly made against Derrida, and in organization studies have been stated forcefully in a recent polemic by Stephen Feldman (1998). Derrida responded to charges of relativism in a recent interview with the following comments:

> What is relativism? ... Relativism is, in classical philosophy, a way of referring to the absolute and denying it; it states that there are only cultures and that there is no pure science or truth. I have never said such a thing ... I take into account differences, but I am no relativist. If I say that there are two zero points here and there, and that you cannot reduce the difference, and if this is interpreted as being relativism, then I am a relativist, and who is not? ... this charge against me amounts to obscurantism, and is issued by people who don't read. My concern would be this: what is their interest and their motivation, what do they want? ... Usually they charge me with saying that the text means anything, a charge made even in academic circles, not only in the media. If I were saying such a stupid thing, why would that be of any interest? Who would be interested in that, starting with me? (Derrida, 1999a: 78–9)

Charges of relativism often emerge alongside the suggestion that deconstruction implies the 'indeterminacy of meaning'. Many, both proponents and critics, suggest that deconstruction shows that the meaning of texts is totally open to interpretation and hence 'indeterminate'. Although in the course of his work he has documented certain moments of *undecidability* in specific texts so as to analyse specific relations of opposition, this has often been overstated into a global claim about the *indeterminacy* of meaning. Derrida insists that it is necessary to distinguish clearly between indeterminacy and undecidability. As he puts it:

> I do not believe that I have ever spoken of 'indeterminacy', whether in regard to 'meaning' or anything else. Undecidability is something else again ... undecidability is always a *determinate* oscillation between possibilities (for example, of meaning, but also of acts). These possibilities are themselves highly *determined* in strictly *defined* situations ... I say 'undecidability' rather than 'indeterminacy' because I am interested more in relations of force, in differences of force. (Derrida, 1988/1990: 148/273–4, emphases in original; see also 127, 144–5/230, 267; 1999a: 79; and earlier 1967/1976: 227/158; 1972/1981a: 72/64)

Derrida is in a potentially difficult position here, which could be seen as a double-bind of the kind that he has spent so much effort analysing. He tries to break with a 'positivist' or 'objectivist' conception of interpretation which denigrates the role of interpretation and reading and finds confidence in obvious-ways readings of texts. But at the same time he seeks to avoid a complete openness or relativity of interpretation. Given the embeddedness of the potentially misleading opposition between objectivism and subjectivism (see Bernstein, 1983; Deetz, 1996), it is hardly surprising, although still inexcusable, that so many have taken Derrida to be endorsing some form of relativism. If we cast this as a double-bind, we might see Derrida to be making efforts to avoid *both* extremes in the opposition. This is not to destroy the opposition, or to imagine that it could simply be surpassed or outmanoeuvred. Instead, a deconstructive strategy would be to acknowledge the difficulties of both poles, and try to remain vigilant of the tendency to fall into one or the other end of it.

In organization studies we can see various shades of relativism amongst those who have taken up deconstruction. While some have argued that deconstruction does not imply relativism (Arrington and Francis, 1989: 3; Boje, 2001: 20; Kilduff, 1993), many writers in organization studies using deconstruction invite such a reading. Others tend to import a relativism into deconstruction, often through misrepresenting issues of undecidability, from overstating Derrida's position or conflating it with 'postmodernism'.

In the early paper by Cooper (1989, discussed above) which frames deconstruction in terms of overturning and metaphorization, undecidability is central to this second movement. In the phase of metaphorization, Cooper explains:

> the relationship between the apparently opposing terms is really one of mutual definition in which the individual terms actually inhabit each other. In other words, the separate, individual terms give way 'to a process where opposites merge in a constant *undecidable* exchange of attributes' (Norris, 1987: 35). (Cooper, 1989: 483, emphasis in original)[9]

This phrase 'constant *undecidable* exchange of attributes', which Cooper cites from Norris, has been taken up by others following Cooper in various shapes or forms. Hassard suggests that in the second movement of deconstruction, metaphorization, 'seemingly unique terms submit to a process which sees them combine in a continual exchange of "undecidable" characteristics' (1993: 11; 1994: 312). The phrase appears once again in a slightly different form in Linstead, who suggests that this phase of metaphorization 'entails the recognition that the positively-valued term at any moment is defined only by contrast to the negatively-valued term and that they interpenetrate and inhabit each other. In Derrida's writing this emerges as a ceaseless moving between terms' (Linstead, 1993b: 112).

On this terrain, undecidability can collapse into indeterminacy. As the determinacy of meaning is called into question, 'knowledge becomes relative, dispersed between multiple, fragmented realities' (Linstead, 1993a: 49; cf. 1993b: 110). Chia, attributing this argument to Derrida, argues that 'indeterminacy inheres in writing's very essence' (Chia, 1994: 784). As part of a project which would outline an alternative ontology for the study of organization which would be based on deconstruction, Chia argues that Derrida shows us that meaning is 'caught in an endless chain of signifiers which therefore makes it unstable and, in the final analysis, indeterminate' (1994: 783).

Possibly the most relativistic reading of Derrida, and certainly the target of attacks on deconstruction such as Feldman's (1998), is offered by those who position Derrida as a 'postmodernist'. Cooper and Burrell, for example, contrast the discourse of modernism with postmodern discourse, by which they refer to the work of Derrida (and also Lyotard, Foucault, Deleuze and Guattari), which, they suggest, 'analyses social life in terms of paradox and indeterminacy' (1988: 91). According to this postmodern discourse:

> terms contain their own opposites and thus refuse any *singular* grasp of their meanings ... Difference is thus a unity which is at the same time divided from itself, and, since it is that which actually constitutes human discourse (Derrida, 1973), it is intrinsic to all social forms. At the very centre of discourse, therefore, the human agent is faced with a condition of irreducible indeterminacy and it is this endless and unstoppable demurrage which postmodern thought explicitly recognizes and places in the vanguard of its endeavours. (Cooper and Burrell, 1988: 98, emphasis in original)

Between these different degrees of relativism in the representation of Derrida in organization studies, we can see a variety of positions ranging from the denial of relativism to what seems to be its overt celebration. While there are very complex subtleties of difference in these arguments, and we are citing selectively here, it should be clear that a great variety of different epistemological and ontological positions are assumed by those using deconstruction in organization studies. So while Feldman's criticism of the relativism of deconstruction in organization studies makes a potentially valuable caution, his argument misses its target on several counts. When condemning the tendency to relativism in the way that deconstruction has been used in organization studies Feldman fails to account for the variety of very different ways in which it has been used. While some have certainly introduced a fairly simple relativism into deconstruction, this is far from universally the case. Feldman has, ironically, been confronted with a situation which is ultimately undecidable – the question: 'is deconstruction relativistic?' – without an account of differences is a close-up example of an undecidable. In 'deciding' that deconstruction in organization studies is relativistic, Feldman has made a series of enormous and weakly grounded assumptions based on the worst protocols of reading. Indeed, Feldman's arguments seem to be aimed at an incredibly naïve caricature of Derrida, which is hardly strengthened by the fact that he fails to cite a single one of Derrida's texts, despite roundly condemning Derrida's relativism.

Late Derrida

Our discussions of method, negativity and relativism raise serious questions about the way that Derrida has been set to work in organization studies. In all three cases it seems that strong arguments can be made against the way that Derrida has been read, but I have tried to make clear here that reading Derrida in these ways might often be *possible*, and might even be invited by a quick reading. Rather than suggesting that these readings of Derrida are impossible, it might be more productive to use these comments here in order to consider other possibilities. Here I have tried to open out these possibilities in order to work with Derrida's repeated invitation to look to the future, to the possibility of a transformed understanding of his possible contribution to organization studies through a reconsideration of the way that his work has been taken up so far.

There is another way in which Derrida's work remains a possibility rather than an actuality as far as organization studies is concerned. Since his earliest writings on phenomenology and what appeared to be a 'programme' of deconstruction in the 1960s, Derrida's work has expanded in a number of directions. Where Derrida's work has been taken up in organization studies the focus has been principally on his earlier works, and the more recent developments in his work remain largely unexamined possibilities in terms of the direction that deconstruction might be taken in organization studies (cf. Calás and Smircich, 1997: xxvi; Letiche, 1998; Willmott, 1998). Here, then, I will attempt to outline certain possibilities suggested by Derrida's recent work. As we have limited space remaining, I will only point towards certain selected directions in which Derrida has moved in recent years.[10]

Periodizing ...

In 1972, shortly after his entry onto the French intellectual scene, Derrida once again published three books in one year, *Margins of Philosophy* and *Dissemination*, both collections of essays, and *Positions*, a short collection of interviews. With the arrival of these three books Derrida's significance as a leading intellectual force was emphatic. It also subsequently seemed to some commentators that after 1972 Derrida's work underwent a change of emphasis. In a series of books, of which *Glas* (1974), *Spurs* (1978), *The Postcard* (1980) and *Cinders* (1982) are possibly the most notable, it appeared that the 'serious' tone of Derrida's early work was giving way to a more playful and adventurous style of writing. For some commentators this change of emphasis was enough to justify talk of a shift from an 'early' to a 'late' Derrida. Richard Rorty, for example, argued that 'as he moves along from the early criticisms of Husserl though *Glas* to texts like the "Envois" section of *The Postcard*, the tone has changed' (1991: 128), and concluded that 'Derrida's work divides into an earlier, more professorial period and a later period in which his writing becomes more eccentric, personal and original' (1989: 123).

Almost predictably – and ironically given Derrida's comments about the role of division and hierarchization – this separation of Derrida's work into early and late periods was accompanied by evaluations, either implicit or explicit, of the merits of the work of the two periods. For Rorty, the early work was 'something of a false start' (1991: 128), and amounted to the work of 'a young philosophy professor, still a bit unsure of himself, making quasi-professional noises' (1996b: 41). On Rorty's reading, the later work is the best of Derrida, while 'Derrida's earlier, less idiosyncratic, more "strictly philosophical" work – and in particular his books on Husserl – were necessary to get him a hearing, necessary to establish himself' (Rorty, 1996a: 17). For others however, this picture is inverted, the early work being the genuine article and the later work being a diversion from an earlier rigour. Thus, writers such as Rodolphe Gasché (1986, 1994) argue for a 'serious' reading and privilege Derrida's early work and treat the work of the later 1970s and early 1980s as the diversion.

While this division into an earlier, serious, philosophical period and a later, playful literary period no doubt reflects the interests of respective readers, some, such as Geoffrey Bennington, have cast doubts on the merits of any periodization of Derrida's work. Bennington argues that Derrida's work

> which is remarkable for its diversity *and* its consistency, its powers of dispersion *and* of gathering, its *formation*, cannot be divided into styles or periods: even the quite widespread idea that there are first of all very philosophical texts and then, after *Glas* (1974), a more 'literary' and less 'serious' tendency, is doubtful as to its empirical accuracy and irrelevant to our understanding. (Bennington, 1991/1993: 16–17/13–14, emphases in original)[11]

Bennington makes a very important warning here, and perhaps we should think of attempts to periodize as a *pharmakon*, as potentially useful and potentially harmful, and to recognize that any periodization cannot and should not be applied in advance of reading. So rather than sketching a matrix of transformation, in this final section I will speak of some of the specific developments in Derrida's work in the 1990s. These developments should be seen simultaneously as tendencies which develop out of Derrida's early work at the same time as they break from it, and it is hence neither continuous *nor* discontinuous with the earlier work.

Marx

Possibly the development in Derrida's later work which has attracted the most attention has been what is widely seen to be a 'renewed' interest in Marx (see in particular Derrida, 1993/1994, 1999b; Derrida and Guillaume, 1997). In Derrida's earlier work we find only rare scattered references to Marx's texts, and when questioned about this in an interview in 1971 he explained that his engagement with Marx was 'still to come' (1972/1981b: 85/62). Twenty years later, when questioned again about his reticence about the texts of Marx in his early writing, his response was almost apologetic: 'I did not read him enough. One never reads enough Marx' (1993b: 195).

The most detailed engagement with Marx came in the form of a lecture delivered in 1993 and now published as *Specters of Marx*. In this book Derrida makes an explicit political gesture, foregrounding the contemporary relevance of Marx. He argues that 'It will always be a fault not to read and reread and discuss Marx – which is to say also some others – and to go beyond scholarly "reading" or "discussion". It will be more and more a fault, a failing of theoretical, philosophical, political responsibility' (1993/1994: 35/13). One of the central themes of this book is the concept of inheritance, and Derrida suggests that it is up to us to decide what we might inherit from Marx. We must continue to ask what this inheritance involves, because inheritance is never passive, is never 'given', but like any inheritance requires us to sort out and sift through what we have been left with. Derrida insists that 'there is no question of a "return to Marx" – which anyway never would have interested Marx nor clear-sighted Marxists – but perhaps something to wait for or to learn from a certain "spirit" of Marx, of a certain manner of refusing, disobeying, criticizing and denouncing, but also of analysing, affirming and promising' (Derrida, 1997: 64).

Although there is something new in Derrida's engagement with Marx, which Derrida explains in terms of changes in the global political economy, he sees 'neither a theoretical break or a political change' with his earlier work (Derrida, 1997: 57). In direct continuation of his earlier work, we find here an extension of the notion of a double-bind or divided duty which draws us in two directions (see also Derrida, 1991/1992b: 75–8/76–80). Thus for Derrida 'Marxism remains at once indispensable and structurally insufficient: it is still necessary *but* provided it be transformed and adapted to new conditions' (Derrida, 1993/1994: 101/58, emphasis in original). Thus, Derrida speaks of

> the necessity of a new culture, one that would invent another way of reading and analyzing *Capital*, both Marx's book and capital in general; a new way of taking capital into account while avoiding not only the frightening totalitarian dogmatism that some of us have known how to resist up until now, *but also, and simultaneously*, the counter-dogmatism that is setting in today, (on the) left and (on the) right [*à droite et à gauche*], exploiting a new situation, to the point of banning the word 'capital', indeed even the critique of certain effects of capital or of the 'market' as the evil remnants of the old dogmatism. (1991/1992b: 56–7/56, emphasis in original)

As might be expected, reactions to *Specters of Marx* have been mixed, but wherever one stands on these debates, it seems clear that Derrida's writings on Marx offer the potential to rethink what it means to read Marx today.[12] They recommend a suspicion with the ease with which certain 'postmodern' writers, and in particular Baudrillard and Lyotard, abandon Marx altogether. They also invite us to ask how it is that not a single author in this volume cites a single work by Marx, despite their willingness to offer 'criticisms' of Marx and of 'Marxism'. They hold the potential to rethink the opposition between deconstruction and critical theory, an opposition of which I indicated certain limits earlier in this chapter, and to see in Derrida's work a clearer and more explicit politics.

Politics

While in some of Derrida's early writing there was a feeling that the concrete realities of the external world dropped out of the picture – a feeling certainly encouraged, if not produced, by certain commentators – Derrida began writing in an explicitly political and almost vanguardist fashion in the 1990s. In the context of the widespread perception of the universality of capitalism and liberal democracy, he offers a scathing 'ten-word telegram' identifying what he calls the plagues of the New World Order (1993/1994: 134–9/81–4). He concludes:

> [A]t a time when some have the audacity to neo-evangelize in the name of the ideal of a liberal democracy that has finally realized itself as the ideal of human history: never have violence, inequality, exclusion, famine and thus economic oppression affected as many human beings in the history of the earth and of humanity. Instead of singing the advent of the ideal of liberal democracy and of the capitalist market in the euphoria of the end of history, culminating in the 'end of ideologies' and the end of the great emancipatory discourses, let us never neglect this obvious macroscopic fact, made up of numerable sites of suffering: no degree of progress allows one to ignore that never before, in absolute figures, have so many men, women and children been subjugated, starved or exterminated on the earth (1993/1994: 141/85).

In works such as *The Other Heading* (1991), *The Force of Law* (1992), *Politics of Friendship* (1994), *Adieu to Emmanuel Levinas* (1997), *Of Hospitality* (1997) and *Of Cosmopolitanism and Forgiveness* (2001) issues of democracy, law, politics and the relation to the other become central themes. Here we find far more direct engagements with the realities of post-communist Europe, with political philosophy and with the depth of xenophobia in Western thought. As he turns to the more traditional concerns of what is usually thought of as 'politics', we might be justified in speaking of a 'political turn' in Derrida's more recent work.

At the same time, however, we should not underplay Derrida's political engagements or the passion which is clearly evident in his early work. Derrida has long been committed to political causes, as is evidenced in his active opposition to the French war in Algeria and the US war in Vietnam, and in his support and petitioning for Nelson Mandela and writers such as Salman Rushdie. Through the 1970s and 1980s Derrida was involved in the formation and leadership of GREPH, the Research Group for the Teaching of Philosophy (*Groupe de Recherches sur l'Enseignement Philosophique*) and the Collège International de Philosophie, which have both waged political battles over the teaching and dissemination of philosophy (see Derrida, 1990a). There is also a clear political passion in his early writing, for example in his condemnation of the tendency to ethnocentrism in Lévi-Strauss, whose idea that the Nambikwara are a people 'without writing' is dismissed as being 'dependent on ethnocentric oneirism, upon the vulgar, that is to say ethnocentric, misconception of writing' (1967/1976: 161/109). It is also difficult to fail to see the political engagement of the young writer who spoke of a future which 'can only be anticipated in the form of an absolute danger' (1967/1976: 14/5) and pointed to 'the as yet unnameable which is proclaiming itself and which can do so, as is necessary whenever a birth is in the offing, only under the species of the nonspecies, in the formless, mute, infant and terrifying form of monstrosity' (1967/1978: 428/293).

Perhaps it would be fairer to say that in Derrida's recent work we can see a more *recognizably* political engagement, that is to say, an intervention into the domains that we generally assume to be the domains of the political. When we frame the issue in these terms we are faced with a question of domains of politicization, and Derrida has certainly insisted on calling into question the narrowness of the demarcation of 'the political' into a small domain neatly separated from the other realms of life and of experience. So when Derrida affirms his commitment to the classical emancipatory ideal of critical thought he insists, at the same time, that we must seek to continuously move beyond this and that 'other areas must constantly open up that at first can seem like secondary or marginal areas' (1992/1994: 28/63). In much the same way, when Derrida suggests that we might retain the name democracy, he seeks to constantly question the same concept, to show how democracy might be rethought, broadened, expanded and radicalized, and thus if we speak of democracy then we must speak of a 'democracy to come' (see, for example, Derrida, 1991/1992b: 76/78).

Here again we find classic deconstructive operations, but engaging in questions of democratic politics. Here the logic of an either/or, a yes/no, a 'for or against' Marx, a for or against democracy, becomes the subject of suspicion. Out of that suspicion comes not inaction nor indeterminacy, but an opening to the future, to new ways of reading and thinking politics. As in Derrida's earliest works, we find ourselves caught in double-binds, where we cannot, and should not, decide between the competing demands. For Derrida this experience of undecidability is not the onset of passive nihilism and the end of politics, as it is sometimes perceived to be, but is the condition of possibility of a democratic politics worthy of the name.

Ethics

In *The Gift of Death*, Derrida takes up the biblical story (Genesis 22: 1–13) in which Abraham is instructed by God to take his son to a mountain in Moriah to offer him there as a sacrifice (Derrida, 1992/1995a; see also Jones, 2003; Caputo, 1993; and more generally Critchley, 1992). Following Kierkegaard's (1843/1985) reading of this story, Derrida frames this as a classic situation of fear and trembling in the face of a call from the other that requires a serious but troubling decision. On this reading, Abraham is potentially governed by two demands, one from his son and one from his God who calls on him to kill his son. If Abraham simply 'decides' without experiencing the difficulty of the conflict between these two demands then he is simply following a formula, and has not experienced the double-bind or 'aporia' and what Derrida calls 'a certain experience of the impossible', a moment of 'not knowing where to go' (see Derrida, 1984/1992: 27/328, 1993a: 12).

This kind of situation is analogous to many situations appearing in Derrida's earlier analyses. It is not dissimilar from the pattern he outlined when discussing how Plato treated writing both as a poison and a cure (Derrida, 1972/1981a: 69–197/61–171), how Foucault treated psychoanalysis variously as a liberating counter-science and a normalizing technology (Derrida, 1996/1998), and as just discussed, the simultaneous desire for democracy and a dissatisfaction with current democratic structures. Derrida exposes the way that we often assume that there are grounds for deciding when we would be better placed to insist on the irreducibility of these competing demands, so that we might see writing as poison *and* cure, psychoanalysis as liberating *and* normalizing, and democracy as necessary but insufficient. What emerges in Derrida's most recent writing is the suggestion that ethics and responsibility do not involve perfect and clear knowledge and absence of such decision-making difficulties, but are themselves emergent in and even defined by the experience of double-binds such as these. For Derrida, responsibility and ethics necessarily involve working with undecidability, with double-binds and aporias. Without an experience of the undecidable, of 'not knowing where to go', there is good conscience but nothing which we could be justified in calling an ethical decision. As Derrida puts it:

> I would argue that there would be no decision, in the strong sense of the word, in ethics, in politics, no decision, and thus no responsibility, without the experience of some undecidability. If you don't experience some undecidability, then the decision would simply be the application of a programme, the consequence of a premiss or of a matrix. So a decision has to go through some impossibility in order for it to be a decision. (1999a: 66; see also 1992/1994: 24; 1992/1995b: 157/147–8)

Further, Derrida argues that the experience of a double-bind does not involve paralysis or inaction but is, paradoxically, the condition of possibility of action, or at least of 'responsible' action. Such a double-bind

> paralyzes [*immobilise*] us because it binds us doubly (I must and I need not, I must not, it is necessary and impossible, etc.). In one and the same place, on the same apparatus, both hands are bound or nailed down. What are we to do? But also how is it that it does not prevent us from speaking, from continuing to describe the situation, from trying to make oneself understood? (1993/1995: 53/22)

Caught between two irreducible demands, there is nothing to decide for us. This is the kind of situation which Derrida has written about from his earliest work. This effort to think through double-binds, of competing demands when there is nothing to tell us which way to go, is particularly distinctive about deconstruction. And while some have dismissed deconstruction on the basis that it involves 'irresponsibility', this charge has now been returned with interest. For Derrida this 'nonpassive endurance of the aporia' is the condition of possibility of responsibility and of decision (Derrida, 1993a: 16). As Keenan, following Derrida argues: 'responsibility is not a moment of security or of cognitive certainty. Quite the contrary: the only responsibility worthy of the name comes with the removal of grounds, the withdrawal of the rules or the knowledge on which we might rely to make our decisions for us. No grounds means no alibis, no elsewhere to which we might refer the instance of the decision' (Keenan, 1997: 1).

Conclusion: possibilities of deconstruction

I have covered a considerable amount of ground here, and in most places have done so far too quickly. We might be tempted to move to a conclusion, and possibly one that might deal with questions about what direction one might take from here. What do we do next? What do we do with Derrida? How do we use Derrida in relation to organization and organization studies? But Derrida does not offer us any easy or satisfying answers to questions such as these. As we have hopefully seen, there is no simple 'programme' of deconstruction that might be followed or 'applied'. This lack of certainty does not have to lead to passive nihilism or to abdication in the face of undecidability. Indeed, it is in exactly this lack of a clear programme and a lack of answers as to what we should do that we might find a position from which we *must* decide what to do, without resort to excuses or formulae. These 'grounds without grounds' might be the basis for a responsible engagement with deconstruction.

Having said this, and *on the other hand*, one can see in Derrida's work a persistent and radical experience of *possibility*, based on an opening or openness to the possibilities of an alternative future. It may seem ironic that Derrida's work, which is largely retrospective in the way that it speaks almost exclusively of existing texts, could be seen as opening possibilities for possible futures. But Derrida's readings are always active transformations, not passive reflections on texts, and his readings do not simply interpret texts but change them. It is this 'performative' aspect of deconstructive reading – which in this chapter I have not managed to avoid setting to work at least once or twice – that recommends deconstruction to a radically transformative politics and ethics.

In terms of possibilities for deconstruction and organization studies, we might see at least two possibilities. On the one hand we could see a broader application of strategies of deconstructive reading to a variety of 'texts'. Despite the range of texts already subjected to deconstruction, this could be extended to a range of 'empirical' texts from organizational life and a range of 'theoretical' texts about organization. This would imply a deep and radical interrogation of texts of organizational life and of the way that organizations have been represented. As I suggested above, deconstruction could be applied in areas where it has been largely ignored, such as in the deconstructive reading of critical analyses of organization.

At the same time we might see the possibility of different ways of understanding deconstruction, of different ways of setting Derrida to work. This would involve not just applying the model of deconstruction that has been used in organization studies to date, but subjecting that model to a careful and rigorous deconstructive reading. Such a reading, to which this chapter has hopefully contributed, would not attack or indict the way that deconstruction has been used in organization studies. It would work in the space that has been opened by the many valuable efforts to introduce deconstruction but would *also* remain dissatisfied and keep an open eye to the possibility of other future efforts to set deconstruction to work.

Notes

1 For example, Derrida writes that 'the facile, demagogic, grave error of confusing my work (or even "deconstruction" in general) with postmodernism is indicative ... of a massive failure to read and analyze' (1999b: 263–4).

2 For more on Derrida's background, and also on the problem of biography, see Bennington and Derrida (1991/1993).

3 The translation of these sections, and particularly of the word *Destruktion* as 'destruction' has contributed to some of the most serious misunderstandings of both Heidegger and now Derrida. Here I follow David Farrell Krell who in his retranslation of the Introduction to Heidegger's *Being and Time* translates *Destruktion* as 'destructuring'. Krell explains this choice: 'Heidegger's word *Destruktion* does not mean "destruction" in the usual sense – which the German word *Zerstörung* expresses. The word *destructuring* should serve to keep the negative connotations at a distance and to bring out the neutral, ultimately constructive sense of the original' (in Heidegger, 1977: 63n).

4 Boje outlines a 'seven-step deconstruction process':
   1. Define the dualities – who or what is at opposite ends in the story?
   2. Reinterpret – what is the alternative interpretation to the story?
   3. Rebel voices – deny the authority of the one voice. Who is not being represented or is under-represented?
   4. Other side of the story – what is the silent or under-represented story?
   5. Deny the plot – what is the plot? Turn it around.
   6. Find the exception – what is the exception that breaks the rule?
   7. What is between the lines – what is not said? What is the writing on the wall? (Boje, 1998: 462; see also 2001: 21)

5 If we were to consider the deconstructive method outlined by Calás, Boje and Martin in deconstructive fashion, we might recover a recognition of the way that some of these dangers (at some level) come back to haunt their simple outlines of method. They all admit, at various points that 'deconstruction is far more than a methodology' (Martin, 1990: 340), that deconstruction 'cannot be considered a methodology in the traditional sense of the word' (Calás, 1993: 307) and that 'Deconstruction is not meant by Derrida to be defined, lest it become a rational and token blueprint of analysis steps' (Boje, 1998: 462). But at the same time, these warnings seem to have to be 'forgotten' or 'repressed' in order to preserve their outlines of deconstruction as a method. Such double-binds are perhaps inescapable.

   For further discussion of the problem of 'applying Derrida' see Brannigan, Robbins and Wolfreys (1996).

6 Carter and Jackson (Chapter 6, this volume) also stress the affirmative character of Deleuze's work, which they trace back to Nietzsche. For further discussion of affirmation in Derrida see Krell (2000).

7 Such comments, and the much-needed deconstruction of the opposition between deconstruction and traditional forms of critique pose serious challenges to a number of writers in organization studies who have argued that deconstruction casts doubts on classic goals such as emancipation. Alvesson and Willmott, for example, argue that after the poststructuralist critique of 'essentialism', the traditional goal of critical theory of emancipation must be re-evaluated. In the place of the classical goal of emancipation must be substituted a far more modest goal of 'microemancipation' (see Alvesson and Willmott, 1992, 1996: 159–87). Derrida has made his views of such revisions clear, when he states: 'Nothing seems to me less outdated than the classic emancipatory ideal' (1992/1994: 28/62). Further, he writes:

> I refuse to renounce the great classical discourse of emancipation. I believe that there is an enormous amount to do today for emancipation, in all domains and all the areas of the world and society. Even if I would not wish to inscribe the discourse of emancipation into a teleology, a metaphysics or even a classical messianism, I none the less believe that there is no ethico-political decision or gesture without what I would call a 'Yes' to the discourse of emancipation … I must say that I have no tolerance for those who – deconstructionist or not – are ironical with regard to the grand discourse of emancipation. This attitude has always distressed and irritated me. I do not want to renounce this discourse. (Derrida, 1996: 82; see also 1991/1992b and 1993/1994, especially 102, 126/59, 75)

8   Calás (1993) has offered a deconstructive reading of certain aspects of Weber's work, and deconstructive moves are at work in du Gay's (2000) reading of Weber even if – unfortunately to my mind – they are not described as such. For the beginnings of a deconstructive reading of Foucaldian organization studies see Jones (2002).

9   Cooper's citation from Norris here is taken from the midst of Norris' discussion of a highly specific section of Derrida's deconstruction of Plato's views on writing. We could note that the way in which Cooper cites Norris here leads to an abstraction from the original argument into an abstract, and presumably universal, principle. Norris' comments are in fact highly local, and emerge as a comment in relation to a specific text by Plato, *The Phaedrus*. To quote the section from Norris which Cooper leaves out, Norris writes:

> …this is not a question of simply *inverting* the received order of priorities, so that henceforth 'writing' will somehow take precedence over 'speech' and its various associated values. More than this, it involves the dismantling of all those binary oppositions that organize Plato's text, to the point where opposition itself – the very ground point of dialectical reason – gives way to a process where opposites merge in a constant *undecidable* exchange of attributes. Thus Plato is unable to define what should count as the 'good' employment of language … (Norris, 1987: 35, emphases in original)

This indeterminacy is not simply an isolated phenomenon which can be found at specific points in specific texts. It is used to characterize the experience of the present epoch, a postmodern world in which uncertainty and indeterminacy are taken to be central experiences. As Legge puts it, the project of deconstruction 'is to reveal and celebrate the ambivalence of *all* texts' (Legge, 1996: 1003, emphasis added).

10 This selection of recent developments in Derrida's work is obviously selective. We could also discuss Derrida's continuing and developing engagement with psychoanalysis, including the shifts and continuities from 'Freud and the scene of writing' (1967/1978: 293–340/196–231) to *The Postcard* (1980/1987) to *Resistances of Psychoanalysis* (1996/1998). Likewise we could have discussed Derrida's recent encounter with anthropology in *Given Time* (1991/1992a), in relation to his earlier writings on Lévi-Strauss (Derrida, 1967/1976: 149–202/101–40; 1967/1978: 409–28/278–93). In terms of what seem to be more novel developments, we could have also discussed Derrida's writings, and responses to his writing, on law (Derrida, 1986/1987, 1992/1994; cf. Cornell, Rosenfeld and Carlson, 1992; Cornell, 1991) and religion (Derrida, 1992/1995a; Derrida and Vattimo, 1996/1998; Caputo, 1997; Caputo and Scanlon, 1999). Due to restrictions of space my discussion here remains largely schematic and will need to be extended at a later date.

11 Responding to criticisms of his division Rorty later admits: 'I have, in the past, made too much of the difference between earlier and later Derrida', and that 'the closer one looks, the harder it is to find any substantial difference between earlier and later work' (1996b: 41; see also Derrida, 1999a: 73).

12 Terry Eagleton accuses Derrida of opportunism and of only turning to Marxism at the point at which it had become marginal, of being 'hardly concerned with an

effective socialism at all' (1995/1999: 37/86, emphasis in original), and describes his political rhetoric as a form of 'slipshod late-Frankfurt swearing [which] contrasts tellingly with the precision of his philosophical excursions elsewhere' (1995/1999: 36/85). Fredric Jameson (1995/1999) offers a more measured critique, working with Derrida's positioning statements, but casting doubt on the haste with which Derrida considers himself able to dismiss certain caricatures of Marxist categories. For more on these debates see the collections edited by Magnus and Cullenberg (1994) and Sprinker (1999) as well as the earlier efforts at an 'articulation' of Marxism and deconstruction by Ryan (1982).

References

Alvesson, M. and Deetz, S. (1996/1999) 'Critical theory and postmodernism: approaches to organization studies', in S. Clegg, C. Hardy and W. Nord (eds), *Handbook of Organization Studies.* London: Sage. Reprinted as 'Critical theory and postmodernism: approaches to organization studies' in S. Clegg and C. Hardy (eds), *Studying Organization: Theory and Method.* London: Sage.

Alvesson, M. and Deetz, S. (2000) *Doing Critical Management Research.* London: Sage.

Alvesson, M. and Willmott, H. (1992) 'On the idea of emancipation in management and organization studies', *Academy of Management Review,* 17 (3): 432–64.

Alvesson, M. and Willmott, H. (1996) *Making Sense of Management: A Critical Introduction.* London: Sage.

Arrington, E. and Francis, J. (1989) 'Letting the chat out of the bag: deconstruction, privilege and accounting research', *Accounting, Organizations and Society,* 14 (1/2): 1–28.

Beath, C. and Orlikowski, W. (1994) 'The contradictory structure of systems development methodologies: deconstructing the Is-User relationship in information engineering', *Information Systems Research,* 5: 350–77.

Bennington, G. (1991/1993) 'Derridabase', in G. Bennington and J. Derrida, *Jacques Derrida.* Paris: Editions du Seuil. Trans. G. Bennington, 'Derridabase' in *Jacques Derrida.* Chicago: Chicago University Press.

Bennington, G. (1994) *Legislations: The Politics of Deconstruction.* London: Verso.

Bennington, G. and Derrida, J. (1991/1993) *Jacques Derrida.* Paris: Editions du Seuil. Trans. G. Bennington, *Jacques Derrida.* Chicago: Chicago University Press.

Bernstein, R. (1983) *Beyond Objectivism and Relativism: Science, Hermeneutics and Praxis.* Oxford: Basil Blackwell.

Bloom, H., de Man, P., Derrida, J., Hartman, G. and Hillis Miller, J. (1979) *Deconstruction and Criticism.* New York: Seabury Press.

Boje, D. (1995) 'Stories of the storytelling organization: a postmodern analysis of Disney as "Tamara land"', *Academy of Management Journal,* 38 (4): 997–1035.

Boje, D. (1998) 'Nike, Greek goddess of victory or cruelty? Women's stories of Asian factory life', *Journal of Organizational Change Management,* 11 (6): 461–80.

Boje, D. (2001) *Narrative Methods for Organizational and Communication Research.* London: Sage.

Boje, D. and Dennehey, R. (1993) *Managing in a Postmodern World: America's Revolution against Exploitation.* Dubuque, IA: Kendall/Hunt.

Boje, D., Rosile, G. A., Dennehy, R. and Summers, D. (1997) 'Restorying reengineering: some deconstructions and postmodern alternatives', *Communication Research,* 24 (6): 631–68.

Brannigan, J., Robbins, R. and Wolfreys, J. (eds) (1996) *Applying: To Derrida.* Houndmills: Macmillan.

Burrell, G. (1988) 'Modernism, post modernism and organizational analysis 2: the contribution of Michel Foucault', *Organization Studies*, 9 (2): 221–35.

Burrell, G. (1994) 'Modernism, post modernism and organizational analysis 4: the contribution of Jürgen Habermas', *Organization Studies*, 15 (1): 1–19.

Calás, M. (1993) 'Deconstructing charismatic leadership: re-reading Weber from the darker side', *Leadership Quarterly*, 4 (3/4): 305–28.

Calás, M. and Smircich, L. (1991) 'Voicing seduction to silence leadership', *Organization Studies,* 12 (4): 567–602.

Calás, M. and Smircich, L. (1997) 'Introduction: when was "the postmodern" in the history of management thought?', in M. Calás and L. Smircich (eds), *Postmodern Management Theory*. Aldershot: Ashgate/Dartmouth.

Calás, M. and Smircich, L. (1999) 'Past postmodernism? Reflections and tentative directions', *Academy of Management Review*, 24 (4): 649–71.

Caputo, J. (1993) *Against Ethics: Contributions to a Poetics of Obligation with Constant Reference to Deconstruction.* Bloomington: Indiana University Press.

Caputo, J. (1997) *The Prayers and Tears of Jacques Derrida: Religion without Religion.* Bloomington: Indiana University Press.

Caputo, J. and Scanlon, M. (eds) (1999) *God, the Gift and Postmodernism.* Bloomington: Indiana University Press.

Chia, R. (1994) 'The concept of decision: a deconstructive analysis', *Journal of Management Studies*, 31 (6): 780–806.

Chia, R. (1996) *Organizational Analysis as Deconstructive Practice.* New York: Walter de Gruyter.

Cooper, R. (1984) 'The other: a model of human structuring', in Gareth Morgan (ed.), *Beyond Method: Strategies for Social Research*. London: Sage.

Cooper, R. (1986/1990) 'Organization/Disorganization', *Social Science Information* 25 (2): 299–335. Reprinted as 'Organization/Disorganization' in J. Hassard and D. Pym (eds), *The Theory and Philosophy of Organizations*. London: Routledge.

Cooper, R. (1989) 'Modernism, post modernism and organizational analysis 3: the contribution of Jacques Derrida', *Organization Studies*, 10 (4): 479–502.

Cooper, R. and Burrell, G. (1988) 'Modernism, postmodernism and organizational analysis: an introduction', *Organization Studies*, 9 (1): 91–112.

Cornell, D. (1991) *Beyond Accommodation: Ethical Feminism, Deconstruction and the Law*. New York: Routledge.

Cornell, D., Rosenfeld, M. and Carlson, D.G. (eds) (1992) *Deconstruction and the Possibility of Justice*. New York: Routledge.

Critchley, S. (1992) *The Ethics of Deconstruction: Derrida and Levinas*. Edinburgh: Edinburgh University Press.

Deetz, S. (1996) 'Describing differences in approaches to organization science: rethinking Burrell and Morgan and their legacy', *Organization Science*, 7 (2): 191–207.

Derrida, J. (1962/1978) *L' Origine de la géométrie, Edmund Husserl*. Paris: Presses Universitaires de France. Trans. J. Leavey, *Edmund Husserl's Origin of Geometry: An Introduction*. Brighton: Harvester.

Derrida, J. (1967/1973) *La voix et le phénomène: Introduction au problème du signe dans la phénoménologie de Husserl*. Paris: Presses Universitaires de France. Trans. D. Allison, *Speech and Phenomena and Other Essays on Husserl's Theory of Signs*. Evanston IL: Northwestern University Press.

Derrida, J. (1967/1976) *De la grammatologie*. Paris: Editions de Minuit. Trans. G. Spivak, *Of Grammatology*. Baltimore OH: Johns Hopkins University Press.

Derrida, J. (1967/1978) *L'écriture et la différence*. Paris: Editions du Seuil. Trans. A. Bass, *Writing and Difference*. Chicago: Chicago University Press.

Derrida, J. (1972/1981a) *La dissémination*. Paris: Editions du Seuil. Trans. Barbara Johnson, *Dissemination*. London: Athlone.

Derrida, J. (1972/1981b) *Positions: Entretiens avec Henri Ronse, Julia Kristeva, Jean-Louis Houdebine, Guy Scarpetta*. Paris: Editions de Minuit. Trans. A. Bass, *Positions*. Chicago: Chicago University Press.

Derrida, J. (1972/1982) *Marges: De la philosophie*. Paris: Editions de Minuit. Trans. A. Bass, *Margins: Of Philosophy*. Chicago: Chicago University Press.

Derrida, J. (1974/1986) *Glas*. Paris: Edition Galilée. Trans. J. Leavey and R. Rand, *Glas*. Lincoln, NE: University of Nebraska Press.

Derrida, J. (1978) *Eperons: Les styles de Nietzsche/Spurs: Nietzsche's Styles*. Chicago: University of Chicago Press.

Derrida, J. (1980/1983) 'Ponctuations: Le temps de la thèse', in *Du droit à la philosophie*. Paris: Editions Galilée. Trans. K. McLaughlin, 'The time of a thesis: punctuations', in A. Montefiore (ed.), *Philosophy in France Today*. Cambridge: Cambridge University Press.

Derrida, J. (1980/1987) *La Carte postale: De Socrate à Freud et au-delà*. Paris: Aubier-Flammarion. Trans. A. Bass, *The Postcard: From Socrates to Freud and Beyond*. Chicago: Chicago University Press.

Derrida, J. (1982/1985) *L'oreille de l'autre: Otobiographies, transferts, traductions*. Montréal: VLB Editeur. Trans. Peggy Kamuf and Avital Ronell, *The Ear of the Other: Otobiography, Transference, Translation*. Lincoln, NE: University of Nebraska Press.

Derrida, J. (1982/1991) *Feu la cendre*. Paris: Editions des Femmes. Trans. N. Lukacher, *Cinders*. Lincoln, NE: University of Nebraska Press.

Derrida, J. (1983/1985) 'Lettre à un ami japonais', in *Psyché: Inventions de l'autre*. Paris: Editions Galilée. Trans. D. Wood and A. Benjamin, 'Letter to a Japanese friend', in D. Wood and R. Bernasconi (eds), *Derrida and Difference*. Warwick: Parousia Press.

Derrida, J. (1984/1992) 'Psyché: Invention de l'autre', in *Psyché: Inventions de l'autre*. Paris: Editions Galilée. Trans. D. Attridge, 'From Psyché: Invention of the other', in D. Attridge (ed.), *Acts of Literature*. New York: Routledge.

Derrida, J. (1986/1987) 'Admiration de Nelson Mandela, ou, les lois de la réflexion', in *Psyché: Inventions de l'autre*. Paris: Editions Galilée. Trans. M. A. Caws and I. Lorenz, 'The laws of reflection: Nelson Mandela, in admiration', in J. Derrida and M. Tlili (eds), *For Nelson Mandela*. New York: Seaver.

Derrida, J. (1988/1990) *Limited Inc*. Evanston, IL: Northwestern University Press. Trans. E. Weber, *Limited Inc*. Paris: Editions Galilée.

Derrida, J. (1990a) *Du droit à la philosophie*. Paris: Editions Galilée.

Derrida, J. (1990b) *Le problème de la genèse dans la philosophie de Husserl*. Vendôme: Presses Universitaires de France.

Derrida, J. (1991/1992a) *Donner le temps*. Paris: Editions Galilée. Trans. P. Kamuf, *Given Time: 1. Counterfeit Money*. Chicago: University of Chicago Press.

Derrida, J. (1991/1992b) *L'autre cap, suivi de la démocratie ajournée*. Paris: Editions de Minuit. Trans. P.A. Brault and M. Naas, *The Other Heading: Reflections on Today's Europe*. Bloomington: Indiana University Press.

Derrida, J. (1992/1994) 'Force of law: the "mystical foundation of authority"', trans. Mary Quaintance in D. Cornell, M. Rosenfeld and D. G. Carlson (eds), *Deconstruction and the Possibility of Justice*. New York: Routledge. French: *Force de loi: Le «fondement mystique de l'autorité»*. Paris: Editions Galilée.

Derrida, J. (1992/1995a) 'Donner la mort', in *L'éthique du don: Jacques Derrida et la pensée du don*. Paris: Metailie. Trans. D. Wills, *The Gift of Death*. Chicago: University of Chicago Press.

Derrida, J. (1992/1995b) *Points de suspension: Entretiens*. Paris: Editions Galilée. Trans. E. Weber, *Points: Interviews, 1974–1994*. Stanford: Stanford University Press.

Derrida, J. (1993/1994) *Spectres de Marx: L'etat de la dette, le travail du deuil et la nouvelle Internationale*. Paris: Editions Galilée. Trans. P. Kamuf, *Specters of Marx: The State of the Debt, the Work of Mourning and the New International*. New York: Routledge.

Derrida, J. (1993/1995) *Passions*. Paris: Editions Galilée. Trans. D. Wood, J. Leavey and I. McLeod, 'Passions: "An oblique offering"', in *On the Name*. Stanford: Stanford University Press.

Derrida, J. (1993a) 'Apories: Mourir-s'attendre aux limites de la vérité', in *Le passage des frontières: Autour du travail de Jacques Derrida*. Paris: Editions Galilée. Trans. T. Dutoit, *Aporias: Dying – Awaiting (one another at) the 'Limits of Truth'*. Stanford: Stanford University Press.

Derrida, J. (1993b) 'Politics and friendship: an interview with Jacques Derrida', in A. Kaplan and M. Sprinker (eds), *The Althusserian Legacy*. London: Verso.

Derrida, J. (1994/1997) *Politiques de l'amitié*. Paris: Editions Galilée. Trans. G. Collins, *Politics of Friendship*. London: Verso.

Derrida, J. (1996/1998) *Résistances: De la Psychoanalyse*. Paris: Editions Galilée. Trans. P. Kamuf, P.A. Brault and M. Naas, *Resistances: Of Psychoanalysis*. Stanford: Stanford University Press.

Derrida, J. (1996) 'Remarks on deconstruction and pragmatism', trans. S. Critchley in S. Critchley, J. Derrida, E. Laclau and R. Rorty (eds), *Deconstruction and Pragmatism*. London: Routledge.

Derrida, J. (1997) 'Quelqu'un s'avance et dit, entretien avec Jacques Derrida', in J. Derrida and M. Guillaume, *Marx en jeu*. Paris: Descartes & Cie.

Derrida, J. (1997/1999) *Adieu à Emmanuel Levinas*. Paris: Editions Galilée. Trans. P.A. Brault and M. Naas, *Adieu to Emmanuel Levinas*. Stanford: Stanford University Press.

Derrida, J. (1997/2000) *De l'hospitalité*. Paris: Calmann-Lévy. Trans. R. Bowlby, *Of Hospitality*. Stanford: Stanford University Press.

Derrida, J. (1999a) 'Hospitality, justice and responsibility', in R. Kearney and M. Dooley (eds), *Questioning Ethics*. London: Routledge.

Derrida, J. (1999b) 'Marx and sons', in M. Sprinker (ed.), *Ghostly Demarcations: A Symposium on Jacques Derrida's* Specters of Marx. London: Verso.

Derrida, J. (2001) *On Cosmopolitanism and Forgiveness*, trans. M. Dooley and M. Hughes. London: Routledge.

Derrida, J. and Guillaume, M. (1997) *Marx en jeu*. Paris: Descartes & Cie

Derrida, J. and Vattimo, G. (eds) (1996/1998) *La Religion*. Paris: Edition du Seuil. Trans. David Webb, *Religion*. Stanford: Stanford University Press.

du Gay, P. (2000) *In Praise of Bureaucracy: Weber, Organization, Ethics*. London: Sage.

Eagleton, T. (1995/1999) 'Marxism without Marxism', *Radical Philosophy*, 73: 35–7. Reprinted as 'Marxism without Marxism' in M. Sprinker (ed.), *Ghostly Demarcations: A Symposium on Jacques Derrida's* Specters of Marx. London: Verso.

Elias, N. (1978) *The Civilizing Process*, trans. E. Jephcott. Oxford: Blackwell.

Feldman, S. (1998) 'Playing with the pieces: deconstruction and the loss of moral culture', *Journal of Management Studies*, 35 (1): 59–79.

Fischer, E. and Bristor, J. (1994) 'A feminist poststructuralist analysis of the rhetoric of marketing relationships', *International Journal of Research in Marketing*, 11: 317–31.

Frug, G. (1984) 'The ideology of bureaucracy in American law', *Harvard Law Review*, 97: 1276–388.

Gasché, R. (1986) *The Tain of the Mirror: Derrida and the Philosophy of Reflection*. Cambridge, MA: Harvard University Press.

Gasché, R. (1994) *Inventions of Difference: On Jacques Derrida*. Cambridge, MA: Harvard University Press.

Genre (1984) Special Issue on Deconstruction at Yale, Spring and Summer, 17 (1/2).

Gergen, K. (1992) 'Organization theory in the postmodern era', in M. Reed and M. Hughes (eds), *Rethinking Organization: New Directions in Organization Theory and Analysis*. London: Sage.

Gowler, D. and Legge, K. (1984a) 'The deconstruction of evaluation research: Part I, the way forward?', *Personnel Review*, 13 (3): 3–13.

Gowler, D. and Legge, K. (1984b) 'The deconstruction of evaluation research: Part II, the way back?', *Personnel Review*, 13 (4): 2–7.

Hassard, J. (1993) 'Postmodernism and organizational analysis: an overview', in J. Hassard and M. Parker (eds), *Postmodernism and Organizations*. London: Sage.

Hassard, J. (1994) 'Postmodern organizational analysis: toward a conceptual framework', *Journal of Management Studies*, 31 (3): 303–24.

Hassard, J. and Parker, M. (eds) (1993) *Postmodernism and Organizations*. London: Sage.

Heidegger, M. (1927/1962/1977) *Sein und Zeit* (Gesamtaumsgabe, Vol. 2). Frankfurt: Vitorio Klostermann. Trans. J. Macquarrie and E. Robinson, *Being and Time*. Oxford: Blackwell. Trans. (partially) D. F. Krell, 'Being and time: introduction', in D. F. Krell (ed.), *Martin Heidegger; Basic Writings*. London: Routledge.

Hoskin, K. and Macve, R. (1986) 'Accounting and the examination: a genealogy of disciplinary power', *Accounting, Organization and Society*, 11: 105–36.

Jameson, F. (1995/1999) 'Marx's purloined letter', *New Left Review*, 209: 75–109. Reprinted as 'Marx's purloined letter', in Michael Sprinker (ed.), *Ghostly Demarcations: A Symposium on Jacques Derrida's* Specters of Marx. London: Verso.

Jones, C. (2002) 'Foucault's inheritance/inheriting Foucault', *Culture and Organization*, 8 (3): 225–38.

Jones, C. (2003) 'As if business ethics were possible, "within such limits"...', *Organization*, 10 (2): 223–48.

Keenan, T. (1997) *Fables of Responsibility: Aberrations and Predicaments in Ethics and Politics*. Stanford: Stanford University Press.

Kierkegaard, S. (1843/1985) *Fear and Trembling*, trans. Alistair Hannay. London: Penguin.

Kilduff, M. (1993) 'Deconstructing organizations', *Academy of Management Review*, 18 (1): 13–31.

Kilduff, M. and Mehra, A. (1997) 'Postmodernism and organizational research', *Academy of Management Review*, 22 (2): 453–81.

Krell, D. F. (2000) *The Purest of Bastards: Works of Mourning, Art and Affirmation in the Thought of Jacques Derrida*. University Park, PA: Pennsylvania State University Press.

Learmonth, M. (1999) 'The National Health Service manager, engineer and father? A deconstruction', *Journal of Management Studies*, 36 (7): 999–1012.

Legge, K. (1995) *Human Resource Management: Rhetorics and Realities*. Basingstoke: Macmillan.

Legge, K. (1996) 'Deconstruction analysis and management', in Malcolm Warner (ed.), *International Encyclopaedia of Business Management.* London: Routledge.

Letiche, H. (1998) 'Business ethics: (in-)justice and (anti-)law – reflections on Derrida, Bauman and Lipovetsky', in M. Parker (ed.), *Ethics and Organizations.* London: Sage.

Linstead, S. (1993a) 'Deconstruction in the study of organizations', in J. Hassard and M. Parker (eds), *Postmodernism and Organizations.* London: Sage.

Linstead, S. (1993b) 'From post-modern anthropology to deconstructive ethnography', *Human Relations*, 4 (1): 97–120.

Linstead, S. and Grafton-Small, R. (1992) 'On reading organizational culture', *Organization Studies*, 13 (3): 331–55.

Magnus, B. and Cullenberg, S. (eds) (1994) *Whither Marxism? Global Crises in International Perspective.* London: Routledge.

March, J. and Simon, H. (1958) *Organizations.* New York: Wiley.

Martin, J. (1990) 'Deconstructing organizational taboos: the suppression of gender conflict in organizations', *Organization Science*, 1 (4): 339–59.

Mumby, D. and Putnam, L. (1992) 'The politics of emotion: a feminist reading of bounded rationality', *Academy of Management Review*, 17 (3): 465–86.

Mumby, D. and Stohl, C. (1991) 'Power and discourse in organization studies: absence and the dialectic of control', *Discourse and Society*, 2 (3): 313–32.

Noorderhaven, N. (1995) 'The argumentational texture of transaction cost economics', *Organization Studies*, 16 (4): 605–23.

Norris, C. (1982) *Deconstruction: Theory and Practice.* London: Methuen.

Norris, C. (1987) *Derrida.* London: Fontana.

Parker, M. (1992) 'Post-modern organizations or postmodern organization theory?', *Organization Studies*, 13 (1): 1–17.

Parker, M. (1995) 'Critique in the name of what? Postmodernism and critical approaches to organization', *Organization Studies*, 16 (4): 553–64.

Peterson, L. and Albrecht, T. (1999) 'Where gender/power/politics collide: deconstructing organizational maternity leave policy', *Journal of Management Inquiry*, 8 (2): 168–81.

Reed, M. (1997) 'In praise of duality and dualism: rethinking agency and structure in organizational analysis', *Organization Studies*, 18 (1): 21–42.

Rhodes, C. (2000) 'Reading and writing organizational lives', *Organization*, 7 (1): 7–29.

Rorty, R. (1989) 'From ironist theory to private allusions: Derrida', in *Contingency, Irony and Solidarity.* Cambridge: Cambridge University Press.

Rorty, R. (1991) 'Is Derrida a transcendental philosopher?', in *Essays on Heidegger and Others: Philosophical Papers*, Vol. 2. Cambridge: Cambridge University Press.

Rorty, R. (1996a) 'Remarks on deconstruction and pragmatism', in S. Critchley, J. Derrida, E. Laclau and R. Rorty (eds), *Deconstruction and Pragmatism.* London: Routledge.

Rorty, R. (1996b) 'Response to Simon Critchley', in S. Critchley, J. Derrida, E. Laclau and R. Rorty (eds), *Deconstruction and Pragmatism.* London: Routledge.

Ryan, M. (1982) *Marxism and Deconstruction: A Critical Articulation.* Baltimore OH: Johns Hopkins University Press.

Simon, H. (1945) *Administrative Behavior: A Study of Decision-Making in Administrative Organization.* New York: Macmillan.

Spivak, G. C. (1999) *A Critique of Postcolonial Reason: Toward a History of the Vanishing Present.* Cambridge, MA: Harvard University Press.

Sprinker, M. (ed.) (1999) *Ghostly Demarcations: A Symposium on Jacques Derrida's Specters of Marx.* London: Verso.

Steingard, D. and Fitzgibbons, D. (1993) 'A postmodern deconstruction of Total Quality Management (TQM)', *Journal of Organizational Change Management*, 6 (5): 27–42.

Steingard, D. and Fitzgibbons, D. (1995) 'Challenging the juggernaut of globalization: a manifesto for academic praxis', *Journal of Organizational Change Management*, 8 (4): 30–54.

Summers, D., Boje, D.M., Dennehy, R. and Rosile, G.A. (1997) 'Deconstructing the organizational behaviour text', *Journal of Management Education*, 21 (3): 343–60.

Thompson, P. (1993) 'Postmodernism: fatal distraction', in J. Hassard and M. Parker (eds), *Postmodernism and Organizations*. London: Sage.

Turner, S. (1983) 'Studying organization through Lévi-Strauss's structuralism', in G. Morgan (ed.), *Beyond Method: Strategies for Social Research*. London: Sage.

Willmott, H. (1998) 'Towards a new ethics? The contributions of poststructuralism and posthumanism', in M. Parker (ed.), *Ethics and Organizations*. London: Sage.

Xu, Q. (1999) 'TQM as an arbitrary sign for play: discourse and transformation', *Organization Studies*, 20 (4): 659–81.

4

Jean-François Lyotard

Hugo Letiche
with the assistance of Juup Essers

Organizing Lyotard in three movements: representation, justice and organization

The task of a chapter such as this is to do justice to Jean-François Lyotard's ideas and demonstrate their significance to organizational thought. But Lyotard doesn't believe that one can, in any such text, do *justice* to someone's ideas. So the task is paradoxical: if one tries to do justice to Lyotard, one has to argue against what he has said. And if one produces a text driven by one's own fascinations and pulsions (will/desire), one 'breaks one's contract' with, i.e. does not meet expectations – of the reader, of the editor or of the other contributors.

Lyotard writes more about writing, speaks more about speaking, thinks more about thinking, than he actually describes, states or posits. Throughout his *oeuvre*, he has distrusted the power of narrative; i.e. of descriptive text, of statements of how things 'are' or of accounts of happenings. Lyotard thinks that 'narratives' are almost never what they appear to be. The 'business case' doesn't simply describe organizational practice but indicates what is right and wrong; the expert report isn't a neutral (so-called 'objective') document but indicates what ought to be done; the summary of a meeting displays the (in-) effectiveness of the participants' rhetoric and persuasion. What appears to be mere narrative is really almost always strongly normative, prescriptive and/or aesthetic. The effort to write narrative – to describe an event, circumstance or practice, inevitably fails. The products of organizational research – texts which seem to be narratives about companies, practices, organizations and businesses – are really disguised tracts about norms and values, attempts to tell us what we should do and/or treatises on the beautiful. Lyotard asserts that normative, prescriptive and aesthetic texts are often disguised as narratives in order to palm them off onto unsuspecting readers. Lyotard's *oeuvre* is (amongst several other things) about the injustices of reading. One cannot read without being manipulated, abused and having chicanery carried out on one. 'Text' is not 'straight' – it is almost never what it claims to be, and is pretty much incapable of giving the reader a consistent and/or accurate account of itself.

What I am trying to do is, thus, really of little avail – I cannot explain the *nature* of my text to you, the reader, and there is no space where we can really meet, have open dialogue or be able to 'do justice to one another'. The space we (co-)accommodate is theatrical: when you opened the covers of this book, you accepted entering a special and strange universe of enactment. Each chapter is a stage, i.e. a space within which something is presented with a persona, the authorial 'I', who addresses you and *you*, the readers, in the audience. When one enters this theatre, one leaves some of the complexity and chaos of the 'real' world behind. One is here to view the 'spectacle'. But how does the 'spectacle' relate to the world outside? Theatrical conventions determine that you will see a tragedy or a comedy, inductive or deductive representation, pure theory or applied thought – but not everything mixed-up or all at once. In the 'theatre of ideas' the representations follow one another in an orderly and purposeful manner. But in our lives outside the theatre, there is no such fixed structure. The theatre reassures us by falsifying complexity – it gives us safe, ordered, easy representations. Nowhere is this so pervasive as in textbooks, which are the highest point of such theatre; they 'represent' what students can (supposedly) easily master and reproduce (in exams) without upsetting or confusing them.

Lyotard's battle cries, then, are 'How false are your representations!' 'How little justice do you do to reality!'. It is clear why so many business students fail miserably in their first job – they actually think that the world resembles the theatre they have experienced in the (business) textbooks. The spectators (readers/students) have learned to confuse nice, neat, safe text with the experiencing of events and the Other. Lyotard has tried to teach students and to write books that open up, rather than close down, perception. How did he tackle this crisis in representation? There are really three answers, in his work, to this question: (1) an early one, wherein he tries to smash his way through conventions, (2) one from the middle of his career wherein he describes a society characterized by representational uncertainty, and (3) one from late in his career wherein he elucidates the crisis in representation and tries to deal with it not by transcending it (or 'solving' it) but by experiencing it all the more fully. In this chapter I will examine each of these three strategies in turn.

But first, an overview of the most important themes in Lyotard's thought, from the perspective of the focus, here, on organizational theory. Lyotard has been pre-occupied, throughout his career, with the theme of *justice*. In his thinking *justice* can best be imagined in terms of a judge who weighs countervailing arguments and takes a decision. Lyotard tends to employ very visual forms in expressing himself. Thus, his use of the metaphor of the theatre to conceptualize how ideas are transferred, or his metaphor of the courtroom with a case to be adjudicated. These metaphors appear, and reappear, over and over again in Lyotard's books and articles. The problem for the judge is to find the right criteria for judgement. What do you do when two claimants appear before you, with totally different forms of logic, discourse and evidence? For example, an Australian judge confronted with Aborigines making land claims, or an American judge confronted by a witness claiming multiple personality disorder.

The Aborigines tell myths, sing religious chants and speak of their spirits. The witness 'speaks' in different voices, and as different identities, which may not agree with one another. How does one 'understand' such 'testimony' and do 'justice' to what is said? How does one judge? What does it mean, here, 'to do justice'? Lyotard is convinced that no judge can 'do justice' – that they are doomed to their prejudices, to the logic of their bureaucratic position and to their limited sense of rationality. Likewise, managerialism (the mind-set learned in almost all business schools) cannot hear 'labour', 'cultural crisis' or the (economically and politically) 'disenfranchised'. The 'judge' (manager) only hears what his logic (point of view, social role) *prepares* them to hear. For instance, the production manager can 'do justice' to what their factory and employees are capable of – but often has no idea what suppliers can and cannot do, or what the market place really 'requires', or what plans exist on a corporate level for the future. Judgement is radically partial and limited to the criteria readily available; injustice, i.e. not 'doing justice to an Other', is inevitable. And *real* injustice – the protest of the totally wronged, the voice of the absolutely taken advantage of, cannot be heard. The logic(s) available to the 'judge' rarely have any ability to hear the voice of the unequivocal victim. The conceptual processes of judgement, i.e. the criteria used to judge, are inadequate to the complexity of circumstance(s). Judging generates injustice. Where does Lyotard's radical assertion of the inability to judge adequately lead us? He confronts us with the inability of our humanist, capitalist, socialist or liberal democratic conceptual apparatus to deal with concrete circumstances. But is this an invitation to irrationalism or to total relativism? Should we give up on trying to judge and act however we feel? Lyotard draws the opposite conclusion – the crisis in judgement doesn't make judgement less important but *more so*. He sets himself the task of clarifying how to make judgement as adequate to the circumstance(s) as he can.

Though Lyotard's thought informs, very insightfully, several recent debates in organizational thought, his radical theory of incommensurability, unfortunately, does not seem to have been considered by the key players in the paradigm incommensurability debate in organizational theory (with the exception of Jackson and Carter [1991]). Lyotard emphasizes the inherent inability of any text to be commensurable with any other. Human mental existence ('thought' 'stream of consciousness'), for Lyotard, is characterized by the one sentence following the other. It is inevitable that there will be sentences and that each sentence will be followed by others. But what links the one sentence to the other? What creates order, coherence, and consistency? Lyotard insists that no 'truth', or first principle, logically underpins the connection(s) between the sentences. Each statement stands alone, followed by other statements. But is there order, logic or purpose to the chain of sentences? No one can be sure, or specify what the nature of that order (political, economic, social or logical) might be. There are various regimes of order – various possible progressions from sentence to sentence; but none is inevitable, or entirely effectively grounded. Between each statement and its successor there is a chasm of possibilities and incertitude. When one hears the one sentence (idea, pronouncement, position), one does not know (for sure) what the next one is going to be. The links between statements are unsure, indeterminate and unclear enough that the succession is not predictable or pre-known. Each sentence is incommensurable with the next – each defines one statement, one point of view, one speech act, that stands alone and separate from the sentence(s) that follow(s). There is no guaranteed continuity, or certain flow. Ideas come as distinct building blocks, each following its own internal logic.

The logic of organization is comparable. Every element stands alone, with a gap between it and the next element. Organization has to get the sentences (elements) somehow to follow one another in a way that 'makes sense'. Lyotard's name for the chasm that stands between each unit of meaning (sentence) and the next, is *différend*. The *différend* characterizes the contemporary crisis in meaning significance and order. Sentences do follow one another. The question, *Will there be nothing or something?*, is really quite irrelevant as there will be something: a succession of statements, sentences and actions. But will this succession make any 'sense', and how so? This is the crux of the (in)commensurability question – does the order of things (ideas, statements, speech acts) make any sense, and if so, how? In organizational theory much of the debate was between thinkers who accepted *perspectivism* (i.e. an 'organization' can be seen from various perspectives and when seen from each perspective it generates another interpretation or description), and those who rejected *perspectivism* (i.e. there is *one* 'truth' to an organization's identity or 'meaning' and organizational [social] science should display it). The debate often hinged on the issue of relativism – does *perspectivism* lead to some sort of *nominalism*, wherein the observer can make any claim about organizational identity that they wish? Does any rigour or control remain, in our narratives (descriptions, analyses) of organizations, if we assume a perspectivist point of view? If any perspective is as good as any other, what is to stop uncontrolled, wild prejudices and speculation? Will there be any justice, i.e. doing 'justice' to the organization, people and situation studied, left after one opens the floodgates to perspectivism?

Though the theme of justice and the issue of representation (*différend*) is crucial to Lyotard's thought, he is better known as the initiator of the so-called postmodernism debate. Lyotard was a writer who abhorred the 'sound bite'. He didn't want to be remembered for a series of clever phrases or attention-catching aphorisms. He distanced himself from the classic tradition of French intellectuals, such as Bergson or Sartre, who were very public thinkers who saw it as their task to get large numbers of people to think about crucial ideas, themes and issues. Lyotard insisted that the classic intellectual's task was to fill empty, vacant, slow-moving time. People used to have plenty of time, time that they could use to reflect. According to Lyotard, that sort of time no longer exists. Contemporary society puts the person under constant pressure to perform, to be economically active and productive. The intellectual who fills empty time (i.e. time free from work or any economic pressure) has no role in the globalized 24-hour economy. One cannot be a point of reference for free thought in a society wherein no free space exists. If one can no longer be an intellectual in the tradition of Bergson and Sartre, what can one do?

Lyotard wanted to be someone who asked critical questions about the preconditions of meaning. He was out to be a 'critical thinker' who ferreted out the assumptions inherent in various points of view, and laid bare the limits and contradictions of ideas. But in addition to his philosophical *oeuvre*, Lyotard wrote some sociology. His sociological texts try to characterize contemporary society – they are (in effect) a narrative about present-day society. In these texts Lyotard 'authored' the term *postmodern/postmodernism*. That name (word, idea) has caught on, and become a touchstone for innumerable debates. The last thing in the world Lyotard appreciated was catchy phrases, which reduce complexity to simple names. He abhorred the reduction of complexity. But his own term *postmodern,* has become the very sort of totalizing term he fought against. Lyotard wanted to teach us that it is impossible to do justice to social or historical reality with any simple, singular assertion. The falsity of humanism, socialism or free market thought was that they all tried to subsume the complexity of circumstances (all the 'sentences' of real life) into one simple statement about the nature of mankind, or the liberation of the working class, or how to maximize economic wealth. Simple truths do extreme violence to diversity and circumstance. That's why all the 'idealisms' turn, de facto, against themselves and become destructive. The 'truths' that reduce history to a single factor, become 'terror' because they suppress reality and do violence to aspects of existence, which do not fit their pattern. Such 'truths' end up more 'machines of repression' than forces for 'freedom' and 'justice'. Lyotard's radical critique of 'grand narratives', i.e. of any single 'truth' that claims to explain history and humanity, applies equally to the (his own) concept of *postmodernism.* Thus we need to critically examine the concept *postmodern,* for instance in organizational theory, to see what effect it has on meaning.

Postmodern society has lost the stable sense of time and space with which modernism was capable of relating personal (private) existence to public (historical) existence. The globalized economy has destroyed the old ideas of space, identity and order. Globalization has brought the issue of culture and identity to the forefront. Is cultural diversity inevitable, desirable and possible? And if there is diversity, how can one deal with it? Lyotard argues that diversity is inevitable, but unmanageable. Each factor, action, voice is impelled to be radically inconsistent (*différend*) with the next. Every effort to create one regime, i.e. to 'manage' the differences, only leads to the suppression of difference. One can only 'manage' difference from a meta-position that pretends to see 'both sides' of the difference and to be able to mitigate them. But no such position can do justice to the differing points of view. The claim of one, if not of both, parties will be submerged to the logic of the judge's 'understanding'. Difference cannot be channeled into a 'system of diversity', without destroying the *différend* involved. But if difference cannot be 'managed', without destroying identity and submerging 'self' to the terror of those in control, how can a diverse and complex society function without falling into totalitarianism? What sort of political solution does Lyotard propose for the evident and real need to deal with (social) difference(s)? Very different groups inevitably will bring different assumptions, meanings, purposes and ideas to their interactions: how does one deal (with justice) with this?

To return to the theme of representation, the social sciences have been confronted during the last thirty years with the dilemma of recognizing that their object of study is linguistic. One can say that one studies 'trust' in organizations, or 'motivation', or 'leadership', or corporate culture, but what does one really study? The terms do not refer to clear matters, with distinct ostensive definitions: i.e. something you can point to and show to someone else. 'Trust', 'motivation', 'leadership' are fairly vague concepts and ideas. For instance, in agency theory some social scientists claim that 'control' exists as the direct opposite of 'trust'. Supposedly there are two managerial possibilities – direct 'control' or management based on 'trust'. But the thinker who is used to taking language into account, immediately realizes that these two terms are not simple opposites, but exist in inter-relationship to one another. Without a concept of 'trust' there would be, in the example, no definition of 'control'. And 'trust', in organizational affairs, is a form of 'control'. 'Control' is most often grounded in one's trust in the predictability of demands and behaviour. Careful linguistic analysis makes simple assertions about social reality impossible. Each term defers to many others, if not all others; language is a web of implications without end. Lyotard wrestled throughout his *oeuvre*, with this problem of the linguistic nature of social reality and understanding. Are any meanings stable, significant and really clear, or is social science and organization studies nothing more than a never-ending form of linguistic regression – every term implicating a series of other terms, which in turn refer to still more concepts?

Thus, the rest of this chapter addresses the three key areas of thought already indicated:

(1) the crisis in representation: in what sense is a positive logic of text, thought or idea possible?
(2) (in-)justice and (mis-)judging: is good 'judgement' possible and if not what does this mean for leadership responsibility or organizing?
(3) the implications of Lyotard's ideas for organization theory and the current debates in organization studies.

Crisis in representation

There are two principal starting points to the examination of Lyotard's thought – one via *Économie libidenale [Libidinal Economy]* (1974) and one by way of *Le Différend [The Differend]* (1983). This section follows the first path and the next the second. *Libidinal Economy* is a scandalous and angry book. In it Lyotard fires a massive broadside at 'semiotics' and Marxism, thereby attacking the two most active intellectual movements of the time. *Libidinal Economy* rejects any synthesis, method or (first) law of thought. It celebrates the *dérive* ('drifting' – something similar to the stream of consciousness), *déplacement* (displacements – ideas or thoughts that nudge out other ideas or thoughts) and temporary *positions* (changing points of view and/or standpoints) (Maggiori, 1998). Lyotard's *oeuvre*, read from this approach, centres on the temporariness of positions, the broken path of intellectual development and the lack of any single key '-ism' in writing. A thinker who declines to 'mean' one thing, who will not be 'accountable' for a single position or point of view, refuses to play the intellectual game according to its established rules. Such a strategy of active nihilism sees knowing and organizing as 'the explosive dissolution of the central organs of domination, that will say of the very means of representation' (Vattimo, 1998). The destruction of representation is driving the writer back into speechlessness, the philosopher back into *not* knowing, and is forcing the judge to revert to incertitude. It is the first step in liberating communication from prevailing structures of repression and injustice.

Lyotard criticizes the discourses of liberation (essentially semiotics and Marxism) for having become texts of totalization and closure. These texts do not open up debate and discussion, but close it down. They are not tools leading to new conjecture and experiential insight, but a force for thoughtless cleverness and intellectualism run wild. Theory stultifies; it is complex to be complex. It is divorced from real life concerns and lived worlds. This cry of despair and protest is fitting for someone who began his intellectual trajectory close to phenomenology, and in particular close to Maurice Merleau-Ponty (Lyotard, 1954). Merleau-Ponty was continually up-dating Husserl's claim that philosophy (intellectual activity) was not opening our eyes to the lived world, but was blinding us to experience. Intellectual activity avoids seeing what happens to *Others*, and ignores pain, crisis and turmoil. For Husserl the crisis in early twentieth-century intelligentsia is to be found in its unwillingness to look and see, and its complex ways of eluding responsibility to the *Other*. Merleau-Ponty's work re-assumed this theme, emphasizing the faults of intellectualizing, objectifying and depersonalized perception. Merleau-Ponty's phenomenology pleads for direct openness and commitment to the immediate, concrete lived-world. What Lyotard has done is to radicalize this line of thought. Merleau-Ponty pleads for perceptual integrity and fundamental openness to the plight of the other; Lyotard attacks the rationalizations that pretend to look to the *Other* but really look away. It is characteristic of the fifties and early sixties in France that the question of the *Other*, i.e. the (un-)willingness to know, understand, respond to the *Other,* is seen to be crucial. Social injustice needs to deny the existence of the *Other*, i.e. to not see the *Other* as human. Having dehumanized *Others*, one is free to exploit and repress them. Direct perceptual veracity, the ability and willingness to acknowledge the existence of *Others*, was seen as the crux of social humanism. This line of thought was shared from Existentialism to Personalism, from Camus to Sartre, from Merleau-Ponty to Mounier. By 1974 a more radical and embittered version of the argument was called for. There was too much theory that claimed to be humanist, i.e. to open perception to the immediate and lived, but that only rationalized and reified thought. For Lyotard, semiotics and Marxism were such 'false humanisms' that pushed the *Other* out of sight more than opening up vision.

Lyotard claimed that semiotics reduced all communication to signs and emptied all interaction of genuine substance. By categorizing and labelling sign systems, the semioticians emptied text of meaning, voice and passion. Semiotics was a way of banishing content and of focusing on mere formalism(s). It deferred meaning, further and further away from reading. Semioticians revealed the text below the surface of the text, and the text below that, etc. etc. This is a process of constant regression, leading further and further back into linguistic analysis, and the study of language structure. By focusing on how language works, they lost contact with meaning and limited themselves to a universe of signs.

Lyotard's critique of Marxism centres on Marx's unrealized and unrealizable effort to capture all reality in theory. For Marxism, no event, occurrence or action is free from, independent of or unanticipated by the theory. Marxism brings theory to its most suffocating, all-deadening level of activity. Marxism creates a theoretical point of zero degree(s) of freedom. The all-inclusive socio-economic theory makes independent, fresh, new observation unnecessary. Marxism creates a total form of theoretical alienation, wherein theory makes perception irrelevant. Despite thousands of pages of text, Marx never actually arrived at the point that there was nothing to see, because everything had been totalized in text. But his project destroys the need to examine the empirical, thanks to the theory's all-inclusive explanatory power, just as in semiotics, theory destroys the real and experienced by forcing thought into constant regression. In Lyotard's view, Marxism fetishizes theory: ideas are presented as empirical reality, making the life-world invisible and irrelevant.

A second objection of Lyotard's to Marxism is that Marx did not correctly conceptualize his first cause, or (primary) source of energy. The proletariat supposedly negates capitalism. But what gives the proletariat the energy needed to change, make or recast history? Why assume that the proletariat (accepting for a moment that such a thing actually exists) would do anything of the sort? Especially since the proletariat's destiny is not derived from its own culture or tradition, but answers more to a theoretical socio-economic necessity, defined by intellectuals such as Marx. Lyotard accepts that a primary source of energy – some sort of will, drive or pulsion, makes activity possible. But this life force is not explained in Marx's thought. For Marx the proletariat provides the energy leading to change. But this assumption is made without explanation. Marxism takes it for granted that some pulsion or energy that comes from outside the theory animates human activity. In effect, Marxism is meta-physical – a system which posits a first cause exterior to the workings of the concrete, material universe. However good (or flawed) Marx's descriptions of capitalism were, socio-economic reality is logically subsumed in it to an assumed source of energy or life force, that permits the proletariat to act and generate change. But what is this primary life force really like? Whatever it may be, it is not a product of the rational laws of capitalism. Thus the more Marx described capitalism, the more he distanced himself from the primary life force, upon which his thought is based. As in semiotics, the thought distances one from the immediate lived force of existence.

Lyotard also objects to Marx because Marx remains, in essence, a 'critical' thinker. For Lyotard criticism is locked into the realm of discourse which it criticizes. Criticism is glued to what it discusses, debates, and opposes. In criticism, one simulates – reproduces, summarizes, states in a narrative the thought that is to be problematized in order to *dis-simulate* it – to distort it, to argue against it and to point to its flaws. *Dissimulation* cannot lead to fundamental renewal or change. It creates an altered version of what has been simulated. For Lyotard, Marx simulated capitalist development and on that basis dissimulated an idea of socialist socio-economic evolution. The theatre of Marxist thought shares the same basic structures as that of capitalism. Thus, the socio-economic powers stage society's industrial politics in a way that leaves most people disempowered observers of forces that totally overreach them. The social machinery may work somewhat differently under Marxism from under capitalism, but it is the same machine. The theatre is the same: the audience is passive, the author (playwright) dominates experience and the staging is over-simplified and over-rationalized. One can extend the metaphor of the theatre ('idea') ever further: lived-experience forced to pretend to resemble the theatre. Under communism this occurred – the 'idea' tried ate up reality. But the 'idea', of course, finally collapsed under the weight of its own absurdity. The (Modernist) theatre of ideas cannot, however hard it tries, actually replace the messy, energized, dynamic world of events. Human action and not the theatre of rationalizations, prevails.

Lyotard thinks that Freud has successfully described the force of human pulsion, in his theory of the *libido*. Freud has not made the same mistake as semiotics and Marxism. Lyotard rejects, in semiotics as well as in Marxism, the suggestion that the 'idea' (*language* in the one case and *proletariat* in the other) replaces the *thing* that it supposedly represents. Lyotard is determined to embrace not a sign that has replaced what it signifies, but *desire*, i.e. the first principle of energy and action. Lyotard has embarked on a quest for intensity. But direct experience is only thinkable *beyond representation*. By getting rid of semiotics' self-absorbed self-conscious approach, and by escaping Marxism's pre-conceptualized theoretical totalization(s), one can hope to return to the experiential lived-world. Lyotard's libidinal economy is made up by the energy or force (pulsion) which wills us to live, create and act. The libidinal economy is the force of the lived-world – it is the energy that makes human activity possible. This economy was only repressed and suffocated by semiotics and Marxism. Lyotard calls its force of human activity and the tension underpinning its ability to create, the *tensor*. The *tensor* is generated by Eros and *Todestrieb* (the death-drive). Lyotard tries to escape the semiotic and Marxist logic that vitiates human energy and makes access to lived-existence impossible. For Lyotard, Marxist and semiotic representation – i.e. the 'world', 'consciousness', and 'text' they create – cannot accede to the life-world, because it is smothered in critical meta-narrative. The narrative's failure to give access to direct circumstance is conveyed by the metaphor of the theatre. Narrative theatricizes existence, alienating the *self* from direct perception, and hopelessly entangling consciousness in symbols and endless regression into explanation and rationalization. Only by overturning the rationalizing power of (semiotic/ Marxist) narrative is escape from the theatre possible. Only then can an identity embedded in dynamic primary processes be possible.

But a simple, primary principle of activity or dynamism amounts to a God-concept. It guarantees activity irrespective of human differences or choices. Lyotard is not looking for such an absolute or a first principle that empties human action of purposiveness. He is looking for a theory of the active human agent independent of a first cause or any predetermined certainty. He searches for a theory of activity or existence without pre-defined purpose(s) or essence. Lyotard latches onto Eros with *Todestrieb*. Eros is the principle of order, organization, constancy and concrete action; *Todestrieb* is the principle of disruption, of the unsettling, and is directed towards infinity. Lyotard isn't searching for a simple principle of *vitalism*, but a logic of conflict and imbalance. *Desire* is the key term: it is what we lack (what is desired) and it is the basic pulsion (a life force). *Desire* is Eros and *Todestrieb*. Together they create tension, indeterminacy and passion – this is the *tensor*. It is tension, created by contradictory forces, pushing and pulling consciousness in different directions, making involvement and enthusiasm possible.

This force is pre-verbal, pre-conscious and prior to representation. It is the fore-structure to an alive, open, involved approach to existence. The libidinal economy is composed both from forces that create an active and alive demeanour and from those that stop or deaden activity. Semiotic and Marxist intellectual strategies, however 'critical' they may be, remain grounded in the regressive logic to representation. They cannot break out of the negative libidinal economy. A positive libidinal economy requires the abandonment of control, and a radical openness to experience. But a positive libidinal economy cannot be defined, because every effort at definition is limited by the rules of representation and the theatricality of rationalization. Examples of the positive libidinal economy include: the polymorphous pervert (the child-like psychology of pleasure, physical delight and positive sensuality) and the metaphor of dancing (the Dionysian passion for joyful abandon [*jouissance*], creativity and expression). But these examples can only be hinted at, so as not to reify them. The will to escape from intellectualism, from the limits of criticism and the entanglement in the logic of representation, are clear. Is there a subterfuge to the endless conceptual regression and repressive theatricality? Can the positive libidinal economy of will, pulsion and desire overcome the negation of critical thought and representation?

Justice and judging/in-justice and mis-judgement

The previous section presented a 'phenomenologized' version of *Libidinal Economy*. Frequent use was made of the notions of the 'subject' and 'experience'. An 'I' or 'subject' was confronted with *an Other* or 'experience', to whom it did or did not (try to) do justice. But Lyotard goes beyond these concepts and questions their meaning. The 'I' is no more stable than its 'this' (place) or 'now' (time), and it changes from context to context. An 'experience' can be almost anything at all. The 'I' that has an 'experience' is not a satisfactory way to ground knowledge. We have no grounds for assuming, on the one hand, a world of event and change (a principle of instability and impermanence) and on the other hand, an experiential consciousness (principle of stability and ground for meaning). Thus, Lyotard rejects the tradition of Merleau-Ponty wherein significance is grounded in the life-world, in the specifics of the 'I' and its 'experience'. Lyotard chooses a more radical form of epistemological scepticism. 'Meaning' and 'knowledge' are not analysed as *human social events* because Lyotard refuses either to *assume* a knowing subject (the 'I') that by definition one can know nothing about, if it really is an *a priori* to all consciousness, or to presuppose a generalizable human consciousness wherein the experiences of the life-world lead, in one and the same manner, to ideas, remembrance, and consciousness ('text'). Lyotard refuses to ground knowing on unknowable assumptions. He follows, thus, the French philosophical tradition of Descartes, wherein the grounds of knowledge are radically questioned. Can we really be sure that we can trust 'knowledge'? Already in *Libidinal Economy,* Lyotard began to question the trustworthiness of 'knowing', the nature of the energy, pulsion and will to create. In *The Differend* he criticizes his previous work, calling it 'transcendental', a solution to the problem of knowing and knowledge dictated from the outside, in a God-like imposition of a 'first truth'. But Lyotard returns, in *The Differend*, to the theme of the importance of the specific and experiential in that he values modest (immediate) narratives and local truths. Was Lyotard epistemologically inconsistent the first time (in *Libidinal Economy)* or the second time (in *The Differend)*, or both times?

In *The Differend* Lyotard turns away from Freud, towards Wittgenstein and Kant. He reinterprets Wittgenstein's idea of 'language games', in an effort to create his own language-based philosophy. He takes the sentence ('phrase')[1] as his point of departure. 'Sentences' are defined in terms of four characteristics. How these characteristics are employed, determines the different types ('regimes') of sentences. These 'regimes', in turn, are assembled into a variety of 'genres' – a 'genre' links sentences from different 'regime(s)' in a prescribed manner. Lyotard spends a lot of time examining the problems involved in linking 'regimes'. 'Regimes' are problematic when the sentences do not (really) follow the rules that they are supposed to, or claim to, follow.

Construction of a 'sentence' entails a sender, an addressee, a referent and a meaning. 'Subjects', 'reality' and 'experience' are produced via the relationship(s) between the four constituent parts of the sentence. Lyotard has opted for hyper-Cartesianism: 'I think, therefore I am' is still too uncertain for him. The only thing we can be utterly certain of is that there are sentences. But the meaning of the sentence can be, and often is, doubted. Many sentences can be used to explain what any one sentence 'means'. The nature of the sentence's *being*, whether it is 'reality', 'fantasy', part of a 'nominal' universe, God-given etc. etc., can be doubted. The *ethics* of the sentence, whether an utterance is wise, generous, or just, can be debated. Every aspect of a sentence can be questioned, but not without first accepting that there really is a sentence. It is a given, over which we have no control, that there are sentences. We cannot choose between a world with or without sentences. All that is certain is that sentences will happen. To the *Arrive-t-il?* (Is it happening?) there is an answer: *There is, it happens* – there are always language events (sentences, regimes and genres) (Lyotard, 1983).

The universe of the sentence is defined by the logic of the *sender* (the *source* of the sentence), the *addressee* (to whom the sentence is *addressed*), the *referent(s)* (*what* the sentence says something *about*) and the *meaning* (*what* the sentence *says* about the referent). Each type or 'regime' of sentence obeys rules;

in the descriptive sentence, the sender and addressee are in symmetrical positions i.e. they are effortlessly able to exchange positions. In a descriptive sentence, such as 'It is nice weather', it makes no difference if the sentence is directed to the one person, or the other (Van Peperstraten, 1991). But in a prescriptive sentence, there is no such symmetry. The *addressee* ought to obey; the *sender* enacts the role of unreachable authority. A descriptive sentence, thus, cannot be freely transposed into a prescriptive one. The descriptive discovery of *favelas* in Brazil does not inevitably lead to prescriptive (for instance, political) action(s). There is no automatic, or even easy, movement from the realm of 'fact' (the 'descriptive') to the universe of 'mores' (the 'prescriptive'). Lyotard's critics claim that he has, hereby, created a philosophy of de-politicization and indifference.

In other juxtapositions of two different types of sentences, similar chasms arise. In the ostensive sentence, the sender attaches him or herself to the referent: 'Right here and now, there is this thing that confirms the validity of what I say'. But in the cognitive 'phrase', the referent is located in a universe of unchanging place and time. The referentials of the ostensive sentence need to be as proximate or close as possible to the sender; those of the cognitive sentence as far away as possible (Lyotard, 1987). Thus, how does one move, in laboratory research, from ostensive sentences ('Here are the data') to cognitive ones (the interpretation of the data and theoretical consideration of their significance)? And in narrative the sender is always implicated in what they describe (the referent) because the description exists on the basis of the sender having seen, witnessed, and known what is described. But the theoretician does not want to be implicated in their referent. Theoreticians keep their distance from their referent, to be able to develop their thought on the basis of reason, logic and analysis – the senders' authority depends on their distance from (neutrality towards) the referent (Lyotard, 1988). Thus, the social scientist who wants to move from observation (narration) to theoretical discussion has to change regimes – but how can one legitimize such a move? Changing from one sentence regime to another is a discursive move that demands explanation and justification. The move from one sort of sentence to another is problematic (i.e. logically doubtful); therefore the purposive (pragmatic) use of thought (sentences) is very difficult.

Only sentences that follow one logic (regime) of sender – addressee – referent – meaning, are logically consistent and thus compatible. If one changes regime, there has to be a bridge, a mechanism justifying the linkage. Otherwise, the change in regime is non-rational and unjustified. Regimes are, thus, irreducible, in the sense that they cannot be easily translated from one to the other (Bennington, 1988). Lyotard scrutinizes how sentences (do not) earn their way from one regime of linguistic action to another. He repeats the analysis on two levels: between *regimes* of sentences and between *genres* of discourse. Different sorts of regimes include the descriptive (He opens the door); the narrative (He opened the door); the prescriptive (Open the door); and the ostensive (This door, here, is open) etc. Different genres include science, philosophy, tragedy and politics.

A phrase (sentence), even the most ordinary one, is constituted according to a set of rules (its regime). There are a number of phrase regimes; reasoning, knowing, describing, recounting, questioning, showing, ordering, etc. Phrases from heterogeneous regimes cannot be translated from one into the other. They can be linked one onto the other in accordance with an end fixed by a genre of discourse. For example, dialogue links an ostensive (showing) or a definition (describing) onto a question; at stake in it is the two parties coming to an agreement about the sense of the referent. Genres of discourse supply rules for linking together heterogeneous phrases, rules that are proper for attaining certain goals: to know, to teach, to be just, to seduce, to justify, to evaluate, to arouse emotion, to oversee, ... (Lyotard, 1984, in 1988 English translation p. xii)

Lyotard isn't a typical language philosopher. His categorizations of regimes and genres are, at best, sloppy, if not downright arbitrary. Furthermore, he isn't really interested in the questions of 'truth' and 'certainty'. In the section in *The Differend* entitled 'Presentation', Lyotard asserts that a sentence is incapable of presenting its own presentation. A sentence can present something, conceptualized structurally as a relationship between a sender – addressee – referent – and meaning, but the sentence cannot present its own rules of presentation (i.e. justify *how* it presents). The reflexivity of the sentence or phrase is very limited. Something other than sentences is needed to understand their presentation. What comprise that something else are (Kantian) Ideas.

What draws Lyotard to Kantian Ideas is not that they form a coherent logic, but just the opposite. For Lyotard, Kant is a source of reflection on judgement and aesthetics. Lyotard's concerns: 'What regimes of sentences can be combined in what sort of genres of discourse?' 'Can empirical and prescriptive genres be linked?' 'How can one get from observation (narrative) to action (politics in the most general sense of the term)?' Lyotard replies in terms of a *dissensus* between description (the empirical) and Ideas (*a priori* assumptions that make thought possible). Philosophy has tried to unite the realm of the concrete/practical/empirical and that of the mind/reason/principles. Philosophy has tried to assert that *What is, is logical,* and *What is logical, is*, whether *'logical'* was interpreted as 'history' (Hegel), 'perception' (Merleau-Ponty), 'pragmatism' (Dewey), in terms of 'Being' (Heidegger), or as human 'will' (Nietzsche). Lyotard ruptures the link so there is a *dissensus* between *being* (what 'is') and *idea* (concepts, principles, sense making). One can try to bridge the gap between basic principles and observations, but there is no guarantee of success. Social Science is so terribly problematic, in Lyotard's opinion, because it has tried to link social (economic) observation with (social) philosophical reflection. These are two very different realms of discourse; the one narrative and demanding empirical evidence, the other theoretical and only indirectly discussible via analogy and metaphor.

The effort to mould the two realms together is very precarious. For instance, Lyotard's critique of Marx is that he seized upon the empirical plight of the labouring class, named it the 'proletariat', and then claimed that the 'proletariat' demanded social justice. Marx transformed an empirical observation into a theoretical actor, shifting from one realm to another in an unwarranted manner. When one moves from one register to another, one has to defend (have very good reasons for) one's action. For Lyotard, the tension between the empirical (narrative) and conceptual (Ideas) cannot be resolved. Lyotard thinks we simply have to live with the conflict, a conflict that produces, in its tensions and difficulties, the experience of the *sublime*. In this idea he follows Kant, not the rules of knowledge, applicable to 'nature' or 'theory', but those appropriate to 'judgement', are here crucial. 'Judgement' is defined as ethical and aesthetic. 'Judgement' is experienced as *sublime* – as the disharmony (*dissensus*) that arises between observation and thought, between bearing witness and the analysis of concepts. Combining, on the one hand, mental creativity, ideational performance, abstract activity and, on the other, pure observation, empirical research, and careful watching, does not lead to harmony. The tension creates a heightened sense of awareness, a need for insight, or what Lyotard calls the *sublime* (Van Peperstraten, 1991). This polarity rather closely resembles Lyotard's earlier description of the *tensor,* but with Eros replaced by 'beauty' (harmony of imagination and observation) and *Todestrieb* by the *sublime* (the dynamic, complicated, struggling relationship between thought and perception).

In *The Differend* Lyotard tries to reveal the logic of (in-)justice. The problem is that real injustice leaves no trace. Litigation or bargaining over (some sort of) restitution, occurs between two parties who share a common regime of sentences. Real injustice occurs between parties who do not share any such common regime, either of sentences or of genres. In real injustice one party silences the other. Auschwitz is such a case of injustice. The philosophical importance of Auschwitz is that it makes it evident that humanity does not necessarily share a common regime of sentences, or use of genres.

Lyotard's universe of sentences is very tentative and provisional. The diverse bits and pieces of language philosophy do not coalesce into a tight system. No transcendent order unites language's sub-systems. Speech ('text') is constantly threatened by incoherence and disorder. There is dynamism, or ample degrees of freedom, in the system. But the fluidity can be abused. In the past, false order has been imposed; all genres have been forced into a closed system, dictated by a totalitarian regime of sentences and of government. Every genre has a totalitarian aspect to it. Each genre claims to be the 'truth' and threatens to shut out all other forms of expression. But as long as a plurality of genres exists, and grappling with their inconsistencies and a complex universe of discourse continues, the totalitarian danger is remote. But as soon as a regime starts to totalize, to get a grip on all genres, the danger of injustice arises.

To reiterate: injustice occurs when a discourse (claim) cannot be heard and a logic (genre) is made inadmissible. Lyotard explains, using the metaphor of the trial. If Australian Aborigines put forward their land claims in their own discourse, the legal system will not acknowledge the claim. Australian law is based on concepts of property, deed, ownership and precedent, that are incompatible with the Aboriginal discourse. Total injustice occurs when power (the state's monopoly over violence) only acknowledges its own discourse, and negates the discourse of the Other. In injustice there is total *dissensus*. The one text refuses to admit the other. Lyotard has tried to show that no discourse (text) really admits the other. The logic of injustice is omni-present. The way to guard against it, is to make sure that discourse takes place in a social field where no one has the power to dominate. Local discourses, about immediate events, produce mini-totalities that do not threaten others too much. For Lyotard there is no solution, in principle, to the problem of injustice; at best we can keep the danger manageable by restricting the power of all claims and claimants.

Lyotard, postmodernism and organization

Neither attention to, nor much knowledge of, Lyotard's philosophical thought has been evident in the postmodernism debate in organizational theory. A perusal of the literature reveals many citations of the *Postmodern Condition*, but a marked lack of references to the rest of Lyotard's work. But the *Postmodern Condition* is more the exception than the rule. It is a text of narration, a sociological description, albeit with philosophical undertones and digressions. Lyotard's critique of grand narratives has been quoted over and over again. The assertion that all the root theories of modernism, Marxism (revolution), positivism (enlightenment), liberal democracy (freedom), and psychoanalysis (self-awareness) have failed to deliver what they promise, draws all the scholarly attention. Lyotard argues that each of these systems produces a totalization of thought and whatever it doesn't encompass it banishes. Seemingly satisfactory explanation is achieved at the cost of exclusion. But the partiality of each of these 'truths' returns to haunt it: what it cannot deal with, it represses and distorts. These explanatory systems do violence to those aspects of life that they do not explain. This theoretical violence translates into practical (political) violence. The partiality of the 'explanation' transforms it into a source of acts of injustice and destruction. This argument is born of Lyotard's opposition to limited and partial genres that pretend to be more than they are. Marxism produces the Gulag, Positivism, the destruction of the environment, liberal democracy hyper-capitalism and performativity.

But Lyotard goes much further than the 'grand narrative' thesis. He describes the de-legitimization of thought and the growing supremacy of hyper-capitalism. The *Postmodern Condition* was written as a report on the (future of the) university, in which Lyotard asserted that the 'entrepreneurial university' has no time for thought and is more a management consulting firm than a place free for speculation. The irony is, that by destroying the legitimacy of the intellectual, one ends up destroying *all* organizational legitimacy. At first, it is merely the critical and reflective practices of the scholar that suffer. The institution, university, continues to exist as a training establishment with the task of preparing persons for 'employability'. But if every person is responsible for his or her own 'employability', there will be less and less management. This, in fact, is the current trend, where so-called 'flexibility', 'down scaling' and 'virtual organization' are de-managing organization. If one associates 'management' with hierarchy and machine bureaucracy, this seems to be an attractive alternative. But if one identifies 'management' with intellectual leadership, innovation, creativity and renewal, it is a disaster. 'Employability' is 'everyone for themselves and nothing for us all'. It leads to the triumph of market mediocrity at the cost of excellence, rigour and investment in long term change and imagination.

The uses of Lyotard in the organizational theory literature are often downright strange. For instance, an article by Majken Schultz and Mary Jo Hatch has as its main tenet, a key thesis that Lyotard *rejects* in *The Postmodern Condition*, while claiming Lyotard as a principal point of reference (Schultz and Hatch, 1996). Schultz and Hatch claim to produce a logic of 'connections' that appears 'when researchers consider postmodern critiques'; and assume:

> ... discontinuity and difference rather than order and similarity. Because there is no pattern of sense to be found, general theories, which Lyotard and others labelled grand narratives, are sentimental illusions. Lyotard (1984) described the attack on the grand narrative as an argument against the modernist drive toward determinacy and consensus, whereas modernist notions of order and patterning neglect discontinuity, passion and rupture. (Schultz and Hatch, 1996)

Schultz and Hatch defend a logic of paradigm interplay, arguing that different paradigms (genres of sentences in Lyotard's terminology) can coexist in a logic of 'both-and' with 'generality' (functionalist and systems theory inspired) and 'contextuality' (case based, interpretative, ethnographic) codeterminant. The researcher is told: (1) to recognize the contrasts and connections between functionalist and interpretative paradigms, and (2) to exploit the interdependence and tension between these contrasts and connections by moving between paradigms. One should flow between paradigms (Schultz and Hatch, 1996).

This epistemic strategy is in total conflict with that of Lyotard. The rhetorical strategy of *The Postmodern Condition* begins by contrasting functionalism or systems theory with critical neo-Marxist social science, the positivist versus the radical (interpretative). Lyotard argues that these modernist polar choices are losing their credibility (Lyotard, 1979). The disintegration of grand narratives (meta-theories attempting to explain the broad course of history and/or humanity: communism, socialism, liberal democracy, capitalism, psychoanalysis) is occurring because the social cohesion which the grand narratives supported is itself disintegrating. Society has become 'a mass composed of individual atoms launched in absurd Brownian movement' (Lyotard, 1979: 31). Schultz and Hatch are calling, in the name of Lyotard, for tolerant, pluriform and multifaceted research based on the liberal democratic grand narrative. Lyotard is arguing that such a thing is no longer realistic or possible. The cutting and pasting of genres (paradigms) that Schultz and Hatch are calling for, goes against the whole thrust of Lyotard's language philosophy. Lyotard has no problem acknowledging that in different regimes of sentences (styles of analysis), there can be common points (i.e. the relationship between the 'referent' and the 'meaning' may be similar), but his whole point is that there are also differences that must not be ignored. If injustice is to be avoided, the 'sender' (researcher) must not have the power to admit or banish data (phrases/sentences) as she/he wishes. This is, *par excellence*, the sort of 'language game' Lyotard dreads, and he optimistically argues that there are fewer and fewer 'senders' (researchers) who want to take on such a position of meta-dominance in relationship to their objects of study.

In Lyotard's terms, the Schultz and Hatch 'regime' is characterized by a 'sender' who determines the terms of reference for 'meaning'. By joining the 'sender' to the 'meaning', the 'regime' cuts out the 'addressee', who is admitted to the text only in so far as the duo 'sender-meaning' choose to acknowledge their presence. Thus, the researcher prioritizes the meta-narrative (paradigm, theoretical point of view, philosophical assumptions), at an enormous cost to the ability to relate to *an Other* (the 'referent' or 'addressee'). This is a prescription for research wherein ideas dominate under the tutelage of the researcher's presuppositions. But Lyotard argues that such research will not get funded because performativity has become all-important. Researchers have to identify with their 'addressee'; the 'addressee' has to be 'better off' thanks to the research. Modernist intellectual activity, wherein the researcher ('sender') was motivated by an ideal of 'progress' and/or 'objective science' ('meaning') is dying. The 'regime' of modernism has been overwhelmed by the demands of hyper-capitalism; intellectual freedom is vanishing under the aegis of performativity. Schultz and Hatch propose a classical modernist research strategy in the name of postmodernism, which is a contradiction in terms for Lyotard.

For (neo-)Marxists and/or labour process thinkers, postmodernism has erred by being too apolitical (for example Parker, 1993). Obviously, I maintain that Lyotard's *oeuvre* is very political because it continually returns to the theme of *justice*. The conflict originates in Lyotard's conviction that robust or powerful theories – i.e. (1) political economy (Marx), (2) bureaucracy (Weber) or (3) the division of labour (Durkheim) to cite those mentioned by Parker – lead to injustice. Meta- (or grand) narratives are, for Lyotard, totalitarian in their 'truth' claim. They can admit of no other 'truth' than their own. Such 'genres', and each of the 'grand' modernist theories defines a research 'genre', identifies a 'sender' (researcher) with a 'meaning' (truth), and for the rest shuts out the phenomenal (lived-) world of the 'addressee' and/or of the 'object of research'. For Lyotard 'justice' is only possible if the story of every plaintiff (person or group who demands justice) can be heard.

As soon as a strong research paradigm is put in place, all the voices that do not speak in terms of that paradigm, and/or contradict its assumptions, are banished. Lyotard argues that *strong research paradigms* do not permit other, marginal, external voices to exist. And *strong research paradigms* influence action – Weber, (de-)bureaucratization; Marx, the struggle over the means of production even to the point of revolution; and Durkheim, attention to *anomie*. Thought, leading to action based on a strong paradigm, is convinced of the 'justice' of its own conduct. When use is made of organized (state or corporate) power, convictions lead to 'totalitarian' action(s). For the research paradigm convinced that it is the 'truth', whatever it does not encompass simply is not 'truth'.

Parker (1993) seems to see Lyotard as a source of fairly irrelevant, speculative thought. Supposedly, in Parker's reading of postmodernism, 'anything goes': its epistemology is completely relativist. Lyotard argues that there are in fact two alternatives to dominance by grand narrative, i.e. to 'totalitarianism' (Lyotard, 1988). In the one, called *'terreur'*, the researcher still believes in their paradigm, as in the strategy of grand narratives, but forswears the use of organized/institutionalized power. Statements leave little room for an Other, i.e. for alternative points of view, but the speaker tries not to attach social (organizational) power to their intellectual 'moves'. Thought is a way of 'taking time', 'taking time' to talk, write and reflect rather than to act. In the contemporary world, where performativity demands a cost/benefit analysis of each use of human resources, the pledge to 'waste time' on reflection is an act of opposition 'politics' (Lyotard, 1984). But *'terreur'* is coercive as its texts claim to state: 'How things really are' and 'What is actually happening'. *'Terreur'* asserts the 'justice' of its truth(s): it imposes itself on the 'addressee'.

In the other strategy to escape 'totalitarianism', the researcher chooses little narratives that resist totalization altogether. Lyotard explains the strategy with descriptions of the Cashinahua Indians. They always begin their story telling (i.e. narratives) with: 'Here is the story of ... as I've always heard it told. I am going to tell it to you in my turn, listen to it!' Their rhetorical structure creates a circular logic between 'sender', 'addressee' and 'referent'. The person who tells the story has previously heard the story ('sender' = 'addressee') and (in principle) is named in the story(-ies) ('sender' = 'addressee' = 'referent'). The legitimacy of Cashinahua discourse is grounded in the unity: (1) of speaking, (2) being spoken to and (3) being spoken about. Injustice is (theoretically) impossible as the logic of the narrative is inclusive (Lyotard, 1979, 1988; Lyotard and Thébaud, 1979). In Cashinahua narrative logic, phrases, text and discourse are grounded in actions of concrete, explicitly *named,* persons. 'Knowledge' is about specific, known and knowable persons and situations. The 'scale' of representation is concrete and immediate. Obviously, Parker may disagree with Lyotard's analysis of 'totalitarianism' (the nature of thought with organizational clout), or of *'terreur'* (statements that impose themselves even though the speaker tries to avoid power), or of 'shared speech' (speech embedded in concrete local existence). But Lyotard's thought certainly contains an extensive discussion of the (epistemological) politics of 'justice'.

Stephen Linstead has stressed the (political/social) limits to focusing as much on epistemology as Lyotard does:

> Lyotard's (1984) focus on knowledge despite his disillusionment with the world as it is, leads to a virtual suppression of ... 'non epistemological' issues as truth and power become more or less indistinguishable. (Linstead, 1993)

Lyotard assumes that philosophy has to commence with sentences (phrases) because they are the only thing we can be certain about. The *Is it happening?* (*Arrive-t-il?*) of language is irrefutable.

> ... his sole addressee was the *Is it happening?* It is to it that the phrases which happen call forth. And, of course, he will never know whether or not the phrases happen to arrive at their destination, and by hypothesis, he must not know it. He knows only that this ignorance is the ultimate resistance that the event can oppose to the accountable or countable [comptable] use of time. (Lyotard, 1984, trans. 1988)

Using time for reflection is a form of opposition to the dominant culture of performativity. For Lyotard 'truth' and 'power' *sentence*, they are concluding phrases spoken by a judge. Is there another sort of 'truth' or 'power', separate from *sentencing*? Does Lyotard's 'turn to language' end up exerting *'terreur'* or even 'totalitarianism' on its 'addressee'? Linstead thinks that it does. And Lyotard claims, that by destabilizing the power of the grand narratives and by avoiding performative hegemony, he defines an oppositional position.

Furthermore, Lyotard's political argument is not only epistemological. Lyotard is very aware that the communication flows of the Postmodern society are the same as its economic ones. Hyper-efficiency, measured in terms of the 'productive use of time', or the total capitalization of lived-existence is the economic side to the postmodern society. It is a society characterized both by the refusal of reflection and the negation of alternatives, by the subjugation of the *différend*. Existence is organized around wealth maximization, economic optimization found in organizational efficiency and effectiveness. There is no Other (alternative) to hyper-capitalism but that of exclusion and impoverishment. The *différend* of all other possibilities has been short-circuited and repressed. What is it that has so nearly totally mastered the *différend*? In Lyotard's terms: What *judge* is it, that defines the (in-)justice to be done? The question is not answered in Lyotard's texts. To answer, we would need a *meta*-narrative of *the rejection of the meta-narrative*; and this would be paradoxical. Lyotard calls epistemological (self-)explanation, 'presentation.' There are, obviously, sentences about sentences. But nothing can be known about a state prior to *sentence-ing* (Lyotard, 1984). (Meta-)meta-narrative is called upon to explain the pre-structure of speech (sentences), but how could you explain the presuppositions needed for speech to exist, with speech? Linstead reveals the logical limit to Lyotard's theoretical 'moves'.

My analysis of Lyotard, as well as of Parker and Linstead's comments, focuses on the social, political and ethical significance of the *oeuvre*. Robert Chia in his article 'From modern to postmodern organizational analysis' points to yet another aspect of Lyotard. What is the significance, for consciousness and the subject, of Lyotard's thought (Chia, 1995)? Chia takes a passage from *Le Postmodern expliqué aux enfants (The Postmodern Explained for Infants)* as his point of departure:

> ... the 'post' of postmodernism instantiates a procedure of analysis that elaborates an 'initial forgetting' in modernism (Lyotard, 1992: 80). In other words, the postmodern is the modern in a nascent state. It is not located nor locatable through the framing of a simple succession of historical periodizations, since this latter idea is itself a pivotal feature of modernist discourse. Rather, modernism is better construed as a consequence or outcome of the systematic suppression and consequent forgetting of its other term (i.e. the postmodern) through the cumulative effects of more than three centuries of privileging a dualistic mode of thought. (Chia, 1995)

In Lyotard:

> Tu comprends qu'ainsi compris, le 'post' de 'postmoderne' ne signifie pas un mouvement de *come back*, de *feed back*, c'est-à-dire de répétition, mais un

procès en 'ana', un procès d'analyse, d'anamnèse, d'anagogie, et d'anamorphose, qui élabore un 'oubli initial'. (Lyotard, 1988: 119)

The suffix 'ana' signifies 'back'/'backwards', which is to say that 'postmodernism' is the recalling to mind (the 'going back') that permits, in an analogy to psychoanalysis, the subject to discover the hidden sense of their life and behaviour. The quote is part of a short passage (seven pages) wherein Lyotard compares three different 'ideas' of the 'postmodern'. The first is from architecture: 'postmodernism' simply follows modernism (1910–1945) and is a style of 'bricolage' that cites previous styles. This architecture is, in effect, 'neo-modernist', as an effort to go back to a degree zero of style, in order to re-begin the process of innovation, is really very modernist. The second idea of the 'postmodern' centres on the rejection of grand narratives, that one cannot reinterpret (in the sense of *aufheben*) *Auschwitz*, (a metonym for modern history) to make it signify progress, freedom or the triumph of the universal rights of man, liberation of society, etc. This failure of the modernist project has led to the current *Zeitgeist* of melancholy. Having seen that history refuses to mean what the modernists wanted it to mean, mankind has entered into a crisis of (all) meaning. 'Postmodernism' may contain a sociological (or narrative) 'truth', but it doesn't provide anything more. Postmodernism cannot account for the destructive dominance of the 'technosciences', it merely describes hyper-reality. Nor can it explain the division of society into an elite threatened by complexification (i.e. a society of small semi-independent units that are difficult to conceptualize, manage or control) and a mass frightened that it may not be able to survive economically. It can only talk about cyberspace and the information 'haves' and 'have nots'.

The third definition focuses on thought that re-seizes the presuppositions of modernism, in order to work through (*perlaboration/durcharbeiten*) what modernism's assumptions repress, let out and distort (Lyotard, 1988). Chia argues that process – act-ing, be-ing, organize-ing – has been sacrificed in modernism. Modernist organizational science reifies structure, strategy, quality, flexibility and (corporate) culture. It studies all these themes as if they were objects. Not the interactions between people, the process of meaning creation and activity, but the objectifications of 'organization' become the 'objects' of study. The subjects, the actors who organize, are forgotten, which makes the process of organizing invisible and bans human activity from organization theory. Chia pleads for the rediscovery of the active verb, to view the world not in terms of 'the tree is green' but 'the tree greens itself', not in terms of 'the monkey is a mammal' but 'monkeys bring forth live young'. His goal is to break with the inversions that make thought 'thin' and 'cold', in order to reinstate action, motion and 'pulsion'. Chia's plea is close to Lyotard's position in *Libidinal Economy* where Lyotard struggles to embrace activity and to escape the deadening grip of representation(s). But it is at great distance from the later Lyotard who is a critical language philosopher.

Between the early and late Lyotard, there is the rejection of the Nietzschian 'will to power' and 'pulsion'. When Lyotard had to choose between a weak ontology that can do little political harm, and a strong ontology that can 'change the world', he chose the former. He argued that efforts 'to change the world' have already done more than enough harm. Lyotard's focus on the prevention of injustice made him into a minimalist who tries to restrain thought's violence and the imposition by the powerful of 'wrongs' on the weak. For Chia postmodernism is the *différend* of modernism. It is a 'regime' of sentences that 'bridges' the difference between different 'regimes' – some sort of floating 'genre' of linkage and movement. Chia calls such a 'regime of sentences' an 'ontology'. For Chia, the difference between the modern and postmodern is a difference between an ontology of linkage (or activity) and of reification. But 'ontology' in Lyotard is 'presentation', that is, on a meta-meta level of 'sentences about "sentences about sentences"'. For Lyotard, first there is 'something' – the '*t-il-arrive*' of expression and of the sentence. Only then can there be cognizance of 'what's happening' where 'meaning' can be developed, explored and commented on. Thereafter can come the desire to understand the *being*-of-the-sentence. This third level is ontological. But Lyotard does not believe that the third level is achievable without *assuming* a first cause – some sort of metaphysics or 'God-trick' wherein one assumes the (ontological) pre-eminence of the meta-narrative and gives credence to the third 'meta-meta' level. Does Chia's effort to interpret Lyotard lead him to ascribe metaphysical assumptions to a thinker who wants to be judged by his effort to stick to the lived-flow of interaction (sentences, phrases)? Perhaps, but in any event, I agree whole-heartedly with Chia's conclusion:

> In most instances, a failure to recognize the radical ... character of postmodern thinking as an alternative thought style, rather than as a different theoretical perspective or social paradigm, has distracted attention away from the postmodern problematic and led to an indiscriminate appropriation of postmodern concepts and terminology into mainstream organizational theory. For instance [in some hands postmodernism] becomes reduced to the all-too-familiar classical organizational question of the 'division of labor' and 'de-differentiation' is ... cast in opposition to it [as 'postmodern']. ... Despite the recent attempts to discredit postmodernism in organizational studies (see, for instance, Thompson 1993; Parker 1993), it is clear that much of this so-called critique has not even begun to appreciate the complex cognitive style underpinning much of postmodern thought. Much of what passes for scholarly debate on modernism/postmodernism, particularly in organization theory, remains firmly rooted in a modernist set of intellectual priorities. (Chia, 1995)

Lyotard's critique of 'grand narratives' needs to be understood in the context of his intellectual 'moves'. Knowledge of Cooper and Burrell's article 'Modernism, postmodernism and organizational analysis' (1988) doesn't suffice. The article summarized the 'grand narratives' thesis and called, within organization theory, attention to Lyotard. But the article was meant as an introduction to Lyotard and not as a reification of his thought.[2] Analysis of the key 'moves' in Lyotard's thought and their significance for organizational analysis really has remained very scant.

Dissensus

Lyotard has become the source to be quoted when attacking 'grand narratives'. His 'sociology' is clever and he had obviously the ability to coin the right phrase at the right moment: 'postmodernism'. But his intellectual 'moves' could contribute much more to the understanding of organization: to

1. research methodology and especially the tension between 'justice' (singularity) and 'generalizability' ('totalitarianism/*terreur*');
2. the relationship between the technosciences and their culture of performativity (linked to the Zeitgeist of 'melancholy'); and
3. the epistemology of theory focusing on the problem(s) of the incommensurability of 'phrases' (paradigms).

Firstly, is 'generalizability' possible without doing injustice to the *Other's* claim? But will there be any research funding without the promise of generalizability? Totally specific and local work will not be 'scientific' in the modernist sense. It cannot claim to be generally or universally valid, nor will it contribute to an ever-increasing 'body of knowledge'. Modernist 'performativity' tries to plan and optimize economic results, preferably on the basis of 'scientific' principles. Purely local 'truths' attack the logic of standard or universal 'truth' by privileging 'unicity': the singular event, activity or person needs to be taken into account if we are to understand organizational occurrence or change. Organization studies grounded on 'performativity' cannot acknowledge lived-experience or the concrete processes of organizing. In effect it is a logic of 'injustice' that rejects the 'story' of the *Other*. Its 'truth' or 'regime of sentences' creates a flow of meanings, texts and decisions that appear to be seamlessly connected. Lyotard questions the 'justice' of bridging the one 'statement' to the other. Can such intellectual 'moves' be socially and politically justified? A rhetorical ability to make a 'text hang together' is not synonymous with intellectual integrity or 'good' research. The incommensurability of paradigms debate that took place in organizational theory, inspired or at least revivified by Gareth Morgan's *Images of Organization* (1986), defined the problem in terms of 'perspectivism'. If one can analyse an organization as a system (functionally), but also as an organism (a biological metaphor), politically (in terms of repression, totalitarianism and *terreur*), and also via autopoesis (self-organization and the logic of emergence), then what remains of 'truth'? Are organizational studies doomed to relativism, or does the discourse need somehow to be restricted? Basically there have been four different positions in the debate:

1. a purely relativist one (there are no firm grounds of choice between the perspectives, 'May the best story win');
2. a positivist one (the objective study of organization can identify causal relationships with which organizational success or failure can be predicted);
3. a (neo-)Marxist (labour process theory) position (it is necessary to view organization from the perspective of value creation – the relationship between ownership and production is crucial); and

4. a pragmatic or praxis viewpoint ('What sort of practice does each perspective reveal?' and 'What best furthers the general well-being?').

Each thesis has its own political and philosophical background: the first draws on Nietzsche, radical psychology and the defence of civil society; the second on the tradition of scientific rigour, research methodology and representational democracy; the third represents (post-)Braverman radical sociology and leftist politics; and the last appeals to humanist psychology and reformist liberalism. In effect, the debate exhausted itself, with no one convincing anyone else of much of anything.

Lyotard's analysis makes it clear that such different regimes of phrases can perhaps be 'bridged' on the surface, but that the 'bridges' are problematic. The intellectual (political and managerial) 'moves', needed to get from the one cognitive position (as an example, a descriptive narrative of social circumstances), to another (to illustrate, a prescriptive statement of policy and plans), remain brittle and vulnerable. Lyotard confronts organizational studies with its inability to resolve the questions it posed itself in the incommensurability debate. The only solutions seem to be either to try and prop up modernism, or to try to create meaning grounded in specific nameable contexts. The incommensurability debate was mainly conducted on the level of high modernism, asking what general principle(s) define(s) an acceptable form of epistemological rigour as well as permit one to take local circumstances and concrete organizing into account. Such a position is self-contradictory. From Lyotard, one can appreciate how radical the epistemological break has to be, if one is going to create a 'postmodern' organizational studies aware of itself and acting in mutual reciprocity with its field of research.

Notes

1   In my 1992 article in *ISMO* I attempted to broaden the 'grand narratives' discussion to encompass more of Lyotard's thought.
2   Translators differ in their use of 'sentence' or 'phrase' – in French Lyotard uses the word 'phrase'. If one wants to emphasize the link between Lyotard and Anglo-Saxon language philosophy, 'sentence' seems more appropriate; if one wants to indicate that 'phrases' may be units of meaning, and not grammatically spoken sentences at all, then 'phrase' seems more attractive. I try to balance between the two options as the context indicates.

References

Bennington, G. (1988) *Lyotard: Writing the Event*. Manchester: Manchester University Press.
Chia, R. (1995) 'From modern to postmodern organizational analysis', *Organization Studies*, 16 (2): 579–605.
Cooper, R. and Burrell, G. (1988) 'Modernism, postmodernism and organizational analysis', *Organization Studies*, 9 (1): 91–112.
Jackson, N. and Carter, P. (1991) 'In defense of paradigm incommensurability', *Organization Studies*, 12 (1): 109–28.

Letiche, H. (1992) 'Having taught postmodernists', *International Studies in Management and Organization*, 22 (3): 46–70.

Linstead, S. (1993) 'Deconstruction in the study of organization', in J. Hassard and M. Parker (eds), *Postmodernism and Organizations*. London: Sage. pp. 49–70.

Lyotard, J.-F. (1954) *La Phénoménologie*. Paris: PUF. [Trans. B. Bleakey (1991) *Phenomenology*. SUNY Series in Contemporary Continental Philosophy. Albany: SUNY Press.]

Lyotard, J.-F. (1973) *Dérive à partir de Marx et Freud*. Paris: Union Générale d'Editions, Collection '10/18'.

Lyotard, J.-F. (1974) *Économie libidenale*. Paris: Minuit. [Trans. L. Grant (1993) *Libidinal Economy*. London: Athlone.]

Lyotard, J.-F. (1977) *Rudiments païens*. Paris: Union Générale d'Editions, Collection '10/18'.

Lyotard, J.-F. (1979) *La Condition postmoderne*. Paris: Minuit. [Trans. G. Bennington and B. Massumi (1984) *The Postmodern Condition: A Report on Knowledge*. St. Paul: University of Minnesota Press].

Lyotard, J.-F. (1983) *Le Différend*. Paris: Minuit. [Trans. G. Van Den Abbeele (1988) *The Differend: Phrases in Dispute*. Minneapolis: University of Minnesota Press].

Lyotard, J.-F. (1986) *L'Enthousiasme: la critique kantianne de l'histoire*. Paris: Galilée.

Lyotard, J.-F. (1987) 'Judiciousness in dispute, or Kant after Marx', in M. Krieger (ed.), *The Aims of Representation*. New York: Columbia University Press. pp. 23–67.

Lyotard, J.-F. (1988) *Le Postmodern expliqué aux enfants*. Paris: Galilée. [Trans. D. Barry (1992) *The Postmodern Explained to Children*. London: Turnaround].

Lyotard, J.-F. (1989) *The Lyotard Reader*, ed. A. Benjamin. Oxford: Basil Blackwell.

Lyotard, J.-F. (1989a) *Témoigner du différend*. Paris: Osiris.

Lyotard, J.-F. and Thébaud, J.-L. (1979) *Au juste*. Paris: Christian Bourgois. [Trans. B. Massumi (1985) *Just Gaming*. Theory and History of Literature, 20. Minneapolis: University of Minnesota Press.]

Maggiori, R. (1998) 'Jean-François Lyotard, postmortem', in *Libération*, 22 April: 37–8.

Morgan, G. (1986) *Images of Organization*. London: Sage.

Parker, M. (1993) 'Life after Jean-François', in J. Hassard and M. Parker (eds), *Postmodernism and Organizations*. London: Sage. pp. 204–12.

Schultz, M. and Hatch, M.J. (1996) 'Living with multiple paradigms: the case of paradigm interplay in organizational cultural studies', *Academy of Management Review*, 21 (2): 529–48.

Thompson, P. (1993) 'Postmodernism: fatal distraction', in J. Hassard and M. Parker (eds), *Postmodernism and Organizations*. London: Sage. pp. 183–203.

Van Peperstraten, F. (1991) '*Inleiding* Het enthousiasme', in J.-F. Lyotard *Het enthousiasme*. Kampen: Agora.

Vattimo, G. (1998) 'Une constante référence', *Libération*, April 22: 38.

5

Julia Kristeva

Heather Höpfl

Of mothers: the maternal body and the organization

Obviously you may close your eyes, cover up your ears, teach courses, run
errands, tidy up the house, think about objects, subjects. But a mother is always
branded by pain, she yields to it. 'And a sword will pierce your own soul too ...'.
(Kristeva, 1987: 241)

'The Holy Trinity' and the mother of the word

Arguably, Kristeva is one of the most important figures in the post structuralist
philosophical movement. However, it is unlikely that Kristeva would ever
identify herself in such terms and especially so since Kristeva has been
primarily concerned with the relationship between language and the self. Her
work came into prominence in the 1970s via the translation of her articles in
journals such as *Semiotext(e)*, *Diacritics* and *Sub-Stance* among others. She
gained increasing recognition in university French language departments both
in the UK and the USA largely through her connection with *Tel Quel*, the
celebrated French journal. In the Spring of 1973, Mary Ann Caw published an
influential article, 'Tel Quel: text and revolution' in *Diacritics*, and this initiated
a series of articles on Kristeva's writings (Oliver, 1993: 165). At the same time,
the writings of Cixous and Irigaray were also gaining recognition in the USA
with their publication in *Diacritics* and other important journals and, in 1978, as
a result of the publication of two articles in *Signs* – Elaine Mark's *Women and
Literature in France* and Carolyn Burke's *Report from Paris* – the three writers
came to be bracketed together as, what Moi has termed, 'the new Holy Trinity'
of French feminist theory' (Oliver, 1993: 163).

Kristeva, Irigaray and Cixous are generally regarded as the leading French
feminist philosophers and, for each of them but in different ways, the task of
reading their work provides a significant challenge. Indeed, in this chapter I
make no pretence of attempting a comprehensive coverage of Kristeva's
themes, giving rather a reading of some aspects of her work in the spirit of her
writing. In part, the challenge of reading any of the 'Holy Trinity' arises
because none of them is primarily a philosopher and to read their writings

requires a considerable appreciation of, at least, psychoanalytical concepts and certainly linguistics. This does not make for a large and receptive audience. Despite this, these writers have a substantial and appreciative following. John Lechte, who was himself a student of Kristeva, says of his task to make her writings accessible that post-structuralist writings are 'extremely difficult and complex, and certainly intimidating and inaccessible to the non-specialist' (Lechte, 1990: 2) and, indeed, the work of Kristeva in particular has been singled out for criticism for its difficulty. Difficult or not, she has come to be considered one of the foremost contemporary French thinkers and her writings have exerted a significant influence on both feminism and postmodernist ideas. This chapter seeks to consider the influence of her work on organization(s).

Annunciation: 'Hail thou who art highly favoured'

We live on that border, crossroads beings, crucified beings. (Kristeva, 1987: 254)

Having said that Kristeva is regarded as a major French thinker, it is intriguing to realize that neither she nor the other two *French* feminists with whom she is associated, Irigaray and Cixous, were actually born in France. Kristeva is Bulgarian by birth and upbringing. Cixous was born and raised in Algeria under French occupation and Irigaray was born in Belgium (Oliver, 1993: 164). Moreover, as Oliver (1993: 164) points out, it is also the case that just as the three are not French, neither are they specifically feminist. Indeed, Kristeva has been extremely outspoken in her criticism of feminism and what she has regarded as their desire to take over phallic power (Kristeva, 1980: 208). She arrived in Paris around Christmas 1965. She was 25 years old, Bulgarian and supported by a French government scholarship (Lechte, 1990: 91; Moi, 1986: 1). She was already disposed to an ambivalence towards French language and literature from her Bulgarian education, already had an awareness of oscillating positions and exclusions. These two constructions alone have had a significant influence on her work. She had come to Paris to study and was at first committed to the communist cause and a supporter of Maoism but she later remained in Paris as an exile from Bulgarian-Soviet communism. Within a year, she was contributing to the most influential and prestigious journals, *Critique, Langages* and *Tel Quel.* In the subversive mood in the Paris of the mid-1960s, Kristeva found a fertile site for her ideas and no doubt gained insights from her own experiences of exile and of difference which gave impetus to her prolific writing during this period. From the start of her studies in Paris, she was to work with some of the leading figures in French structuralism. She was particularly influenced by Roland Barthes who, as one of the foremost champions of structuralism, had sought to reveal the ways in which bourgeois ideology was embedded in French language and literature. Barthes was one of the '*New Critics*' and a semiotician. This concern with semiotics and the implicit regulation of language was significant in terms of the development of Kristeva's writings although it is clear that she was already forming a dialectical relationship to these ideas even in her early writing. Barthes himself acknowledges Kristeva's influence when he says that she 'changes the order of things ... (that) ... she subverts ... the authority of monologic science and filiation' (Moi, 1986: 1).

'A stranger in a strange land'

> A mother is a continuous separation, a division of the very flesh. And consequently a division of language – and it has always been so.
> (Kristeva, 1987: 254)

Kristeva had gone to Paris to study Bakhtin. She had been schooled in Marxist theory, spoke fluent Russian and had lived under the strictures of Eastern European communism. She had a formidable intellect, knew Latin and Greek, spoke French, Russian and German as well as her mother-tongue Bulgarian, and, at the same time, she carried powerful experiences which, with simplification, one might set against her intellectualism. Clearly such tensions find expression in her ideas and in her writing. She was a foreigner and a foreigner exiled from her native land; estranged from her own country and estranged from the theoretical ideas to which she was exposed in her adopted one; another vacillation between the appeal of semiotics and her own theoretical position. The notion of *strangeness/estrangement* was to play an important part in the development of her ideas. Not only this but also, in the mid-1960s, Kristeva was a woman in the masculine world of French intellectuals. It seems that in virtually every respect Kristeva was confronted by repressive structures, by alterity and by estrangement. Yet, it is precisely these experiences which provided the tensions from which her ideas spring. It is as if the more emphatic the restriction, the more emphatic the resistance. Her writing is *seminal* [ME, fr MF, fr L seminalis, fr semin-, semen seed] to the extent that it disrupts and disturbs the phallogocentric order. This is an achievement indeed and one which is considerably threatening to male construction. It also gives emphasis to another of Kristeva's recurrent themes and one, which in various ways, she has tried to relate to political praxis: the concept of revolution. So, together with estrangement and exile, there is the notion of subversion and revolution in Kristeva's writing. There is also the border. The border plays a very important role in Kristeva's ideas. Given her background and experiences, this is not particularly surprising and her concern to examine the borders of subjectivity seem, not least, to relate to her own homelessness and exile. There is a refusal in Kristeva's writing which is *experienced* on reading the text and, while it is there, implicit, in the writing, it seems more powerfully present in the sense of the resistance which powers the ideas, obscures the writing and seeks to evade capture in the phallogocentric project of language.

Mastery

> A woman will only have the choice to live her life either *hyper-abstractly* (original italics) ... in order thus to earn divine grace and homologation with the symbolic order; ... or merely *different* (original italics), other, fallen ... But she

will not be able to accede to the complexity of being divided, of heterogeneity, of the catastrophic-fold-of-being. (Kristeva, 1987: 248–9)

It would seem that Kristeva writes from the position of a woman restrained by the regulation of the Name-of-the-Father. Anyone who has attempted to read Kristeva's work will acknowledge that there is a curious tension: a contradiction which is difficult to accommodate which presents as dialectic and then breaks down into elusive indeterminacy. Kristeva, for example, in *Stabat Mater*, seeks to achieve a poetical movement or perturbation within the text:

Words that are always too
distant, too abstract for this
underground swarming of
seconds, folding in
unimaginable spaces. Writing
them down is an ordeal of
discourse, like love. (Kristeva, 1987: 235)

However, on other occasions, her writing is formidably theoretical, dense and insistently patriarchal in its trajectory. As a reader, I have been intrigued by the ways in which Kristeva can alienate (I suspect principally the female reader and by this I refer to Kristeva's *abject daughter* [Kristeva, 1984a: 137]) by her sometimes relentless *science*, to the extent that Oliver has put forward the view that her writing 'seems to make Kristeva herself a paradox, an anomaly, or a "man"' (Oliver, 1993: 107). Certainly, this is the effect of Kristeva's writing on me. I am *disturbed* by her ambivalence and her stylistic ambiguities. I am *rendered ab-ject* (thrown-off) by her line of thought. Her writing is not easy to read and so her interpreters and reviewers have themselves been reduced to fairly *impenetrable* accounts of her work. Kristeva's writing is frequently obscure, full of double meanings and idiosyncrasies of style. Sometimes her work appears to display an extraordinary degree of *mastery* of the text. Yet this perturbation she achieves is one of the most significant contributions which she makes to the destabilization of the subject. This is important because it acknowledges the significance which Kristeva places on the *production* of writing as opposed to writing as reproduction (Moi, 1986: 4).

However, it would be wrong to suppose that these aspects of her writing arise merely from attempts to wrestle with difficult and elusive concepts. On the contrary, her style is predominantly a product of her desire to subvert the phallocentrism of the Cartesian logos. Of course, this is both a delight and an irritation. The acquisition of *mastery* of a text is highly valued in pedagogical terms. At the same time, the acquisition of mastery achieves precisely what the term implies, the imposition of a phallogocentric logic. It is this that Kristeva's writing seeks to problematize since, according to her theorizing, it is in language that oppression originates. Specifically, she is arguing that it is in the logos of social organization, in the production of meaning, that such oppression is found (Palmer, 1994: 376). However, for the reader, the problem is whether or not she is transferring her own perturbations, oscillations and indeterminacy to the reader, albeit within the protective framework of a coherent theoretical position, or whether it is precisely this perturbation which she seeks to achieve. To some extent both positions are true, and this is a further characteristic of her writing. Kristeva's ambivalence as theorized, say, in her study of the mother as the abject *and* the sublime (Kristeva, 1984a: 157) but also as a considerable dimension of her work as a whole, seems to have recourse to oppositional structures and with vacillations between them. What this contributes to organizational theory is the capacity to make transparent the effects of the production of meaning and to make the notion of trajectory, strategy and purpose problematic. Coherent and purposive membership is dissolved by such ambivalence. So Kristeva oppresses with the replication of mastery and subverts via the insinuation of the poetic.

The maternal container

> Nights of wakefulness, scattered sleep, sweetness of the child, warm mercury in my arms, cajolery, affection, defenceless body, his or mine, sheltered, protected. A wave swells again, when he goes to sleep, under my skin – tummy, thighs, legs: sleep of the muscles, not of the brain, sleep of flesh. (Kristeva, 1987: 246–7)

Always present in her writing is the pervasive melancholy of one who has experienced isolation, estrangement, the sense of being alien(ated), being an outcast/cast out, being a woman and mother both abject and sublime, a desire for the restoration of the repressed other, for her Motherland, for the poetry of her Mother tongue, the desire for the security of boundaries and the notion of the boundary as disturbing precisely because of its ambiguity – its indeterminacy. I find I am oppressed by reading Kristeva because I am not only required to bear the weight of her patriarchal language, her mastery, but also to bear the pain of her lived experience, her poetics, if I am to engage with the text. It is the power of her work that throws the reader into the tensions of abjection and desire: the reader is repelled by her excess, at what is expelled from her body, and at the same time the reader is drawn to the compelling idea, the powerful ambivalence, the vacillations. However, the abject and the sublime need to be reunited and Kristeva argues that this can only be achieved through the Father, that is to say, via the need to symbolize (Kristeva, 1984a). To read Kristeva is to experience the fact that her writing cannot be separated from her being. Now, to some extent this is her *jouissance* in the profound experience of alterity in which the mother embodies otherness. The mother carries the child as otherness within her being. Her *alterity is within* as Kristeva puts it: simultaneously one and the same, other and different, joy and pain. It acknowledges the considerable analysis she has undertaken of the role of the mother and the careful distinction she has made between the mother and, in particular, the mother as representation with all the regulatory functions that this implies, and woman as subject in process.

Yet Kristeva herself is in labour to give birth and it seems she is reluctant. To give birth would require her to expel everything that her labour represents to her, those things one might suspect she would prefer to hold in, to contain within herself where they are protected. That is to say, not to allow the Word to become Flesh through her agency.

> ... Although it concerns
> every woman's body, the heterogeneity
> that cannot be subsumed
> in the signifier never the less
> explodes violently with pregnancy
> (the threshold of culture and
> nature) and the child's arrival
> (which extracts woman out of her
> oneness and gives her the possibility
> – but not the certainty – of
> reaching out to the other, the
> ethical). Those particularities of
> the maternal body compose woman
> into a being of folds, a catastrophe
> of being that the dialectics of the
> trinity and its supplements would
> be unable to subsume.
> Silence weighs heavily none the less ...
> (Kristeva, 1987: 260)

There is so much pain in her writing: the paroxysm of labour approaches its conclusion and yet to give birth would be to face another separation, the expulsion into the world of all she holds dear to herself, to establish a boundary between herself and her child, the fruits of her labour. Consequently, the space of the uterus, regulated by male order and phallogocentric text, is the maternal container into which she puts her experiences and loss in order to contain and protect them from their inevitable alienation post partum. It is not, perhaps, surprising then that Kristeva values *the loving Father* so highly nor that she appears to find no contradiction in her mastery of the phallogocentric text. Construed in this way, the loving father protects the experiences which she wishes to contain in the sense that the uterus, as the container of symbolically structured experience is already transgressed, and now phallogocentric language is the custodian of its contents. However, Kristeva is in spasm. 'Who calls such a suffering jouissance?' (Kristeva, 1984a: 250 ; Moi, 1986: 175). The loving father is needed should the containment of alterity fail and the contained otherness be expelled from the body by the route by which it entered. All that has been nurtured and changed, in itself both sublime and abject, needs to be given up to paternal support if the mother is to be rendered neither abject nor sublime and the child, itself, not become abject.

The abject daughter

Concerning that stage of my childhood, scented, warm and soft to the touch, I have only a spatial memory. No time at all. Fragrance of honey, roundness of forms, silk and velvet under my fingers, on my cheeks. Mummy. Almost no sight – a shadow that darkens, soaks me up or vanishes amid flashes. Almost no voice

> except in her placid presence. Except, perhaps, more belatedly, the echo of
> quarrels: her exasperation, her being fed up, her hatred. Never straightforward,
> always held back, as if, although the unmanageable child deserved it, the
> daughter could not accept the mother's hatred – it was not meant for her.
> (Kristeva, 1987: 256)

Kristeva (1980: 6, 39) talks of the position of the not-yet-subject and the way in which abjection functions in order to protect *the abject* from the primal narcissistic identification with the Mother. The child becomes the abject in order to avoid both separation from and identification with the maternal body (Oliver, 1993: 60). The mother's body evokes feelings of anxiety and disgust, fear and anger and, for the male child, the problem that he came from a woman's body and yet must become a man (Kristeva, 1980: 39). Does this, perhaps, reveal what Kristeva fears for her own text, that without the aid of a loving father, the products of her labour will not be able to find a secure identity, to constitute themselves within the symbolic order. In which case, it would be safer to produce male children and give them into the care of their fathers: to reproduce. To produce male texts and hand over their care to male authors would ensure that such texts find a secure identity within a male trajectory of language. Organizations might, likewise, reproduce themselves through male heirs. Without the loving father, the texts become orphans, homeless and abject. To some extent, one might say that Kristeva, like all women writers, has been able to give birth to sons (her biological son was born in 1976). Sometimes she has attempted to give birth to sons with more feminine traits (for example, *Stabat Mater, Powers of Horror*). However, to produce daughters is an altogether different proposition. For Kristeva (1984a: 137), a daughter must abandon her mother as a love object in favour of the father and, in doing so, must render her mother abject in order to reject her; in the process she herself becomes abject (Oliver, 1993: 61). To constitute herself in language, the daughter must give herself up to the symbolic order. To consider the implications of this more generally and for organizations in particular, is to acknowledge that it is difficult for organizations to have daughters, to have to admit women, since women, by their very being, introduce ambivalence.

Kristeva has talked about the way in which the daughter might carry the 'living corpse' of the mother's body which no longer nourishes (Kristeva, 1980: 137) or, alternatively, might take up the cause of the symbolic order as a means by which to do battle with the mother (Oliver, 1993: 62). That is to say, Kristeva is concerned with the problem created by the representation of the mother as carried within, and also with the rejection of the mother via the pursuit of male power. The only solution to this is matricide. To surrender the mother is to enter into language, in other words, to negate the mother in order to reconstitute her in language (Kristeva, 1987: 43). However, Kristeva makes the point that this matricide is a form of suicide. For Kristeva to produce daughters she has to reconcile herself to immolation. The wonderful daughters of her text would have to negate her to secure their identity and might, after all that, become the *mere playthings* of the phallogocentric text. Daughters in this scheme of things could never confer identity on the mother. The female text must kill off the representation of the mother which regulates it. Only sons could bring confirming identifications. It is not then surprising to find that despite her poetics, Kristeva has little sympathy with the feminist cause per se, nor that she seems to draw almost entirely on the authority of male literature to support her assertions, nor that she appears to do so little to explore the potential of the poetic. And yet, her work has extraordinary power and her text is replete with the poetic. Kristeva is an extremely frustrating writer since she consistently refuses to locate herself in the structures which she appears to create for her own accommodation and protection and, whilst this approach produces some degree of recognition in the reader, it affords little intimacy. Consequently, the reader might resent the fact that so much is compressed in the text that it is experienced as repressive: where is the *return* of the repressed which she seeks? She seems to prefer estrangement and isolation and, perhaps, the possible consolation that the imaginary loving father might restore love to the text. Of course, I must acknowledge that this is a personal response to Kristeva and part of a particular frustration I have with her work. She refuses to become the mother or, perhaps, is reluctant to give birth to daughters. Now, of course, it may be entirely to her credit to resist categorization, but is there nevertheless a problem with her *mastery* of language?

Poetic language

> ... motherhood destines us to a demented *jouissance* that is answered, by chance, by the nursling's laughter in the sunny waters of the ocean. What connection is there between it and myself? No connection, except for that overflowing laughter where one senses the collapse of some ringing, subtle, fluid identity or other, softly buoyed by the waves. (Kristeva, 1987: 255–6)

The problem which the question of *mastery* presents concerns the relationship between Kristeva's theoretical position and her praxis. Undoubtedly, the theoretical structures she has created are elaborate, conceptually sophisticated, the product of a considerable intellectual and extremely recondite. In 1969 she published *Semeiotike* in which she argues that the self is not a stable entity, but rather constituted by language. In *Revolution in Poetic Language* (1974 in French, 1984a in English) she took the view that what she termed poetic language puts the subject in crisis and disrupts the unity of the symbolic. The poetic thus subverts the dominant social discourse to challenge order, rationality and patriarchal regulation.

More specifically, Kristeva is arguing that what is generally encountered as *the real* is a product of the *symbolic order* and, for Kristeva, the symbolic order is phallogocentric. In brief, Kristeva (1984a) argues that the notion of a unified subject supposes a unified consciousness and this, in turn, requires an ordered mind. An orderly mind requires an ordering mechanism and this, according to Kristeva, is achieved via syntax. Poetic language can achieve the disruption of this order and ordering at both the literary and the social level.

For Kristeva, the regulation of the individual is achieved by controlling the physical and psychic rhythms which are normalized by social learning from the pre-linguistic flux which Kristeva terms the *semiotic*. This is distinct from the ordered, regulated rationality of the adult world which Kristeva refers to as the *symbolic*. Hence, the symbolic uses the semiotic material and gains '*mastery*' (Kristeva, 1984a: 153; Selden, 1989: 83) over it. The symbolic relies on the semiotic for its signification. The symbolic functions to locate subjects, to place them and provide the material for the construction of 'identities'. Yet the sounds and rhythms of the semiotic resist subjection and seek expression through the subversion of the symbolic order.

In simple terms, the symbolic is equated with regulation and the semiotic with the unorganized flux of the physical and the psychic. This provides a basis for an understanding of the mechanisms of control and for an appreciation of what is being controlled. Ambivalence is not merely within the semiotic flux, but its resistance to and memory of regulation. This has led Kristeva to the view that the subject is not the *source* of meaning but the *site* of meaning, a line of thought which is compatible with the argument presented here. She views 'woman as the silence of the unconscious which precedes discourse' (Selden, 1989: 150). Woman embodies the poetic. However, the semiotic is not presented as the unique province of women. The subversion of the patriarchal law is achieved by resistance to syntax and, hence, is related to the rediscovery of the mother and liberation from the authority of the patriarchal text. Clearly, this has political connotations which, on more than one level of analysis, are concerned with phallogocentrism.

Having said that, the poetic is not solely the concern of women. The 'culturally constituted symbolic order' (Sampson, 1989: 14) provides women with a multiplicity of complementary and contradictory images and symbols of selfhood which make the construction of self problematic. This is no less so for men but men have more props to support and maintain a stable construction. By repressing desire for the mother under the threat of castration, the male child can identify with the father (in Kristeva's writings, the imaginary loving father) and assume a masculine identity. It is more difficult for women to assume a feminine identity because of a fundamental and continuing ambivalence towards the mother. Kristeva advocates *matricide* as the necessary condition for the assumption of feminine identity. The power of the mother, the representation of the mother, must be killed off in order for women achieve their identity.

This is my body, broken for you

> The love of God and for God resides in the gap: the broken space made explicit by sin on the one side, the beyond on the other. Discontinuity, lack of arbitrariness: topography of the sign, of the symbolic relation that posits my otherness as impossible. Love, here, is only for the impossible. (Kristeva, 1987: 261)

Kristeva's attitude to feminism is one which receives considerable attention from her biographers (Lechte, 1990; Moi, 1986; Oliver, 1993) and reveals a great deal about her praxis. She is in varying degrees critical of feminism in her writing. In part, her criticism relates to the very specific objectives of what she sees as bourgeois feminism seeking bourgeois ends within the framework of a bourgeois state. Moreover, she has been highly critical of the organized French feminist *movement* for these reasons and of those feminists who seek to enter combat over phallic power. She characterizes the feminist movement as *hysteric* (Kristeva, 1984b: 511), in the psycho-analytical sense, in arguing that the feminist movement represents a hysteric split between the body and its drives, its *jouissance* on the one hand and the patriarchal law on the other. As Moi puts it, 'The problem is that as soon as the insurgent "substance" speaks, it is necessarily caught up in the kind of discourse *allowed* by and *submitted to* by the Law' (Moi, 1986: 10, emphasis added). The desire to confront this problem of inevitable capture is fundamental to Kristeva's work and yet she acknowledges that to attempt to use language against itself is to create an untenable position: a position which is all too familiar to women writers when they attempt to deviate from the notion of mastery.

In *Stabat Mater*, she *breaks the body* of the text in order to allow her personal reflections on motherhood to enter and subvert the text. However, her text is constructed to represent these two positions – her own writing on the Virgin Mary and her own reflections on motherhood in dialectical opposition: two columns running down either side of the page to represent, on one level, the Body on the left (the sinister) and the Law on the right (the right-hand *of God*). The Body speaks of rupture, and tearing, and blood. The Law speaks of regulation and representation, of rational argument and rhetoric trajectory. The Body and the Law are both Kristeva in her vacillation between embodied experience and her mastery of language. Her writing splits the Body of the Text, rends the page. This is the mirror of the rupture of the hymen, the rupture of the tympanum: the intrusion of the phallus and the intrusion of language. Kristeva *breaks the body of the text* and, in doing so, recapitulates the breaking of the physical body of God the Son (who sits at the right hand of God the Father, who is the Logos, the Word made Flesh, the Son who redeems). The rupture of the text is remembrance of the breaking of the body both in physical and in representational terms. In the liturgy of the Mass, the eucharistic host is broken and the priest says, 'This is my body which is given for you'. The broken host is then distributed to the congregation, 'The Body of Christ, The Body of Christ', the body of Kristeva. The Word made Flesh is now transcendent.

   ....**What is loving, for a woman, the same thing as writing. Laugh. Impossible. Flash on the un- nameable, weavings of abstrac- tions to be torn. Let a body venture at last out of its shelter, take a chance with meaning under a veil of words. WORD FLESH. From one to the other, eternally, broken up visions, metaphors of the invisible**. And yet, the humanity of the Virgin mother is not always obvious, and we shall see how, in her being cleared of sin, for instance, Mary distinguishes herself from mankind. But at the same time the most intense revelation of God, which occurs in mysticism, is given only to a person who assumes himself as 'maternal'. Augustine, Bernard of Clairvaux, Meister Eckhart, to mention but a few, played the part of the Father's virgin spouses ... (Kristeva, 1987: 235)

And, all this in the spaces in between: in the unsaid. The Body and The Text: 'The Word Made Flesh'. The *breaking of the waters* and the separation from the mother, the birth and the rupture of separation, of a pain which is more than physical and without respite, Kristeva opens herself to the reader in the conjunction and disjunction of the Body and the Law. This is her offering, her sacrifice. She is broken apart in her being in order for us to encounter her as mother and as father, and as the experience of the space between: a space which is abundant presence, a conjunction of Flesh and Word. This is her praxis: her Body which *is given up*, her transubstantiation into pregnant Being in the space between the words – words of the Law and words of the Body, but words nonetheless. The religious imagery I use here might seem excessive if it were not the case that Kristeva herself has drawn some of her inspiration for her advocacy of a praxis of love from St Bernard and St Thomas, major theologians of the Catholic Church (Kristeva, 1987). She has given specific emphasis to the importance of love and ethics in psychoanalytical practice. In *Tales of Love* (1987) she outlines her views of the ethics of psychoanalysis and the role of love and argues for a new ethics, *herethics*, which she has based on a new approach to motherhood and love.

Maternal love and practice

Archaic maternal love would be an incorporation of my suffering that is unfailing, unlike what often happens with the lacunary network of signs. In that sense, any belief, anguished by definition, is upheld by the fascinated fear of language's impotence. Every God, even including the God of the Word, relies on a mother Goddess. (Kristeva, 1987: 252)

Clearly, with the work of someone as abstruse and as prolific as Julia Kristeva, it is difficult to do more that point to a few interesting themes that emerge from her work. There is also the problem that to introduce the unfamiliar reader to Kristeva is a different task from that of exploring her ideas. Unlike Derrida, who seems to make a free gift of his ideas to his readers, and who seems not to have a particular trajectory of ideas in mind, often writing in a poetic and non-rhetorical way (although this absence is, in itself, a form of rhetoric), Kristeva seems to make specific demands on her readers, to have a point to get across and to exhibit an extraordinary trajectory of thought even when she is at her most disruptive. Ultimately, she lays the blame for the breakdown of sociality on the *representation* of the mother and the failure of maternal love. The image of the Virgin, she argues, is the empty vehicle through which the paternal word is conveyed (1987: 374) and she says that the mother is not a woman. Yet, it seems these are precisely the criticisms that are made of Kristeva herself. She is the instrument of the Word made Flesh to the extent that through her the phallogocentric text is transubstantiated. She produces sons. However, it would be unfair to leave the comment there. Whenever I take a research supervision with my female doctoral students I am conscious that I am asking them to *master* the text. I am also producing sons. Yet Kristeva calls to another way:

> Women doubtless reproduce among themselves the strange gamut of forgotten body relationships with their mothers. Complicity in the unspoken, connivance of the inexpressible, of a wink, a tone of voice, a gesture, a tinge, a scent. We are in it, set free of our identification papers and names, on an ocean of preciseness, a computerisation of the unnamable ... the community of women is a community of dolphins. (Kristeva, 1987: 257)

And, one might add, the task is not undertaken without the smile of irony.

On the lack of the maternal

> ... this motherhood is the fantasy that is nurtured by the adult, man or woman, of a lost territory; what is more, it involves less an idealized archaic mother than the idealization of the *relationship* that binds us to her, one that cannot be localized – an idealization of primary narcissism. (Kristeva, 1987: 235)

It is interesting to follow Kristeva's suggestion that, contrary to common belief, it is perhaps the case that feminism emerged in Protestant countries precisely because it represented a lack rather than a freedom, that is to say, the absence of the cult of the Virgin. In Catholic countries, the role of the Virgin Mary plays a significant part in the apprehension of motherhood and the representation of the Mother. Mary is Queen of Heaven, Mother of the Church. Kristeva, following Warner (1976), talks of the humanization of Christianity through the cult of the mother. The mother intercedes for mankind and offers her tears for humanity, her milk for its succour. The image of the Mater Dolorosa which has dominated the image of motherhood since the fourteenth century is, according to Kristeva (1987: 236–9), a metaphor for non-speech, for the *return of the repressed* in monotheism. The Virgin Mary 'adds to the Christian trinity and to the Word that delineates their coherence the heterogeneity they salvage', (Kristeva, 1987: 237). She goes further to say that the Mater Dolorosa, as Virgin Mother, knows no masculine body other than that of her dead son for whom she weeps. However, Kristeva asks why Mary sheds tears for her son when, as Mother of God, she knows there is resurrection. Is it that Mary wants to experience the death of a human being for herself since 'her feminine fate of being the source of life spares her' (Kristeva, 1987; Moi, 1986: 175) the knowledge of death which is a male preoccupation? The Mother is the fount of love. She has looked on death and seen immortality. She has looked on mere mortal man with profound compassion. All beliefs in resurrection, Kristeva says, are based on mythologies which are characterized by a mother goddess.

This is important because if Christianity relies on the role of a mother goddess to confer immortality, albeit via a displacement, the role of feminine representation in social life as a whole and organizations in particular deserves some comment. It seems that survival, immortality and the transcendence of death, is in some sense implicit in the feminine. The mother knows that via birth and reproduction, that as the source of life, she overcomes death. The mother can die because she knows death from the moment of birth and separation and because she knows life as continuity through her being. This, according to Kristeva, is an experience which men, who cannot reproduce themselves, lack. It is a question of mortality and immortality but it is also a question of order and disorder. If women by their very being represent the intrusion of disorder and subversion, it raises the question of how the feminine can fulfil the maternal function but not pose a threat to male order. In effect, this was achieved in the Church via the elevation of Motherhood and its conflation with Virginity. The Virgin is only sensuous and physical in ways which serve the needs of men and regulate the activities and experiences of women. The Virgin is subject to the Word and gives birth to the Word made Flesh.

Likewise Kristeva's work, and for that matter feminine experience and writing, is neutralized by the Assumption. In the notion of the bodily Assumption of Our Lady, the *body and soul* of Mary are taken up into heavenly glory where she is 'exalted by the Lord as Queen over all things, so that she might be more fully conformed to her Son, the Lord of lords and conqueror of sin and death' (Libreria Editrice Vaticana, 1994).

> In giving birth you kept your virginity; in your Dormition you did not leave the world, O Mother of God, but were joined to the source of Life. You conceived the living God and, by your prayers, will deliver our souls from death.
> Byzantine Liturgy, Troparian, Feast of the Dormition, August 15th (Libreria Editrice Vaticana, 1994, Lumen Gentium 59)
>
> She is the exemplary realization (typus) of the Church.
> Catechism of the Catholic Church, 1994: 208 (Libreria Editrice Vaticana, 1994)
>
> In a wholly singular way she cooperated by her obedience, faith, hope and burning charity in the Saviour's work of restoring supernatural life to souls. For this reason she is a mother to us in the order of grace.
> (Libreria Editrice Vaticana, 1994, Lumen Gentium 61)

Kristeva, in her writing, poses a threat to male order, by her bodily Assumption into the male text she is 'more fully conformed to her son', in this sense, the *son* being her writing: in Derrida's terms, the 'miserable son' (Derrida, 1981: 145). The suffering Mother and the miserable Son to whom she is conformed more fully are the emblems of the *incorporation* of the Mother into the text. In order to say and to overcome the 'anxiety of influence' suffered by every writer when it is 'his (sic) turn to wield his language (his pen)' (original parentheses) (Todorov, 1981 in Bloom, 1982: 24) Kristeva, as experience and as writing, is received body and soul into the trajectory of the male text: honoured and yet disavowed. She is made Virgin in order to make the elevation possible. This is a bizarre transgression by which the appropriation is by what is conferred rather than by what is taken. By rendering real women into mere representations their real power is neutralized and made safe. If the feminine threatens to subvert the text, then the move to affirm the notion of the Assumption, bodily and spiritual subjection to the Law, is the reversal of that potential for transgression. The feminine is *incorporated* into the text and, via its elevation, made part of the

Word: inseparable from the Word. In this way, women and their work, the feminine and its ways of being, are made to conform with the phallogocentric order.

In organizational terms, all that is feminine is other, is sensuous, is excluded by this subjection. Since the feminine must enter the organization without bringing contamination – of menstrual blood, of breast milk, of pregnant bodies – it must enter as representational. However, the feminine might equally well enter as the representation of the Whore. The argument here is confined to motherhood and the mother. As representational, the image of the Virgin thus becomes an instrument of regulation and the instrument of phallogocentric power. The Virgin mediates between man and God but she is created to serve the Father. In organizational terms, one might see this in the way in which, for example, the concept and practice of 'customer care' came into prominence in the 1980s. Care in this sense was about serving the interests of the organization by a greater attention to its customers. What might have been seen as the physical and embodied practices of caring for individuals in any genuine sort of way by men and women was displaced by a notion of care which was mediated through the representation of the feminine: an appropriation and an abstraction. Care, viewed in this way, might be seen as homologous to the Virgin's earthly powers as Mother of the Church. As Mother of the Organization, the representation of the feminine has been constructed and manipulated in the service of the organization: that is to say in the service of the trajectory of the phallogocentric discourse.

The Virgin being *Alone of All Her Sex* (Warner, 1976; Kristeva, 1987) then becomes complicit in the repudiation of other women since she herself is unique, the virgin-mother, the human being who is without sin. The representation of Motherhood offered by the image of the Virgin removes her from association with all other women. So, in organizational terms, by valorizing those aspects of the mother which serve the organization, women themselves are excluded from the valorization of the organization. Worse, since the Virgin Mother, as the representation of Motherhood to the organization, is a status impossible to attain, *mere* woman has only two roles to play: the virgin or the whore. Hence, women as 'untainted symbolic vessels' and women as witches and prostitutes provide complex positive and negative metaphors of 'womanhood' (Hoch-Smith and Spring, 1978). The problem is one of representation: the imposition of the symbolic order and the suppression of difference.

In the manipulative and appropriative styles of culture change in organizations of the last two decades, the violence of the phallogocentric trajectory has changed its emphasis. Male authority has been reinforced by the appropriation and manipulation of the feminine – and hence, of the Virgin – in the pursuit of an authoritative, complete, male self. However, what is achieved is the construction of a travesty of all that is feminine: a grotesque parody of the feminine parading its lack. Docherty writing about modern authority points to the importance of the feminine reminiscent of Kristeva when he says 'Woman exists as a kind of "boundary", at the margins or extremes of the male self; yet she is also construed as central, not peripheral at all' (Docherty, 1987: 130–1).

Women then are either angelic or the locus of death, the means of salvation by enabling authorship or symbolized as an archetype of betrayal. 'Woman ... is the condition of male writing and authority' (Docherty, 1987: 132). If this means that organizations, as phallogocentric trajectories, are lacking the Mother, then it is also the case that the construction and elevation of feminine attributes to the status of the representation of the Mother, the counterfeit mother, the Virgin, will not resolve the difficulties. The ambivalence of the masculine resides in the desire for the mother and the simultaneous desire to repel her (Schwartz, 1997). There are two aspects to this. Kristeva has been critical of the desire for *phallic power* which she sees as the result of distortions of the mother–daughter relationship. She sees the pursuit of what men have as futile and misplaced. Schwartz (1997) has carefully and, in the current climate of political correctness, bravely analysed the implications of this type of feminine behaviour for organizations. In a sense, the daughter becomes a son in order to fight for her inheritance. This is not surprising since 'Nothing reassures, for only the Law sets anything down', (Kristeva, 1987: 250) but it is a great cost for women. On the other hand, the daughter can discover herself as a woman: can become a mother, or become *her* mother, can delight in the joy and pain of being other, different, woman, mother.

From her position as a revolutionary Marxist in the 1960s, Kristeva has moved through marriage and motherhood to a radically different point of view on political praxis. This has not made her popular with Marxists nor with bourgeois or androgynizing feminists. However, she has taken great pains to convey her ideas in both the form and content of her writing. The issue of praxis is important here since, above all, it seems that this is where she feels the expression of her being human is translated into action. Likewise, in translating her work into an organizational context it is perhaps best to consider her contribution to the micro activities of day-to-day practice and interaction with others. This is her resistance to 'the wealth of signs that constitutes the baroque (which) renders belief in the Mother useless by overwhelming the symbolic weakness where she takes refuge, withdrawn from history, with an overabundance of discourse' (Kristeva, 1987: 253). Rather than be crushed into silence by the weight of the symbolic, Kristeva *is*. Her radical contribution to practice is based on the role of love in the psychoanalytical context. The cure for the patient can only be found in transference and, for Kristeva, this means love. This is her ethical position: her *herethics*. It is a radically different way of being from that conventionally associated with organizational behaviour.

Of mothers

Nothing, however, suggests that a feminine ethics is possible, and Spinoza excluded women from his (along with children and the insane). Now, if a contemporary ethics is no longer seen as being the same as morality; if ethics amounts to not avoiding the embarrassing and inevitable problematics of the law but giving it flesh, language and *jouissance* – in that case its reformulation demands the contribution of women ... Of mothers. For an heretical ethics separated from morality, an herethics, is perhaps no more than that which in life makes bonds, thoughts, and therefore the thought of death, bearable. (Kristeva, 1987: 262)

What then, in summary, is Kristeva's influence on organizational theory? In part, it is to do with borders and their demarcation, exile and homelessness, strangeness, estrangement, the boundary of the body and sociality and love; it concerns ethics and motherhood. These are complex issues which deserve a thorough reading in her work. Maternity, motherhood and the maternal body play a significant part in the dynamics of her psychoanalytical writing. Kristeva sees motherhood as a mode of love which is directed towards ultimate separation and she uses motherhood as the model of love which governs psychoanalytical practice where the client–patient relationship is rooted in love and characterized by what she terms 'herethics of love', (Kristeva, 1987: 263) an implicit ethical practice. Perhaps this would provide a fruitful ground for further investigation. However, just as Kristeva herself seeks to resist capture as the Mother so perhaps Kristeva should be protected from capture by management theorists. There is probably some analysis which could be made of the Organization as the Maternal Body and, in particular, its capacity to produce sons who both fear and loathe it and, at the same time, make it sublime. Moreover, this same analysis has much to contribute to the ways in which organizations regard women.

Lechte (1990: 208) says of Kristeva's work that it is largely individualistic and concerned with micro-practice. Kristeva has moved from the politics of revolution to the interpersonal politics of psychoanalysis and one might look critically at why she might not want to produce daughters (as text, as experiences, as maternal music and language). She is, perhaps after all, a loving Mother. Undoubtedly her work on the heterogeneity of language is a significant achievement. However, perhaps her greatest contribution is her embodiment of such dialectical and dissolving ideas: her text and her subversion of it. Even her name, by some spurious etymology seems to suggest a conflation of the masculine and the feminine: the Word made Flesh, Krist (the Christ) and the sensual Eva (Eve) who subverted the primal order, Krist/eva. Perhaps her mastery is an inevitable and radical achievement. She is irritating and contradictory. She reminds me of my Mother.

Stabat Mater: a footnote at the crossroads

As I was writing this piece, I became aware of the two photographs that I have on my desk. On the right hand side is my mother who died in 1978, her eyes regard me with her great compassion – and, I remember the warmth of her body, the way she held me to her, her love, her kindness, a memory in the flesh. My anamnesis. On the other side, is a photograph of my husband – clever, intense, a scholar. He looks out at me with a curious intensity as if in pursuit of an elusive idea. Another memory of the flesh but as much of contest as of consummation: passion and power. Mothered and mother, my own children smile down from their school photograph on the bookshelf. 'Christianity is perhaps also the last of the religions to have ... the bipolar structure of belief: on the one hand, the difficult experience of the Word – a passion; on the other, the reassuring wrapping in the proverbial mirage of the mother – a love. (Kristeva, 1987: 252)

Note

Extracts from this chapter appear in 'The suffering mother and the miserable son: organizing women and organizing women's writing', *Gender, Work and Organization,* Vol. 7 (2): 98–105.

References

Bloom, H. (1982) *Agon: Towards a Theory of Revisionism.* New York: Oxford University Press.
Derrida, J. (1981) *Dissemination.* London: The Athlone Press.
Docherty, T. (1987) *On Modern Authority.* Brighton: The Harvester Press.
Hoch-Smith, J. and Spring, A. (1978) *Women in Ritual and Symbolic Roles.* New York: Plenum.
Kristeva, J. (1980) *Powers of Horror,* trans. Leon Roudiez. New York: Columbia University Press.
Kristeva, J. (1984a) *Revolution in Poetic Language.* New York: Columbia University Press.
Kristeva, J. (1984b) *Desire in Language: A Semiotic Approach to Literature and Art,* trans. T.S. Gora, A. Jardine and L. Roudiez. Oxford: Basil Blackwell.
Kristeva, J. (1987) *Tales of Love,* trans. L. Roudiez. New York: Columbia University Press.
Lechte, J. (1990) *Julia Kristeva.* London: Routledge.
Libreria Editrice Vaticana (1994) *The Catechism of the Catholic Church* (authorized English translation in Canada). Ottowa: Canadian Conference of Catholic Bishops Publication Services.
Moi, T. (ed.) (1986) *The Kristeva Reader.* Oxford: Blackwell.
Oliver, K. (1993) *Reading Kristeva.* Bloomington: Indiana University Press.
Palmer, D. (1994) *Looking at Philosophy: The Unbearable Heaviness of Philosophy made Lighter.* Mountain View, California: Mayfield Publishing Company.
Sampson, E. E. (1989) 'The deconstruction of the self', in J. Shotter and K. Gergen (eds), *Texts of Identity.* London: Sage.
Schwartz, H.S. (1997) 'The power of the virgin: the psychodynamics of sexual politics and the issue of women in combat', paper presented at the CSOC Colloquium in Organizational Psychodynamics, University of Missouri-Columbia, September, 1997.
Selden, R. (1989) *A Reader's Guide to Contemporary Literary Theory.* Hemel Hempstead: Harvester Wheatsheaf.
Todorov, T. (1981) *Introduction to Poetics.* Brighton: Harvester Press.
Warner, M. (1976) *Alone of All Her Sex: The Myth and Cult of the Virgin Mary.* New York: Knopf.

6

Gilles Deleuze and Felix Guattari

Pippa Carter and Norman Jackson

A 'Minor' Contribution to Organization Theory

Let us make things clear at the outset: Deleuze and Guattari *could* be seen as the first postmodern organization theorists. This is probably a provocative and contentious claim, but the intention of this chapter is to explore their work and, by so doing, to substantiate it. In the process it will be seen that their writing represents radically different thinking about the nature and function of organization in contemporary society, a challenge to all the principles and tenets of conventional Organization Theory, offering in their place a complex but rigorous new agenda for social and organizational relations. Deleuze and Guattari redefined what the subject should be about.

That the work of Deleuze and Guattari is deeply implicated in the development of postmodernism is generally uncontested, though its precise relationship to postmodernism is a matter of considerable debate (see, for example, Bertens, 1995; Harvey, 1989; Jameson, 1991; Lash, 1990). Yet 'both were scornful of the notion of "postmodernity"' (Goodchild, 1996: 2), and some commentators regard one of the principle focuses of their work as to provide a critique of postmodernity (for example, Goodchild, 1996; Massumi, 1992). That this does not contradict our initial contention concerns issues which lie at the very heart of their work. In the absence of any generally agreed definitions of the terms postmodernism and postmodernity, it would be unconstructive to try to resolve the apparent contradiction, but it is possible to make some suggestions. If postmodernism/postmodernity is taken as a description of current conditions – in Jameson's (1991) phrase, 'the cultural logic of late capitalism' – then, given the political commitments of Deleuze and Guattari, one could safely assume that they would be hostile to it, while not denying its ontological status. But if one understands postmodernism as an epistemological critique of modernism – reductively defined as 'the flight from rationality' – then this would not only be entirely congruent with their work, but also that work could be seen as a significant contribution to the development of such a critique. Deleuze and Guattari 'were not celebrants of postmodern playfulness' (Goodchild, 1996: 2). If the flight from rationality leads only to a relativism in the context of which nothing can be said about anything, and, in particular, conditions of morality and criteria for judgement are invalidated, this would, certainly, bring scorn from their pens. If, however, it leads to a rigorous critique of the idea of an authorized, objective truth and includes an exploration of the conditions of possibility for morality and judgement in this 'new' world, this would be entirely consistent with their own project. If relativism reflects only a sense of despair and the abdication of responsibility, it generates a tragic impotence. But, if postmodernism can be seen as more than the abandonment of rationality for relativism, can offer a radical way forward and generate a praxis, it contains a utility lacking in relativism alone. In a claim perhaps reminiscent of Deleuze and Guattari, Lawson (1989: xii) says:

> If relativism initiated an unsettling of truth and objectivity post-modernism is an attempt to engage in the complete dismantling of the edifice. To this extent post-modernism is a radical version of relativism. While relativism can be described as the view that truth is paradigm-dependent, post-modernism might be described as the view that meaning is undecidable and therefore truth unattainable.

What Deleuze and Guattari despised about postmodernism was its retro-perspective, its neo-conservatism and its lack of rigour, disguised as eclecticism. What they appreciated was the infinite potentiality offered by liberation from the oppressive framework of a transcendent rationality. They would argue, however, that no such potentiality has been realized, notwithstanding celebrations to the contrary, because any potential for freedom so generated has been colonized, limited, filtered by the dead hand of capitalism.

One thing about which there is no debate is that Deleuze and Guattari were poststructuralists, and their work provides some of the most challenging writing of the poststructuralist movement. Before working together they had each established independent careers, dating from the 1950s, Deleuze as a philosopher and Guattari as a psychoanalyst and political activist: Deleuze was Professor of Philosophy at the Université de Paris VIII, Guattari worked at La Borde Clinique. In 1972 they published *Anti-Oedipus* (first translated into English in 1977[1]), which created an 'intellectual sensation' (Massumi, 1987: xi) in the context of post-war France in general, and of the May 1968 upheavals in particular. Both had been involved in the events of May 1968, though Guattari more deeply than Deleuze. Both were concerned to understand the failure of the 'uprisings' of that time, and the subsequent *malaise d'esprit* and intellectual doldrums which, in some respects, characterized the 1970s. But although perhaps prompted by such concerns, *Anti-Oedipus* is much more than this, heralded as a primary text of poststructuralism, a political analysis of the conditions of existence in contemporary 'postmodern' society, described by Foucault in his Preface to the book as 'a book of ethics' and 'an Introduction to the Non-Fascist Life' (1984: xiii). In 1980 they published *Mille Plateaux,* translated into English in 1987 under the title *A Thousand Plateaus.* This book was, in effect, Volume 2 of *Anti-Oedipus.* Although they wrote other texts together these two remain the best known and can be seen as representing the epitome of their thinking. Both works bear the subtitle *Capitalism and*

Schizophrenia (which gives a clue to their potential relevance to organization theory). Their relationship was dissolved by the untimely death of Guattari in 1992 from a heart attack, followed in 1995 by Deleuze's suicide.

This intellectual partnership was in no sense simply a matter of convenience, as is so often the case. Deleuze and Guattari also published independently of each other, Deleuze, in particular, being known for his innovative studies of philosophers, including Hume, Spinoza, Bergson and Nietzsche, as well as texts developing more directly his own thinking, such as *Difference and Repetition* (1968).[2] *Anti-Oedipus* and *A Thousand Plateaus* bear many traces of ideas which each had worked with prior to their partnership. But they were not simply bringing together their thinking. This act itself produced an explosive mix which both recognized could not have been achieved independently (see, for example, Surin, 1997: 19). It contributed to texts of extraordinary integration, diversity, complexity, breadth and power. The mix of philosophy, psychoanalysis and political commitment gave birth to an exegesis of poststructuralist analysis of the organization of the social, of the psyche and of their interrelations, which has as much significance, and power to inspire, now as it did when new.

While in some arenas of knowledge production Deleuze and Guattari are ranked alongside Foucault, Derrida and Lyotard in terms of the significance of their contribution, they have made much less impact than these in organization theory. At one level it might be suggested that there are obvious reasons for this: not only is their work full of complex technical terminology, complex in thought, articulation and style, but it is also deliberately and overtly infused with political commitment, offering a critique of capitalism which, if taken seriously, implies a revolution, not least in thinking about the role of capitalism in the contemporary world and about the ways in which we organize. Yet even among those who do seek to examine the impacts of poststructuralism and postmodernism for organization theory, Deleuze and Guattari's work is rarely present (though, of course, and especially given their pre-eminence in the poststructuralist movement, its absence does not necessarily imply that it is overlooked). Thus, for example, in Cooper and Burrell's series in *Organization Studies*, 'Modernism, Postmodernism and Organizational Analysis' (starting in 1988), Deleuze and Guattari do figure, but only peripherally, and in Burrell's *Pandemonium* (1997), perhaps the most sustained attempt to date to integrate postmodernism into organization theory, while Foucault, Derrida and Lyotard do feature, Deleuze and Guattari do not (though Deleuze does get a mention on his own). Certainly, some of the arguments in Deleuze and Guattari's work can be connected with arguments in Foucault, Derrida and Lyotard (without trying to specify who influenced whom), yet still they bring a unique vision to poststructuralist concerns and, we would suggest, to thinking about organization.

Fortunately, there are, though few in number, some excellent books on the work of Deleuze and Guattari, if not on their relevance to organization theory, that aid access to their ideas (for example, Bogue, 1989; Goodchild, 1996; Massumi, 1992). Our own interest in Deleuze and Guattari's work was first aroused in the mid 1980s (Jackson and Carter, 1986) by the

'Spinozan' question posed by them:

> Even the most repressive and the most deadly forms of social reproduction are produced by desire within the organization that is the consequence of such production under various conditions that we must analyze. That is why the fundamental problem of political philosophy is still precisely the one that Spinoza saw so clearly … : 'Why do men fight *for* their servitude as stubbornly as though it were their salvation?' How can people possibly reach the point of shouting: 'More taxes! Less bread!'? … (A)fter centuries of exploitation, why do people still tolerate being humiliated and enslaved, to such a point, indeed, that they *actually want* humiliation and slavery not only for others but for themselves? (Deleuze and Guattari, 1984: 29, emphasis in original)

Their startling 'conclusion' is that it is not feasible to answer this question by saying that people are just fooled (ibid). This, of course, cuts right across most conventional Marxist-inspired critique, which sees the capitalist manipulation of class interest through false consciousness as the primary explanation of the compliance of the oppressed in their oppression. Even in the sophisticated analyses of the members of the Frankfurt School, such as Adorno and Marcuse, and those of its later exponents, such as Habermas, oppression is still seen as, ultimately, unwanted and, often, supersedable by political action. Even in the work of Habermas, the Critical Theorist perhaps most influenced by poststructuralist thinking, oppression will be overcome, for example, by the displacement of distorted communication by communicative competence (for example, 1984). The idea that people actually desire to be repressed[3] seems at once outrageous and unthinkable. The key to this claim lies in the argument that Deleuze and Guattari make about the nature of desire – indeed, *Anti-Oedipus* has been described as a political analysis, or a philosophy, of desire (for example, Goodchild, 1996: 1).

Theories of desire have a long tradition and central position in post-war French philosophy and social theory, expressed, especially, in the exploration and development of the work of Freud, most particularly by Lacan – Guattari himself was trained as a psychoanalyst by Lacan and was a sort of lapsed Lacanian. Lacan's theory of desire was that it was characterized by *lack* and that all motivation (which would include motivation to work), is rooted in the unachievable desire to fill this lack – metaphorically, to regain a 'lost prior unity', lost through the differentiation that constitutes identity. Deleuze and Guattari not only rejected the notion of lack but also turned Lacan's thesis on its head:

> Desire does not lack anything; it does not lack its object. It is, rather, the *subject* that is missing in desire, or desire that lacks a fixed subject; there is no fixed subject unless there is repression. (Deleuze and Guattari, 1984: 26, emphasis in original)

In other words, it is repression which 'fixes' our identities, which disregards, dissolves, limits our inherent complexity and, above all, potentiality. Nevertheless, we desire such fixed identity, thus desire our own repression. (The reasons why we desire it will be explored later.)

For us, that question remains the central concern in Deleuze and Guattari's work, and the key to their potential contribution to understanding organization. However, as one might expect from a poststructuralist approach, the question itself is nested in a web of other arguments and, indeed, prognoses, which can, at times, seem oblique, obscure and very fluid. In order to try to illuminate the connections between Deleuze and Guattari's work and thinking about organization(s), therefore, we have chosen not to attempt the daunting, and probably impossible, task of giving a linear-logical synopsis of their work. Indeed, no commentator on their work seeks to do this, not least because it would be contrary to the very spirit of that work (again, more on this later). Instead, we pursue a limited number of themes which seem to us to aid the task.

The road to *Anti-Oedipus*

It has already been suggested that it is possible to see Deleuze and Guattari as organization theorists, in so far as they share the common meta-level concerns of all organization theorists: 'externally', the relations of and between organizations and society, the polity, the economy and so on, and 'internally', the processes, productions and relationships, material, human and symbolic, which constitute organization. In Deleuze and Guattari's terms, however, this is a deeply artificial distinction, since each is immanent in the other. What also distinguishes theirs from conventional approaches to understanding organization is their conception of what is relevant and significant in this process of understanding. They were revolutionaries, not just politically, but also in that they did not share the ontological assumptions about the nature of the world which characterize conventional organization theory. By 'conventional organization theory' we mean the dominant, orthodox form of theorizing about organizations. Deleuze and Guattari would refer to this as *majoritarian*, which Goodchild's useful glossary defines as 'of the perspective belonging to the majority, the norm' (1996: 218). Such theory is, typically, conservative and regulatory. Importantly for this comparison, it has two other characteristics: on one hand, it treats organizations as discrete, identifiable entities which can be examined independently of their social context, and, on the other, it is suffused with the notion that organizations, in terms of some specific but usually unarticulated criteria, are perfectible. Both of these characteristics are antithetical to a Deleuze and Guattari perspective.

Not only is conventional organization theory riddled with the notion of perfectibility, but so too are the best established critiques of it, albeit very different perfections. Let us suggest that there are three general attitudes to the notion of perfectibility (whatever it may consist in). *Firstly*, there is the approach which assumes that perfectibility is just around the corner and that what is required is a bit of marginal adjustment to achieve it (conventional organization theory). *Secondly*, there is the approach which sees perfectibility as distant and different, but achievable, not through regulation but through reform (conventional critiques of conventional organization theory). For example, it is typical of approaches based in Critical Theory that they assume that it is possible to achieve a state of social/organizational relations in which those aspects which currently oppress are absent – for instance, the removal of surplus repression (Marcuse, 1956) would lead to an emancipatory praxis; communication in the absence of power (Habermas, 1984) would, similarly, generate emancipation. The *third* approach, however, views the very notion of perfectibility as meaningless. In this approach we are understood to be only ever in a state of becoming and emergence. Perfection cannot (literally, is not possible to) be prescribed. Moreover, the very concept implies the desirability of a stasis, which is unachievable. It is this approach which informs the work of Deleuze and Guattari in particular and poststructuralists in general. Approaches (1) and (2) can both be seen as products of the Enlightenment in that they are conditioned by belief in the achievability of a transcendent rationality, the purging of mysticism and mythology from knowledge, the uncovering of universal truths which will govern social relations. In other words, both share a faith in the signifiers science and rationality, though they differ profoundly on what the signifieds of these signifiers are. Approach (3), however, does not share these Enlightenment assumptions. It has no faith in transcendent, or even putatively transcendent, rationality. It rejects the notion that the world exists only to facilitate the achievement of human betterment. It rejects the Enlightenment teleology of progress. To the poststructuralist, existence is ambiguous, undecidable, complex, chaotic. There is no end point towards which everything tends.

Conventional organization theory (Approach 1) derives much of its inspiration from the work of (late) Marx, though, interestingly, rarely explicitly and always as a template of dystopia, progress towards the antithesis of which is the measure of progress towards perfection. Critical Theory (Approach 2) is explicitly informed by, and committed to (early) Marxist theory, not as something to avoid but as something which, in terms of both critique and prescription, provides a basis for social analysis and progress. However, this perspective is extended through an equivalent interest in Freudian theory – the attempt at the well-known, if problematic, Marx-Freud synthesis. (Freud's work has never had any significant impact on conventional organization theory, nor could it have, since it introduces the essentially metaphysical concept of 'the unconscious'.) Poststructuralism (Approach 3) also includes in its formative influences the work of Marx and Freud, but adds to this the anti-Enlightenment and heterodox work of Nietzsche. Nietzschean thinking has achieved little penetration in Anglo-Saxon theorizing, and has, indeed, often been treated in that context with distaste if not contempt. But Deleuze (1983: ix) suggests

> (i)t is perhaps in England that Nietzsche has been most misunderstood ... They [the English] did not need the detour through Nietzsche's very special empiricism and pragmatism which ran counter to their 'good sense' ... Nevertheless Nietzsche is one of the greatest philosophers of the nineteenth century. And he alters both the theory and the practice of philosophy.

Deleuze's study of Nietzsche substantially contributed to the establishment of Nietzsche's significance in poststructuralist thinking, as well as to his rescue from the allegation that he was a forerunner of fascist thinking – and, in the hands of Deleuze and Guattari, Nietzsche's work was to provide the 'missing link' in the Marx-Freud synthesis. For poststructuralists the exploration of social relations involves two central issues: power and desire, the former conventionally related to society, the latter to the individual. A classic Marxist analysis sees power in structural terms, rooted in class interest and deriving from ownership of the means of production. A classic Freudian perspective sees conscious rationales of action as to be distrusted in favour of unconscious motivation manifested as desire. The fusion of the two perspectives was found in Nietzsche: structural relationships represent a temporary resolution of forces which manifest themselves as power, the determination of which Nietzsche expresses as the will to power; power, therefore, is not to be understood in purely structural terms but as an object of desire. What Deleuze found in Nietzsche's work, and which had a major impact on his later work with Guattari, was the emphasis on the active and affirmative, rather than the reactive and negative:

> Affirmation remains as the sole quality of the will to power, action as the sole quality of force, becoming-active as the creative identity of power and willing. (Deleuze, 1983: 198)

What he found in Nietzsche, also, was a celebration of multiplicity, becoming and chance. (See also Bogue, 1989; Descombes, 1980; Goodchild, 1997.)

Guattari had been working on the Marx-Freud synthesis for many years before he met Deleuze in 1969. As a left-wing militant, Guattari was interested in the role of capitalism and its organizations in the repressive shaping of social relationships, and he had developed a psychoanalytic and political theory of groups (Bogue, 1989). As a psychoanalyst it is not surprising that Guattari would be seeking to understand these structural concerns as they impacted on mental health. Historically, his interests coincided with those of the anti-psychiatry movement led by Laing (see, for example, Boyers and Orrill, 1972), with which Guattari had an 'uneasy relationship' (Massumi, 1992: 3). Both were convinced, for instance, that mental illness, schizophrenia in particular, was primarily the product of oppression/repression by social institutions, and of the poverty of conventional psychoanalytic practice in providing remission. These convictions informed Guattari's own psychoanalytic practice at La Borde Clinique. Where he differed profoundly with Laing was in his belief that the problem lay not in social institutions generally, but in capitalist institutions and in 'the vital tool of capitalist repression', Oedipus (Guattari, 1984: 54).

What came out of the fusion of these pre-existing concerns was a radical reconceptualization of the immanent relations of people and capitalist society and its institutions (organizations). The will to power which articulates the resolution of forces was reconceived as *desire*. Desire

> is shaped by the actual relations, conventions, and meanings that exist in society ... (D)esire is the social unconscious ... If desire naturally seeks multiplicity and creation, the problem then arises of how social formations come about that prevent desire's own autoproduction. Deleuze and Guattari separate instinct, need, want, and interest, [the common currency of conventional organization

theory] which are produced with the appearance of having a fixed status and metaphysical pre-existence in certain social arrangements, from desire. The former are real, but they are a product of a certain machinic social arrangement; desire, by contrast, is the arrangement itself. (Goodchild, 1996: 5)

In Deleuze and Guattari's terms it might be said, with apologies to Pascal,[4] that capitalism has its organizations which organization theory knows nothing of! Organization theory is not organization theory per se, but organization theory within what Foucault (1980) called the capitalist 'régime of truth': although representing itself as non-ideological, capitalism is an unquestioned and unquestionable context. Conventional organization theory admits no need to question because it seems axiomatic that capitalism is (not neutral but normatively) benign. But in the view of Deleuze and Guattari capitalism is a social order which operates, for its own survival, to repress desire, since, unrepressed, desire challenges and questions it. Capitalism channels desire so that desire desires its own repression. Against our interests we are manufactured to desire only what capitalism can provide. But

(t)here is not one ... aspect – not the least operation, the least industrial or financial mechanism – that does not reveal the insanity of the capitalist machine and the pathological character of its rationality ... (T)he capitalist machine does not run the risk of becoming mad, it is mad from one end to the other and from the beginning, and this is the source of its rationality ... Except in ideology, there has never been a humane, liberal, paternal, etc., capitalism. Capitalism is defined by a cruelty having no parallel in the primitive system of cruelty, and by a terror having no parallel in the despotic régime of terror. (Deleuze and Guattari, 1984: 373)

Clearly, this can claim to be of supreme relevance to understanding organization(s). Equally, conventional organization theory can have nothing to offer to such an understanding, since Deleuze and Guattari construct a model with which conventional organization theory is not authorized to deal because such a view exists outside its régime of truth. Taken seriously, Deleuze and Guattari's work presages a radically different understanding of the function and purpose of organization(s).

Schizoanalysis

The common subtitle of both *Anti-Oedipus* and *A Thousand Plateaus*, it will be recalled, is 'Capitalism and Schizophrenia'. While the relevance of capitalism to organization theory is obvious, that of schizophrenia is less immediately clear. Although the psychoanalytic foundation of Deleuze and Guattari's use of the term is undoubtedly clinical, its relevance and significance transcends this, into 'ordinary life'. Massumi (1992: 179 n.76) usefully points to the distinction:

A SCHIZOPHRENIC in the clinical sense is someone who attempted an escape from identity-undifferentiation, but was thwarted by society or otherwise failed. 'SCHIZOPHRENIA' in Deleuze and Guattari is not a malady;

it is a process (that of becoming).

Elsewhere (1992: 1) he says 'The "schizophrenia" Deleuze and Guattari embrace is not a pathological condition .... Schizophrenia as a positive process is inventive connection, expansion rather than withdrawal. Its twoness is a relay to a multiplicity.'

Capitalism's need to control and channel meaning, in order to remain unquestionable, is operationalized through the capture and control of the signifier. Multiplicity of meaning is proscribed, meanings are specified, purged of contradiction, in conformity with the logic of capitalism. This logic is totalizing and normalizing – to question it becomes an act of madness because it is to question 'self-evident' truths. Who dares question the ontology of the market, or the causality of customer demand, or the superordinacy of economic efficiency, or the sanctity of profit? Though many may debate the process of such concepts, it is rare to see the principle itself challenged. Indeed, within the capitalist régime of truth there is no mechanism for mounting such a challenge. To do so, thinking would have to escape the régime, be able to adopt a position where it can break down alleged truths, make other connections, think the unthinkable. This is what *schizoanalysis* promises. It is a process of unmasking apparent homogeneities, problematizing the taken-for-granted, discovering repressed potentialities and possibilities, thinking what is other than/to capitalism. Schizoanalysis celebrates multiplicity through breaking out of the authorized codes of signification to the infinity of possible states of social relations beyond. It is open-ended and expansive.

It is possible to draw parallels here with, for example, Foucault's use of disjunction and discontinuity to explore the development of discourses; Derrida's deconstructive challenge to the authority of authorship; Lyotard's argument for the 'liberation' of victims, made victim by the colonization of signifiers. It is not so easy to draw parallels with organization theory, even within the critique of conventional approaches – though there are some 'honourable exceptions'. It might be suggested that an embryonic schizoanalysis was represented in Burrell and Morgan's (1979) model of incommensurable paradigms. This opportunity has been foregone, however, in the main, by treating the model as a typology rather than a taxonomy and by denying incommensurability (Jackson and Carter, 1991). Treating the model as a typology implies that, even though theorists are in different paradigms, they are all studying the same phenomenon (that is, a unified concept of organization). Denying incommensurability denies real differences between perspectives and allows for the re-emergence of a homogeneous organization theory (as predicted by Burrell and Morgan, 1979: 397) authorized by the capitalist régime of truth. The reluctance (or refusal?) of organization theorists to challenge the capitalist régime of truth is instrumental in the incorporation of dissent – in Deleuze and Guattari's terms, its reterritorialization – and the elision of difference, with profound consequences for the understanding of social/organizational relations in the contemporary world. Through reterritorialization of putatively critical paradigms, the possibilities they might offer for achieving non-exploitative processes of organization are lost.

Schizoanalysis offers a dynamic of becoming, undoing the repression of difference, creating the multiple from the singular, and opens up the realization of potentialities apart from what is. This is not the linearity of simple causal relations: if A then B, if I enrich your job then you will feel satisfaction. This is the totality of possibilities that exist at the point at which change begins to occur. Another important parallel with Deleuze and Guattari's work that can be seen is in theories of chaos and complexity. Thus Prigogine and Stengers (1985), exploring a rapprochement between randomness and determinism, argued that, while systems in or about equilibrium might exhibit predictable characteristics, systems which are not stable can be triggered into a state of change with an infinity of possible, and random, outcomes. Once one is 'selected', a path is followed which leads to another set of near-equilibrium conditions and largely deterministic behaviour. (This is a very appropriate description for the genesis of capitalism, see later.) For Deleuze and Guattari, as for Prigogine and Stengers, and contrary to the assumptions of conventional organization theory, equilibrium is not, however, the norm. It is transitory and illusory. Chaos is the norm. The aura of stability which seems to characterize capitalism is not innate or natural to that particular set of social relations, but is only possible as an outcome of the colonization of signifiers into its own logic and the denial of alternative meanings informed by different logics. Stability is only ever artificially sustained:

> The closest thing there is to order is the approximate, and always temporary, prevention of disorder. The closest thing there is to determinacy is the relative containment of chance. The opposite of chance is not determinacy. It is habit. (Massumi, 1992: 58)[5]

Habit is the closest we can get to the appearance of a steady state. The machine of the steady state is culture, which prescribes 'habits' and justifies what we are required to do. But, Deleuze and Guattari argue, culture and cultural formations, supposed to be a product of the collective and an expression of shared values, traditions and so on, and for the collective benefit, neither represents anything chosen by 'the people' nor benefits the majority of them. Culture is rules which constrain, not liberate. '"Culture" as a selective process of marking or inscription *invents* the large numbers in whose favor it is exerted' (Deleuze and Guattari, 1984: 343, emphasis added). Another term they use to describe this situation is the mechanosphere. Goodchild (1996: 59) elaborates:

> The Mechanosphere: *Homo sapiens*, that tool-making animal, becomes a slave of its own creations ... Technical machines, military machines, industrial machines, economic machines, communication machines, fantasy machines, entertainment machines, media machines, computing machines, consumption machines, and governmental machines – each operates to produce an effect designed by a human, but to serve an end that no human has chosen.

So, this steady state is artificial and sustained by (structural) power, and, as Massumi (1992: 6) notes, 'Power is the domestication of force [in its Nietzschean sense]. Force in its wild state arrives from outside to break constraints and open new vistas. Power builds walls.' It is because equilibrium is only a transitory 'escape' from chaos, because ruptures occur at which change is possible, even inevitable, that schizoanalysis does offer a (perhaps, the) way out of this domination. It is feasible to escape the capitalist régime of truth. The process of schizoanalysis is what Deleuze and Guattari call *nomad thought*. Massumi, (1992: 5–6), again:

> 'Nomad thought' does not lodge itself in the edifice of an ordered interiority; it moves freely in an element of exteriority. It does not repose on identity; it rides difference ... It synthesizes a multiplicity of elements without effacing their heterogeneity or hindering their potential for future rearranging. The modus operandi of nomad thought is affirmation, even when its apparent object is negative.

Nomad thought is the plain (plane) of infinite possibility and randomness. It cannot be known in advance what will transpire from nomad thought. It is deterritorialized and resists immuring.

Another favoured metaphor, especially in *A Thousand Plateaus*, is the *rhizome*:

> ... (t)he rhizome connects any point with any other point, and none of its features necessarily refers to features of the same kind ... The rhizome doesn't allow itself to be reduced to the One or the Many ... It has neither beginning nor end, but always a middle, through which it pushes and overflows ... The rhizome proceeds by variation, expansion, conquest, capture, stitching ... (T)he rhizome is an a-centered system, non-hierarchical and non-signifying, without a General, without an organizing memory or central autonomy, uniquely defined by a circulation of states. (Deleuze and Guattari, 1983: 47–9)[6]

The rhizome not only lacks, but resists, identity. It is a process of becomings, future-oriented. This mirrors the belief of Deleuze and Guattari (amongst others – see, for example, various philosophies of non-identity in writers as disparate as Adorno, 1973; Bataille, 1988; Lyotard, 1988), that people, too, should be understood as in a constant process of becoming. The sense we have of a fixed identity and of its desirability, given to us by our social relations, is, Deleuze and Guattari argue, yet another intended consequence of the colonization of the signifier that is exercised by capitalism. This impression of fixed identity is essential for our governability; it fixes us also in our relation to the social and to power. But identity is merely an attenuator, to be escaped. This point is nicely captured by Deleuze and Guattari in the opening of *A Thousand Plateaus*. We, along with all commentators, have labelled (given identity to) Deleuze as a philosopher and Guattari as a psychoanalyst. They, however, resist such labelling when they point out: 'The two of us wrote *Anti-Oedipus* together. Since each of us was several, there was already quite a crowd' (Deleuze and Guattari, 1988: 3).

Why Oedipus?

Deleuze and Guattari's thinking was, as we have already noted, informed by a clinical understanding of schizophrenia but their work, while providing an illumination of the conditions of contemporary existence, also performed the function of a critique of the role of psychoanalysis in capitalism, focused on the formative influence of the Oedipal relationship. In Freudian terms the Oedipal relationship can be seen as the triangle of relations between the (male) child, the mother as object of desire and the father as authority figure, intervening between desire and its object. Freud's original, and now largely discredited, formulation of the Oedipal relationship in terms of psychosexual development was reconceptualized by Lacan in psychosocial terms, an elaboration of Freud's work which became very important in the poststructuralist canon. Freud's 'literal' view was replaced in Lacan's work by a generalized processual model of structure, in which desire becomes the pursuit of the 'lost object' and entry into language effects the internalization of rules of social living. This generalized model represents the social arrangements for the management of desire. While, broadly speaking, accepting the structural model of the Oedipal relationship, Deleuze and Guattari are at odds with Lacan over the nature of desire. Lacan argued that lack exists at the centre of being, which creates the desire for it to be filled, even though this can never be achieved: desire is desire to fill the lack, but the lack is unfillable, not least because its root is differentiation, and differentiation is the basis of identity. Deleuze and Guattari (1984: 28) argue that lack, rather than existing naturally and inevitably, is

> created, planned, and organized in and through social production ... It is never primary; production is never organized on the basis of a pre-existing need or lack. It is lack that ... propagates itself in accordance with the organization of an already existing organization of production. The deliberate creation of lack as a function of market economy is the art of a dominant class.

Deleuze and Guattari, therefore, reject the notion that desire is a secondary function to lack, arguing that desire is the primary, that desire does not lack anything, it just is. Given this nature of desire, the main objective of capitalism can be seen as regulating and/or repressing it, not least by channelling it towards those things that capitalism can provide, that it sanctions, and from which it will benefit.

Deleuze and Guattari argued that, far from there being a single formative influence to achieve this Oedipalization, the family is only one institution within capitalism that operates to regulate desire through encouragement or proscription. The Oedipal structures of capitalist society are produced and reproduced through its organizations: 'Everybody has been oedipalized and neuroticized at home, at school, at work' (Seem, 1984: xx). Moreover, the family should not be understood solely in its conventional domestic sense. As Massumi (1992: 81–2) notes,

> The family is not a closed microcosm ... It opens directly onto the social field ... The family is a microcosm of society only to the extent that Oedipal processes at work throughout the social field collapse categories belonging to other levels of organization into family categories (equating for example, foreman with father...).

In other words, capitalist organizations per se reflect an Oedipal structure modelled on the family: they function to channel desire and to promote the internalization of authority. One might suggest, for example, that the very structure of organizations mimics that of the family, with the emphasis on groups (such as departments), and people in authority over these who are in control, not just of what *is* done, but also of what *can/cannot* be done. A well-recognized aspect of management is the moulding and manipulation of behaviour, achieved through the control of rewards and punishments. The manager both assesses what is worthy of reward (and how much reward), and defines what the 'desired' reward ought to be: that which it is in the power of the organization to offer and which is sanctioned as appropriate. At a different level, it is common for organizations to take on a role analogous to that of a caring parent, guiding and instructing the employee on self-development (in ways that are useful to the organization), health and welfare, culture and values.

Ironically, the language of the family is prevalent in some forms of organization theory, where it signifies benign paternalism, harmony and unity. This language of the family implies but masks the authority relationships of organizations in representing the family as a comfortable, homely milieu. It is a language stripped of the semiotics of the normalizing, controlling Oedipal role that families have in capitalist society. For Deleuze and Guattari capitalism is not a protective system which exists for the benefit of those who inhabit it, but a system whose institutions and organizations shape our very concept of what it means to be human. Thus work organizations, for example, are not just functional arrangements for the efficient production of goods and services, they are mechanisms for the creation of 'self' and an immanent part of the Oedipalization of society.

Desire

Any understanding of organization must be predicated on an understanding of their Oedipal function. Attempts to understand organizations as discrete, functional, abstracted entities cannot penetrate the significance of organization, since these are merely epiphenomena of a more fundamental process. This undoubtedly explains much of the sterility of conventional organization theory, and its tendency to repeat descriptions and prescriptions that have already failed adequately to explain organization or to solve organizational problems. Based on Deleuze and Guattari's analysis, such an organization theory constitutes the equivalent of a medicine based on humours: pre-scientific, and rooted in an epistemology of myth, ritual, folk wisdom, unconsciously based in ignorance.

Given the significance of Oedipalization, it follows that desire is also of major importance, but this is another concept which is absent from organization theory. In so far as organization theory has a concept of the individual, it is one rooted in behaviourism rather than psychoanalysis. Guattari (1984: 52 n.6) describes it thus:

> Behaviourism is a theory from the beginning of this century that reduced psychology to the study of behaviour, defined as the interaction between external stimuli and the responses of the subject. The neo-behaviourism of today tends to

reduce all human problems to problems of communication and information, ignoring the socio-political problems of power at every level.

Much of conventional organization theory tends to focus on needs rather than desire, especially the delineation and satisfaction of so-called innate needs, whether extrinsic or intrinsic. Thus needs satisfaction becomes self-fulfilling: the need is manufactured, the means to satisfy it is specified, and what satisfaction means is also specified *a priori*, all independent of experience but based on the requirements of capitalism. In contradistinction to need, desire, in Deleuze and Guattari's terms, does not require an object, it just is, an 'unbound, free-floating energy', not acquisitive or oriented to lack but productive (Bogue, 1989: 89). 'Desire is not bolstered by needs, but rather the contrary; needs are derived from desire: they are counterproducts within the real that desire produces' (Deleuze and Guattari, 1984: 27). Moreover, whereas need implies interest – that is, we satisfy a need to serve our own self-interest – desire is independent of any notion of functional utility. This is why desire can work against, and be encouraged to work against, self-interest: 'Desire can never be deceived. Interests can be deceived, unrecognized or betrayed, but not desire' (ibid: 257).

Deleuze and Guattari are fond of linking the concept of desire (that is, hyphenating it), with the concepts of machine and production, though in later work than *Anti-Oedipus*, notably *A Thousand Plateaus*, the machinic concept is usually replaced by that of assemblage. It is worth noting that neither machine nor production is used in the way that the terms are commonly used in conventional organization theory. The machine or assemblage denotes a collection of interacting components that produce something and, by so doing, serves a function. But this function is nothing to do with the efficient production of goods and services. This is a function in terms of desire's desire, that is, sufficient unto itself. The concept of the *desiring-machine* is part of Deleuze and Guattari's reconceptualization of the unconscious and is used to denote 'the working components of the unconscious' (Goodchild, 1996: 218). They

> object to the psychoanalytic conception of the unconscious as a source of representations, and hence as an object of interpretation. The unconscious represents nothing, creates no symbols or signifiers, no veiled or distorted wishes that call for interpretation. The unconscious produces, and what it produces need only be described … (T)he only question is whether the heterogeneous connections produced by the unconscious open up new pathways or block the further proliferation of desire. (Bogue, 1989: 108)

Machines produce and what is produced is the process of becoming. This is relevant to both concrete machines (technological apparatuses) and abstract machines (desiring machines).

> All molar functionalism is false, since the organic or social machines are not formed in the same way they function, and the technical machines are not assembled in the same way they are used, but imply precisely the specific conditions that separate their own production from their distinct product … The desiring-machines on the contrary represent nothing, signify nothing, mean

nothing, and are exactly what one makes of them, what is made with them, what they make in themselves. (Deleuze and Guattari, 1984: 288)

Capitalism

The key to understanding Deleuze and Guattari's argument lies in their conceptualization of capitalism. It is common to describe capitalism as a morally neutral process of money making money, or as a socio-economic model based on ownership of the means of production and class interest. The end-of-history model sees the teleology of history as the intertwining of capitalism and liberal democracy and this as the summit of human achievement. Deleuze and Guattari's understanding of capitalism, while rooted in a Marxist model, places emphasis on psychological aspects of capitalism as a system. One way into this is through a spatio-temporal model. In a schema not dissimilar to that of Foucault (1979), Deleuze and Guattari posit three societal machines, primitive-territorial, barbarian-despotic and civilized-capitalist. The primitive-territorial may be described as, basically, tribal, pre-state. The barbarian-despotic represents the imperialistic colonization of the primitive-territorial by the imposition of 'the "megamachine" of the State, a functional pyramid that has the despot at its apex, an immobile motor, with the bureaucratic apparatus as its lateral surface and its transmission gear, and the villagers at its base, serving as its working parts' (Deleuze and Guattari, 1984: 194). The civilized-capitalist is the supersession of this through the elevation of capital beyond the limits of the state, and focuses on flows of exchange and equivalence.

> The tendency of capitalism is to substitute for fixed and limiting relations between men and things an abstract unit of equivalence that allows free exchange ... of everything for everything. Not only are equivalences established between goods in an open market, but bodies, actions, ideas, knowledge, fantasies, images function as commodities which can be translated into other commodities ... (Bogue, 1989: 100)

Capitalism is seen as the universal limit, not in the end-of-history sense, not as a necessary limit, but one that comes about through contingency and chance, though 'predictable' because of capitalism's infinitely flexible capacity to control and channel desire. This limit is self-defining, because the logic of the capitalist régime of truth controls thought: it both implies that there is nowhere else to go and, through flexible reconfigurations which incorporate dissent, presents barriers to change.

Deleuze and Guattari start from a fairly conventional Marxist position, which denies the moral neutrality of capitalism. Thus Guattari argues that 'Capitalism exploits the labour capacity of the working class and manipulates the relations of production to its own advantage, but it also insinuates itself into the desire system of those it exploits' (1984: 62), and 'The working class are the prime victims of capitalist techniques to manipulate desire' (ibid: 70). However, capitalism does not achieve this through power conventionally understood, but semiotically (controlling and defining signifiers/signifieds) and organizationally (generating particular forms of social interactions). By reducing everything to money, capitalism destroys any notion of social relations, meanings and so on, apart from those which it alone specifies, for its own perpetuation.

> The language of a banker, a general, an industrialist, a middle or high-level manager, or a government minister is a perfectly schizophrenic language, but that functions only statistically within the flattening axiomatic of connections that puts it in the service of the capitalist order. (Deleuze and Guattari, 1984: 246)

The language of organization only functions in so far as it serves capitalism. Thus it subjectifies, but portrays subjection as inevitable, or denies it.

> The wage regime can ... take the subjection of human beings to an unprecedented point, and exhibit a singular cruelty, yet still be justified in its humanist cry: No, human beings are not machines, we don't treat them like machines, we certainly don't confuse variable capital and constant capital ... (Deleuze and Guattari, 1988: 457) [See also Alliez (1997: 86) on hypercapitalism, societies of control and business régimes in Deleuze and Guattari's work.]

Capitalism operates by liberating all flows and exchanges from any kind of social and political constraint – in the terms of Deleuze and Guattari, decodes and deterritorializes. But these freedoms are not absolute, because capitalism then reterritorializes, resignifies all meaning in terms of what will benefit its own acquisitiveness and prevent challenges. Thus are we seduced into desiring not only conformity, but even our own repression.

> By destroying all *ties*, capitalism should have created the conditions for the blissful nomadism of a detached and *absolute* individual, as a consequence of 'deterritorialization'. However, in this liberation of all flux, it has produced a world of nightmare and anxiety ... '(D)eterritorialization' is accompanied by a perpetual 'reterritorialization'. Capitalism postpones the limit towards which it tends (nomadism) by restoring artificial 'territorialities' (beliefs, forms). (Descombes, 1980: 176–7, emphasis in original)

Capitalism subjectifies everyone, even the capitalist, but, while the capitalist defines this subjectivity, others are subjected to it. The role of the state is merely to provide and establish the infrastructure whereby this process is operationalized – the state is simply a tool of capitalism. The state's institutions, therefore, cannot be understood simply as institutions which mediate the achievement of a free and mature society. For example:

> It may appear that all that is happening in a university is the transmission of messages, of bourgeois knowledge; but we know that in reality a lot else is also happening, including a whole operation of moulding people to fit the key functions of bourgeois society and its regulatory images. (Guattari, 1984: 34)

Any organization theory which ignores that organizations are capitalist organizations and are established to satisfy the requirements of capitalism, irrespective of whether these benefit the social or the individual, cannot begin to understand either the process or the practice of organization(s). Nor can it adequately conceptualize organizational problems, let alone provide appropriate solutions. Nor can it evaluate the significance of organization(s). Organizations do not exist simply to provide goods and services as efficiently as possible in response to customer demand, they exist to channel desire into the production and consumption of capitalism's outputs, and to disable the potential for desire to desire anything beyond, or alternative, to this.

> Desire is repressed, even under capitalism which proclaims that 'everything is permitted' (understood: *to whoever can pay*), because it is incompatible with social existence. Thus it only becomes socially acceptable once it is disfigured, distorted and transformed, for example, into Oedipal desire ... (Descombes, 1980: 178, emphasis in original)

To do otherwise jeopardizes the very survival of the capitalist machine itself.

> If desire is repressed, it is because every position of desire, no matter how small, is capable of calling into question the established order of a society: not that desire is asocial, on the contrary. But it is explosive; there is no desiring-machine capable of being assembled without demolishing entire social sectors ... (N)o society can tolerate a position of real desire without its structures of exploitation, servitude, and hierarchy being compromised. (Deleuze and Guattari, 1984: 116)

The Beginning?

Capitalism is bad for us, yet its existence is not maintained through coercion. We are free individuals, yet we desire the continuation of a system that is repressing us. And things are not getting better.

> You no longer have to believe in the legal system to be a lawyer, or in the government to be a civil servant or politician. A businessman doesn't have to believe, even pretend to believe, that capitalism is a force for human betterment. All a body need do is desire – and subordinate its desiring to earning and consuming ... The only correlation it [society] demands of everyone is between buying power and image consumption. The only correspondence it requires is with the credit card company. (Massumi, 1992: 136)

So where do we go from here? What is needed is a revolution, but not a political revolution in which one dominant discourse simply replaces another. The revolution that is needed is one of *thinking*.

Deleuze and Guattari posit two universal conditions: chaos and order (immanence). As Goodchild (1996: 67) points out 'Chaos is not merely an absolute, indeterminate, undifferentiated morass ... for it is defined in relation to another limit of critical philosophy. Any metaphysics of chaos must explain the appearance of order in the world.' According to Deleuze and Guattari (1994: 201–2) 'We require just a little order to protect us from chaos ... But there would not be a little order in ideas if there was not also a little order in things or states of affairs, like an objective anti-chaos ...' Chaos is the non-coherence of order. Moreover, '(c)haos is not an inert or stationary state, nor is it a chance mixture. Chaos makes chaotic and undoes every consistency in the infinite' (ibid: 42).

Conversely, order (immanence, complexity) is the result of a sort of anamorphism of chaos, a *temporary* 'sieving' of chaos to allow a *perceived* consistent residue of order. Forms of order – Deleuze and Guattari's preferred term is *'planes of immanence'* – take their 'determinations' from chaos. There is not just one plane, and each plane 'has its own way of constructing immanence' (ibid: 50). Thus it can be argued that some planes of immanence have better explanatory power than others. There is, Deleuze and Guattari maintain, a difference in the quality of thought, and a difference in utility, between philosophy (concepts) and opinion. Opinion gives a *sense* of certainty – 'a sort of "umbrella", which protects us from chaos' (ibid: 202) – but that is all. Opinion, they suggest, is really no better than chaos. By contrast, rigorous thinking – a concept 'is not a set of associated ideas like an opinion ... it refers back to a chaos rendered consistent, become Thought, mental chaosmos. And what would *thinking* be if it did not constantly confront chaos?' (Deleuze and Guattari, 1994: 207–8, emphasis in original.)

Order/organization is only a momentary achievement snatched from chaos, filtered through some 'sieve' – ideology, *a prioris*, assumptions, a régime of truth – which includes/excludes, bounds, prioritizes, to create an illusion of consistency. The 'process by which chaos gives rise to consistency and influences the course of events' (Goodchild, 1996: 217) is what Deleuze and Guattari call *chaosmosis*. But, to be 'true' to chaos, this process must be based on the infinity of all possibilities, not just one possibility. This is the difference between the realization of potentiality and the appropriation, exploitation and repression of desire. In the contemporary world, Deleuze and Guattari argue, the latter is the case, because the 'sieve' is capitalism and capitalism, through its appropriation of signification, channels desire so that all that appears to be desirable is what capitalism can offer. But, by desiring the 'products' of capitalism, we come to desire our own repression: our interest would be served by the liberation of desire to potentiality but, by accepting the régime of truth of capitalism, we become slaves of the system, rather than its masters, its victims rather than its beneficiaries. But capitalism is not *the* order out of chaos – indeed, in Deleuze and Guattari's terms, it is possibly no more than opinion. It is, at best, *a* sieve, not *the* sieve.

The relations of chaos and order cannot be resisted, nor should they be. Rather, they re-present the 'pool' of possible potentialities which can be thought and through which we can become. It is only by acknowledging chaos that we can even begin to hope that we might extract order/organization which could overcome the unnatural, managed, engineered conflict between desire and interest. We need to, and we can, think our way out of capitalism, to consider the infinity of possibilities that can be thought. This is what 'nomad thought' and the 'rhizome' can do. For Deleuze and Guattari, thinking is the *sine qua non*. It is, perhaps, to be seen as the primary form of practical action (Jackson and Carter, 1997).

The analysis of capitalism and its system of organizing and organizations that is offered by Deleuze and Guattari seems, at first glance, to present it as omnipresent, omniscient and omnipotent. But not so. One reason for this stems from the role of signification in capitalist hegemony. However much control of the signifier is sought, it can never be absolute, and there is always the potential for meanings to escape the authorized versions. Another reason lies in the immanent force of desire, which 'resides' in us all and is the reservoir of potentiality and becoming. This also can escape the grasp of the capitalist machine. The work of Deleuze and Guattari is not just a diagnosis, there are also lines of flight, means of escape. Some of their critics claim that what they propose is just anarchy. This seems at least simplistic in the face of their explicit political position. In any case, the whole of their work is premised upon a conception of the social and the individual as immanent, to the extent that it is not meaningful to treat them as separate, or to talk of them in distinct terms – the word 'individual' rarely occurs in their texts. Thus it can be argued that, while advocating a radical transformation, this does not imply a non-organized society. What it does imply is that we can think rationales for organizing other than the capitalist machine.

It is a truism, especially in the work of Deleuze and Guattari, that organization always has a purpose. In contemporary incarnations this purpose is capitalism, but this is not inevitable. Organizations do not have to be the way they are, other purposes could inform our mode of organization. For example, we could choose to organize in ways which prioritize ecophilosophical principles. We could have a radical reassessment of what organizational outputs are necessary for social survival, betterment, independent of the implications of this for a capitalist system of values. What is needed is for us to develop our capacity for thinking and action which is active and affirmative, rather than reactive, passive and negative. Because we, as individuals, have an immanent relation with the social, this would inevitably become distributed throughout society, offering alternative ways of thinking about organization based upon the infinity of possibilities and potentialities. What Deleuze and Guattari advocate is a politics of multiplicity and creativity, unfettered by any dominant discourse. As Goodchild (1996: 104) concludes, 'Any transformation of society ... begins with a transformation of the subjectivity of the thinker.' Nevertheless, from our present perspective this must have a detotalizing quality. It is in the nature of genuinely radical transformations that one cannot predict what will happen, where we will alight next. The consequences of real change are always unknowable in advance. But, again, not just any old change will do. The system of Oedipalization in contemporary society generates a situation in which the only criterion by which we can judge and evaluate change is whether it is good for capitalism. In Deleuze and Guattari's terms, change must be judged and evaluated according to the extent to which desire, multiplicity and creativity are emancipated, to which the outcome is social relations which exist for the betterment of us all, rather than just for the favoured few.

In Deleuze and Guattari's work there is another important concept, that of the *minor*: minor literature, minor philosophy, and so on. Minoritarian expresses a process of becoming, or transformation:

> A minor philosophy, asking the reflexive theoretical question, aims to make its own mode of existence into the deterritorialized plane of desire. It disinvests desire from its previous social assemblages, so that desire can begin to operate as a liberated and spontaneous plane. This revolution or liberation of desire is also the creation of desire, its condition of possibility. (Goodchild, 1996: 58)

It is also a philosophy characterized by collective values and in which everything is political. Minor philosophies, literatures and so on, are those which resist appropriation and signification. The work of Deleuze and Guattari is itself part of this minority, is itself rhizomic. It is possible to make connections with the work of other writers. But Deleuze and Guattari's work is not really like that of anyone else. In particular, this work has qualities and characteristics which actively resist translation into a language already appropriated by capitalism. In other words, it is not possible to make a conventional organization theory out of Deleuze and Guattari's analysis of organizations. Neither can their work be assimilated into conventional organization theory to add, say, explanatory power. Majoritarian thought may be the norm, but it inevitably serves interests other than its own. Consequently, to think difference a minor philosophy is necessary. This is what Deleuze and Guattari offer – *new* thinking on organization(s).

Notes

1   All references to *Anti-Oedipus* in this chapter refer to the translation by R. Hurley, M. Seem and H.R. Lane, published by The Athlone Press, 1984.
2   Deleuze had what might be seen as a more 'traditional' academic career, and this probably explains the irritating tendency of some commentators to refer to the joint work of Deleuze and Guattari as if it is the work of Deleuze alone.
3   The terms 'repression' and 'oppression' are often used by different authors to mean, apparently, the same thing. The general distinction here is that repression signifies the act, while oppression signifies the experience.
4   Pascal's epigram, from *Pensées* (1670) is: The heart has its reasons which reason knows nothing of.
5   Several commentators link the work of Deleuze and Guattari with theories of chaos. Massumi (1992: 178 n. 73) particularly links them with Prigogine and Stengers, seeing this connection as more appropriate than one with, for example, Derrida. Elsewhere (ibid: 165 n. 32), he notes that Prigogine 'expresses an affinity with Deleuze' although 'the passage in question is not included in the English book based on this work, *Order Out of Chaos*'.
6   Also in *A Thousand Plateaus* (1988: 21), but translated somewhat differently by Massumi.

References

Adorno, T. (1973) *Negative Dialectics*, trans. E.B. Ashton. London: Routledge and Kegan Paul.
Alliez, E. (1997) 'Questionnaire on Deleuze', trans. P. Goodchild and N. Millett, *Theory, Culture and Society*, 14 (2): 81–7.

Bataille, G. (1988) *The Accursed Share*, trans. R. Hurley. New York: Zone Books.

Bertens, H. (1995) *The Idea of the Postmodern*. London: Routledge.

Bogue, R. (1989) *Deleuze and Guattari*. London: Routledge.

Boyers, R. and Orrill, R. (eds) (1972) *Laing and Anti-Psychiatry*. Harmondsworth: Penguin.

Burrell, G. (1997) *Pandemonium: Towards a Retro-Organization Theory*. London: Sage.

Burrell, G. and Morgan, G. (1979) *Sociological Paradigms and Organizational Analysis*. London: Heinemann.

Cooper, R. and Burrell, G. (1988) 'Modernism, postmodernism and organizational analysis: an introduction', *Organization Studies*, 9 (1): 91–112.

Deleuze, G. (1983) *Nietzsche and Philosophy*, trans. H. Tomlinson. London: Athlone (Original 1962).

Deleuze, G. (1994) *Difference and Repetition*, trans. P. Patton. London: Athlone. (Original 1968).

Deleuze, G. and Guattari, F. (1983) 'Rhizome', in G. Deleuze and F. Guattari, *On The Line*, trans. J. Johnston. New York: Semiotext(e).

Deleuze, G. and Guattari, F. (1984) *Anti-Oedipus: Capitalism and Schizophrenia*, trans. R. Hurley, M. Seem and H.R. Lane. London: Athlone.

Deleuze, G. and Guattari, F. (1988) *A Thousand Plateaus: Capitalism and Schizophrenia*, trans. B. Massumi. London: Athlone.

Deleuze, G. and Guattari, F. (1994) *What Is Philosophy?* trans. G. Burchell and H. Tomlinson. London: Verso.

Descombes, V. (1980) *Modern French Philosophy*, trans. L. Scott-Fox and J.M. Harding. Cambridge: Cambridge University Press.

Foucault, M. (1979) 'Governmentality', trans. R. Braidoth, *Ideology and Consciousness*, 6: 5–21.

Foucault, M. (1980) 'Truth and power', trans. C. Gordon, L. Marshall, J. Mepham and K. Soper, in C. Gordon (ed.), *Michel Foucault: Power/Knowledge*. Brighton: Harvester Press. pp. 109–33.

Foucault, M. (1984) 'Preface', in G. Deleuze and F. Guattari, *Anti-Oedipus*. London: Athlone. pp. xi–xlv.

Goodchild, P. (1996) *Deleuze and Guattari: An Introduction to the Politics of Desire* London: Sage.

Goodchild, P. (1997) 'Deleuzean ethics', *Theory, Culture and Society*, 14 (2): 39–50.

Guattari, F. (1984) *Molecular Revolution: Psychiatry and Politics*, trans. R. Sheed. Harmondsworth: Penguin.

Habermas, J. (1984) *The Theory of Communicative Action*, trans. T. McCarthy. London: Heinemann.

Harvey, D. (1989) *The Condition of Postmodernity*. Oxford: Blackwell.

Jackson, N. and Carter, P. (1986) 'Desire versus interest', *Dragon, the Journal of SCOS*, 1 (8): 48–60.

Jackson, N. and Carter, P. (1991) 'In defence of paradigm incommensurability', *Organization Studies*, 12 (1): 109–27.

Jackson, N. and Carter, P. (1997) 'The phantasy of the perfect system', paper presented at the International Conference on 'Uncertainty, Knowledge and Skill', Limburg, Belgium.

Jameson, F. (1991) *Postmodernism Or, The Cultural Logic of Late Capitalism*. London: Verso.

Lash, S. (1990) *Sociology of Postmodernism*. London: Routledge.

Lawson, H. (1989) 'Stories about stories', in H. Lawson and L. Appignanesi (eds), *Dismantling Truth: Reality in the Postmodern World*. New York: St Martin's Press. pp. xi–xxviii.

Lyotard, J.-F. (1988) *The Differend: Phrases in Dispute*, trans. G. Van Den Abbeele.

Manchester: Manchester University Press.

Marcuse, H. (1956) *Eros and Civilisation*. London: Routledge and Kegan Paul.

Massumi, B. (1987) 'Translator's foreword: pleasures of philosophy' in G. Deleuze and F. Guattari, *A Thousand Plateaus*. London: Athlone. pp. ix–xv.

Massumi, B. (1992) *A User's Guide to Capitalism and Schizophrenia: Deviations from Deleuze and Guattari*. Cambridge, MA: MIT Press.

Prigogine, I. and Stengers, I. (1985) *Order Out of Chaos*. London: Fontana.

Seem, M. (1984) 'Introduction', in G. Deleuze and F. Guattari, *Anti-Oedipus: Capitalism and Schizophrenia*, trans. R. Hurley, M. Seem and H.R. Lane. London: Athlone. pp. xv–xxiv.

Surin, K. (1997) 'The "epochality" of Deleuzean thought', *Theory, Culture and Society*, 14 (2): 9–21.

7
Jean Baudrillard

Hugo Letiche

More Baudrillard than Baudrillard:
Baudrillard (subject) meets Baudrillard (object)

The text normally to be expected of me in a chapter such as this would recount who Jean Baudrillard is, what he has accomplished in his writings, how his ideas have developed, and (again, but on another level) what significance this all has for organizational (management) studies.[1] I would be supposed to reduce my subject (or is it, perhaps, the object?) of the chapter, in customary fashion, to a more or less comprehensible, conceptual construct. It would be assumed that there is something, i.e. a persona, hidden in a series of texts; and someone, i.e. the person, who wrote and 'sign'-ed those 'texts', that could be called 'Baudrillard'. My job supposedly would be to fill-in the 'identity' of the name, so that you, the reader, 'knows' who 'Jean Baudrillard' is and what that signifies. Obviously this is a very rational (logo-centric) and linear (Modernist) agenda. But when confronted by the writings of Jean Baudrillard (i.e. the texts that are branded 'Baudrillard'), this plan meets resistance. Firstly, his ideas do not really develop that much at all. He has for thirty years been saying more or less the same thing(s). What makes matters sometimes a bit tedious is that he has even said them in different books and articles (not to mention interviews), in exactly the same words, inclusive of the same illustrations and cynical comments ('jokes'). Reading a lot of Baudrillard, at once, as I did to write this chapter is, frankly, frustrating – it really put me off Baudrillard. His books succeed one another like a series of ocean waves; there is motion but really very little movement. To a large degree, wave after wave of energy passes through the (same) water, over and over again. Yes, each wave is a bit different from the last one, and things do get added and subtracted; but there is a lot of repetition. Don't get me wrong: in the basic ideas there is a concept of the consumer society that is well worth studying. But those ideas I can (and will) summarize in a few pages.

The problem is that Baudrillard is a disciple of McLuhan and embraces McLuhan's interpretation of *the medium is the message*. Thus, the form of his text is at least as important, if not more important than his content. But in a chapter like mine, Baudrillard's style more or less disappears and my own style takes over; the form isn't Baudrillard's. If we assume that language is a window on reality, and that our goal is really to see whatever is outside that window, then language (form) isn't a problem. But if we assume that the text could be a distorting mirror – a pretended window of media hype or advertising for (my)self – then what the text is, and how it appears, becomes crucial. And in Baudrillard appearances are important. By making the way the text is written more important than what the text *communicates*, Baudrillard opts for a very radical textual strategy, one he would probably call *fatal* (Baudrillard, 1983).

Throughout his *oeuvre*, Baudrillard continually wants to escape the existent. What *is* just won't do. One needs to go faster than fast, to create more innovatively than the most innovative, to be more radical than the most nonconformist. Baudrillard's strategy is one of constant excess; he assumes that only by being the advocate of the *more* to any form of *being*, can he escape whatever it is he is trying to escape. And that is one of the mysteries of Baudrillard – just what *is* it that he is really trying to escape? He has leftist origins – he began his career in the French Freudian-Marxist intellectual milieu. But there is no crisis of (an)Other in his work – he is not impassioned by the question of how to do justice to Others. Despite having begun his writing in the entourage of Sartre and *Les Temps Modernes*, Baudrillard is not a thinker of the Other at all. Nowhere in his *oeuvre* is the existential (i.e. experiential, immediate, interactive) or the question of the relationship between the self and other, presented. In fact, Baudrillard's strategy of self is very paradoxical. He denounces the self as encapsulated in the falseness of the consumer society. Thus, evidently, what is wrong with the self is its inauthenticity. But he does not accept the distinction authentic/inauthentic. He refuses to think authenticity – it is for him unthinkable, unacceptable, totally unwanted. But all his writing rotates around polarities, and the rejection of the Hegelian (dialectical) treatment of just such polarities. If we posit stasis (a conformist, inactive, afraid, pole of action) and activism (an innovative, energetic, 'will'-ed, pole of action), Baudrillard insists there is *no* transcendence of the polarity. Thus a conflict between stasis and activism cannot lead to shared-action, possessing the energy of activism and the care of stasis. Baudrillard's rejection of dialectical logic is metaphysical – he provides us with no empirical evidence or epistemological argumentation for his choice. Contrastingly, Sartre grounds his assertions existentially, that is he circumscribes what can be experienced, and because what there is to be experienced is (at least in part) defined, what mankind has to contend with can be discussed (Sartre, 1977). Alternatively, Lyotard grounds his thought epistemologically; it is based on definitions of what one can know, say or express consistently and centres on what the nature of knowing, language and expression makes it possible to know and/or state, rigorously. But Baudrillard is a *pataphysicist* – he *makes it up as he goes*.

Baudrillard's goal is to formulate imaginary solutions that surpass known repertoires of response. But why engage in pataphysics? It may be an extreme form of creativity for creativity's sake, but why opt for it? When cornered by the demand to ground his ideas, Baudrillard seems to go for the Platonic solution; he tells a story about the gods. (Sinaiko, 1965) A story he tells, to answer the sort of demand I am now putting on his text, is that of the *shadow*. It describes the person who tries to escape their shadow – to elude their identity, 'self' and the consequences of what they do; in the story the person is inevitably punished. Only via a pact with the devil (evil) can one escape one's shadow; but the bargain always turns sour and the shadow strangles/overwhelms the self (Baudrillard, 1990b). So why attempt the doomed flight from identity? Baudrillard's answer is *because there is no choice*. The paradox is that pataphysics (the science of imaginary solutions) appears to be the highest point of voluntarism, but is seen by Baudrillard as some sort of determinism. Baudrillard does not see imagination as free or willed. Because the consumer society has destroyed all 'reality', there can *only* be imagined solutions. There is no reality left upon which one can base any other solutions.

Once the hypothesis is made, that any and every sort of realism is historically impossible, the form of cognition that remains possible is inherently pataphysical. Obviously the logic is paradoxical – the reality of history determines that no realism is sustainable. And the human spirit, which somehow remains, is divorced from any traditional realist ground and continues (evidently) to function by writing, thinking and speaking. This spirit is, evidently, the objective realization of history – the product of the reign of objects – determined by the consumer society. Thus, Baudrillard's epistemology looks to be very Hegelian, being based on the welding of the logic (spirit) of history and that of consciousness. He posits that the existing social order (defined in materialist terms), somehow determines (the possibilities of) consciousness. Social (economic) reality makes a subject-based epistemology impossible – the only thought possible is determined by the logic of the object(s). And the logic of objects leads to *pataphysics*.

For Baudrillard we are not free to be realists – he has replaced 'God is dead' with 'the real is dead'. In Sartre, the lack of a metaphysical grounding to consciousness leads to the claim of necessary freedom; the person has to choose, because no first cause will do it for him/her (the choice, not to choose, is also a choice). In Baudrillard, the existential condition as conceived of by Sartre is abandoned and the logic is reversed. The subject is determined by the metaphysics of the real, which makes it impossible to take (mental) possession of the *real*. A pataphysical, enforced creativity, remains the only possibility for consciousness to survive. There is no *free* subject; history has overwhelmed all *freedom*. But the *reality*, which has overwhelmed all existential freedom, possesses a power, creativity, dynamism that humans can imitate. Humans, by trying to be more object than the object, can try to take repossession of the principle of activity. *Objective* freedom (that is the freedom of the material man-made world), is Baudrillard's model of activity. Baudrillard is a materialist, but it is a materialism grounded in the man-made, virtual world.[2] There is none of the Marxist materialist tendency to scientism or natural philosophy. The material that acts as a key point of reference is produced by state-of-the-art capitalist companies. Baudrillard's economy is based on information and communication technologies; it is a knowledge economy. Not the physicist's version of matter but the high-tech company's products form the basis of his reflection.

Baudrillard responds to the supposed primacy of the material, by trying to reproduce on the level of theory what he thinks is the logic of materialist change. His thought claims to go even faster in the direction of the object (materialist change) than does the object itself. He claims to try to escape the grip of economic reality by out-pacing it. His intention is to be more performative than the most performative; more dynamic than the most dynamic; more powerful than the strongest power. Escape is supposedly possible from the logic of the material by out-doing it. But what sort of escape is this? Baudrillard's pataphysics does not imagine every possible solution, but only those solutions that outstrip material (economic) trends by exaggerating them. According to Baudrillard, the frantic version of the consumer society is not merely hyper-consumerism, but catastrophic consumerism. But why would we want to achieve catastrophic hyper-reality?

Throughout his career, Baudrillard has followed the same (textual) pattern. He takes a trend or assumption, and exaggerates it until it collapses from the weight of the overstatement.[3] His most important conceptual success has been achieved by hyperbolizing the principles of the consumer society (consumerism) in a *genealogy* of modern society. But he has also, I think less successfully, followed the same textual strategy in his consideration of the subject/object relationship (arguing that all freedom and dynamism comes from the object) as well as in his perusal of sexuality (arguing that seduction is a first cause to activity and the genital, in whatever form, is secondary and derivative).

Baudrillard practices an idiosyncratic sort of social economic and/or materialist deconstruction. He reduces social action to principles of anti-humanist pulsion, prioritizing the *object* and/or *unfreedom*; and then argues that the exaggeration of this logic can lead to some form of imaginative renewal. A humanist/anti-humanist polarity is, supposedly, to be tapped in order to find the energy needed to prevail by writing. Baudrillard's ultimate goal does not seem to be political, economic or social but aesthetic. He wants to preserve the ability of consciousness to exist and act in a hostile world. His objective appears to be to preserve the significance of consciousness and awareness as signified in text. His goal is to see things, write them up and thereby maintain experiential *being*. Thus, his thought really does come full circle, and rejoin Sartre's, much more than has been realized. Baudrillard is a theoretician of the literary persona; he explores the possibilities, strategies and difficulties of creating living text in our world.

It follows, from what I have argued, that I will explore Baudrillard further, firstly by examining his analysis of consumption and all its ramifications and secondly by looking at his textual strategies and his achievements as text-producer. Finally I will reflect on the (possible) significance of Baudrillard for organizational studies.

The consumer society

Baudrillard's 'theory' of the consumer society was created by stringing together a whole series of other writers' concepts. It is not a systematic theory. Baudrillard weaves others' ideas together into his own, often original, patterns.

But there is no synthesis, or over-arching philosophy, guiding the procedure. For instance, Mauss's anthropology is crucial to Baudrillard's theory of the consumer society. But exactly why he chose Mauss is never revealed. Other possible choices are never compared to the one adopted. Nor is any original empirical evidence provided to justify the choices. Baudrillard assembles his sources in order to make his statements. Why these specific sources, or exactly this (and not another, though similar) statement, is not clarified. Readers of Baudrillard familiar with the work of Georges Bataille will recognize that it is Bataille's reading of Mauss as outlined in his theory of general economy that is the dominant influence on Baudrillard, but Bataille is not even mentioned in *The Consumer Society* – not even in Ritzer's introduction. Indeed, Bataille's influence is not acknowledged formally until several years later, in *Symbolic Exchange and Death*. The dominant form of argumentation is rhetorical – Baudrillard tries to carry the reader along with him on the basis of the passion of his prose and the power of his exaggerated (Baroque) style.

Baudrillard's theory of the consumer society is formulated as a sort of answer to the Marxist sociology of the sixties. The cornerstones are:

1. Mauss's anthropology of the gift, and the principle of reciprocity, mediated through Bataille
2. Foucault's concept of genealogy with an analysis in three steps (representation, production, simulation)
3. McLuhan's differentiation between hot and cool and the assertion that 'the medium is the message'
4. American sociological theories, especially the 'end of ideology' and 'post industrialism' (Bell/Riesman)

All of this is meant to function as an answer to the (French) Freudian-Marxist description of society.

The initial point of departure is his rejection of Marx's concept of production. In the Marxist analysis the means of production (infrastructure) determine, and have always determined, the superstructure (culture, government and management). The history of the infrastructure has, supposedly, moved from the feudal (essentially agricultural) economy to the early modern (with trade and cities beginning to flourish), onto the capitalist (with factory production) form. It is claimed that the inability of capitalism to make full use of its infrastructural potential, manifests itself in intermittent economic crisis, underproduction and the impoverishment of the working class. Furthermore, capitalism determines conditions of work that are alienating, wherein workers have no control over their means of production. And it is the cause of a fetishized pattern of consumption wherein most consumers (the labouring class) value objects more than themselves and experience society's material wealth as dehumanizing (not of themselves). Baudrillard criticizes the absolutization of production in all this. However accurate Marx's description of nineteenth-century social relationships may be it does not provide a correct portrait of pre-capitalist society. Pre-capitalist society was based on entirely different relationships, within which production played no role. There was no production in pre-capitalist society. Baudrillard uses Mauss's description of the gift to describe pre-capitalist society. It was a social order wherein material goods were produced in response to demand. There was no logic of productivity (the principle of wanting to make more with the same, or less, labour) or of surplus value (the accumulation of wealth via control of the infrastructure). Things were produced when they were perceived to be required. One did not produce more than was needed, or try to produce cost effectively. Goods were produced in a logic of reciprocity – the needs of the one were related to the needs of the other, in (fairly) direct exchange relationships. People made things in social structures of interdependence based on what they expected of one another. Society was not driven by an abstract logic of profit, but by a concrete logic of relationships. Exchange was comparable to the process of gift giving, as described by Mauss. The preservation of equality and of stable relationships, was the key to the making and exchanging of objects. Objects symbolized interdependence and the stable logic of the social order. Things were made and exchanged, in what was perceived to be a natural order of human relationships. The balance of giving and taking was an exteriorization of the natural, social and metaphysical order. Production, as a product of capitalism, destroyed all this. Society was split into those who controlled the economic infrastructure, and those who could only sell their labour (power). Production was not a law of social and metaphysical balance, but a principle of imbalance and inequality. The anthropology of balanced exchange, and the social mutuality of pre-capitalism, has disappeared.

Just as capitalism destroyed the logic that preceded it, a post-capitalist phase is destroying the regime of production. Social economic policy, since 1929, sees production and consumption as an integrated system. Production as a single economic principle no longer exists. Corporations are just as aware of the necessity to create and/or maintain demand, as they are aware of their need to produce. A company that was solely focused on production, would today have limited chances of survival. In the contemporary consumer society, traditional industrial labour is less and less important. A clothing manufacturer, for instance, may retain design, marketing, international contracting and logistics, for itself and outsource all production. The actual making of things is no longer at the centre of value production. For the corporation, production can be a rather marginal cost, with (for instance) all the major costs in marketing, product innovation and design. In Marx's universe, wages were closely linked to the value necessary for labour to reproduce itself. In our society, the corporation often can pay any old wage (subject to national minima), since its labour costs may actually be very minor to its cost price. Furthermore, the logic of fetishism has changed. Material goods no longer face the labouring class as the embodiment of their disenfranchisement. Quite the opposite; the contemporary Western working class is a consuming class. It *realizes* itself in the market place. Identification with one's own labour has become all the more difficult: (1) as the production process has been rationalized into ever smaller and more absurd actions; and/or (2) corporate action has become so complex and varied that no one is able to oversee it. Increasingly, work is something one has to have, to belong, but which has little inherent value. One works to consume, and one works to see others (be social). The focus of work is not on what one does with ones hands or head: work has little or no intrinsic value or satisfaction. Marx's labourers, who are alienated because capitalism has robbed them of their craftsmanship, are creatures of the distant past. In a consumer society, it is crucial to ensure that demand is maintained, that an unlimited supply of needs continues to exist. Material goods in such a society do not exist to fill basic needs (the reproduction of labour power), but to keep the cycle of production and consumption afloat. The economy does not respond to a principle of scarcity but to one of affluence.

This analysis is based on a comparison of the succession of three logics: a pre-capitalist economy which was semiotically centred on representation, a capitalist society centred on production, and the post-capitalist society based on simulation. This logic is that of a genealogy (Nietzsche, Foucault) but its content is mainly drawn from Walter Benjamin's analysis of representation and (re-)production. In an industrial society one almost endlessly reproduces objects. One Ford automobile is much the same as any other. Objects, in society, loose their originality – the *original* Ford is a prototype that is not for sale. All the Fords on the market are reproductions. In the pre-industrial, pre-capitalist society all objects were originals. An artisan had an idea or a model in his/her head, which he/she then realized materially. Making things was based on a logic of representation – an abstract design leading to its realization in fact. Objects were products of human action. But in the industrial society, objects became alienated from their designers – the original has retreated behind the logic of the factory. The market place has been flooded by *copies*. Objects have lost contact with a human creator; the object world and the world of human labour are totally alienated from one another. Mankind lives in a material world, unconnected with purposeful, direct human action. Production is alienated from all human purpose. No-one close to the production process decides what is to be made or how it is to be made. The relationship between making things and designing things has been sundered. Objects have lost their individuality, their *humanity* – they have taken on a life of their own. But this fetishized world has already been surpassed as we now live in a civilization of *simulation*.

Most of the economy never produces any objects at all, but only so-called services. An enormous financial world (of options and futures, of insurance and investment for example) exists with apparently no relationship to the real economy (of production) at all. The economy rotates around a symbolic universe of marketing and finance, information and communication without ever producing any objects. Economic existence is totally alienated from the material. There is *no* original – only a flow of information. There is no product, only software. This virtual economy runs on digital code – everything is reduced to some sort of logic of plus and minus. Its metaphor is DNA/RNA – protein capable of carrying all the information necessary for life, which is faultlessly communicated. There is no distance between the code and the next realization of the code; there is, in effect, no communication but a sort of cloning. This is a logic of absolute *sameness*, within which there is no original or copy, but only the proliferation of the code. All differentiation, all individuality, is destroyed in the logic of the digital. Codes of plus and minus engulf all difference. Multiple choice tests (plus and minus codes) replace learning; opinion polls (plus and minus ratings) trample politics. In the logic of digitality there is no reproduction (a model with so many copies), but only simulation (the endless repetition of pattern[s]). Digital society has no individuality: there is nothing specific. It is merely the endless repetition of code. Baudrillard asserts that, increasingly, we live in such a universe of simulation (code). Everything is digitized – images, knowledge, communication, the financial world. Objects are not made by unique human action (as in representation), or even within a logic of the original and its reproductions. There is only the logic of code and of its endless processes. A society grounded in the logic of code is hyper-alienated, more alienated, that is, than alienated. In such a logic, the human agent disappears and the logic of the code pursues its own ends independent of human agency.

From McLuhan Baudrillard gained his assessment of what the logic of simulation means for human interaction. The key distinction is between *cool* and *hot* media. *Hot* media (in Baudrillard's interpretation of McLuhan) possess a high degree of specificity (high definition), and lead to strong individual involvement (low empathy). *Cool* media are characterized by low-definition information (vagueness of content) and intense involvement (an exceedingly social and participative way of sharing). Reading is *hot* – it is based upon the discipline of the book. The individual has to work through the meaning of the text. The relationship between the author and the reader is at a distance, and is relatively rational. The gap between what the writer wants the reader to do, think or feel, and what the reader actually does, is large. In a *cool* culture, the gap between suggestion and response, passion and action is small. Exactly what the medium says (the content communicated) is less important than is the relationship created (the interaction). Different technologies are more or less cool or hot, and lend themselves to particular sorts of relationship(s). Nevertheless, Baudrillard warns us not to be too simplistic in our analysis as there are a variety of different sorts of involvement possible with each medium. After all, one can listen intently to and study a TV interview (for instance, with a writer) as well as be disoriented and mindlessly swept along by a programme (for instance by MTV).

The industrial culture of production was based on linear organization. The organization of factory production was modeled on the same principles as those of the book, with chapters and paragraphs (sections and subsections), clarity of procedure and clear hierarchical differentiation between major and minor issues, for example. The society of production imposed labour discipline on its work force. It demanded social literacy, based on understanding order, structure and procedure. Much Marxist analysis catalogues the displeasure of the masses at having a hot culture imposed on them. A cool culture is much more social, participative and emotional than a hot one. In it more is shared and less is analysed, there is more spontaneity and fewer rules. McLuhan's point is that the new (communication) technologies are reversing the development from cool to hot. The rational, linear society of production is being deconstructed by a post-production society of simulation. In simulation, everything is contemporaneous – there is a cacophony of images, noises and sensations. The ordered and structured social order of the nineteenth century (wherein everyone knew their place) has been replaced by an energized field of action, wherein there is no clear order or social place left. The famous dictum 'the medium is the message' of McLuhan indicates that the nature of the technology used in a society is socially more powerful than are its specific uses. Thus a society, tied together by the telegraph, is different from one without electronic communications. The development of the telegraph leads to fundamental social adaptation, irrespective of whatever specific messages are carried. Centralized, hub and spoke forms of governance, are only possible with electronic communications in place. Likewise, the automobile which made the growth of suburbs possible, was essential to the maturation of the consumer society. Thus a means of communication determines a set of social possibilities.

But what are the characteristics of the social possibilities currently emerging on the basis of ICT (information and communication technology)? Baudrillard argues that we are returning to the cool society. Society is becoming less literary and more oral. Email has nothing of the formality and style of letter writing – emotive and impassioned results (flaming, for example) are evident. There is no time for carefully reasoned or strongly analysed decisions in an instantaneous civilization. Managers have to act quickly before electronic markets act for them. The (neo-)cool of our times has all the characteristics of the immediate and pulsional tension of the past but it is institutionalized on a global scale. While the cool society of the pre-capitalist period was intimate, organized on a human scale, the cool society that is now emerging is abstract and unknowable. Current forms of cool generate the one simulacrum after the other. Images succeed one another, without the audience being able to identify the one as more real than the other. Highly evocative communication takes place, without it being grounded in concrete or specific circumstances. There is communication without context; emotion without clear significance; images without explanation.

The cool threatens consciousness with an impossible task – to make sense of a flow of images without any means of doing so. Unable to know what it is that one sees, one is forced into a form of superficial perception. One can only skim the surface of the images. Cognition is limited to the vaguest outlines of what is communicated. Information overload, image exhaustion and perceptual fatigue result. It is an economy based on simulation (an economy of code, where wealth is generated via electronic bits and bytes, without originals) and a culture on simulacra (a parade of images where the audience is unable to differentiate between them). Baudrillard's division, based on the distinction between the work of an artisan ('originals'), factory production (the product is a reproduction of an originatory model) and simulacra (images without originals), divides history into three periods and adds depth to the genealogy based on the division between pre-modern, modern and post-modern. Nevertheless, it is important to note that via these distinctions a form of technological push has been assumed which distinguishes Baudrillard from his sources. The objects (technology) characteristic of an economic and cultural period evidently structure the possibilities in that period for human *being*. Baudrillard's categorization assumes the primacy of the objective above the subjective. It is not what the subject desires or wills, but what the material structure of his/her existence determines that counts.

In what sense is this, specifically, a sociological analysis, that is to say what does Baudrillard's thought really owe to sociology? His analysis of the consumer society and its link to ICT is not especially out of the ordinary in contemporary terms. If we compare Baudrillard to Castells, for example, the biggest difference (leaving style aside) is to be found in the role of the object. Objects or objectality (the object as first cause) is crucial to Baudrillard. Thus in his analyses of (potential) agency (that is, circumstances wherein the human will could assert itself), he stresses the powerlessness of human action. His interpretation of politics and the role of the masses is probably his most sociological theme. For Baudrillard, politicians have no grasp on *events*; they are mere simulacra. And the masses merely refuse to be what the politicians want them to be. The strategy of the masses is one of refusal: of the work ethic, of political engagement, of the cultural, pedagogical and intellectual demands made of them. There is no silent majority that can be defined by its lack of this or that, but there is a strategy of the masses to frustrate and defeat the impostures made upon them.

If sociology researches the logic(s) of social determination, for example how social structure governs human action, Baudrillard is not much of a sociologist unless we interpret objectality as a form of social structure. Should objectality be interpreted materialistically or symbolically? If we interpret it symbolically, then Baudrillard can be thought of as some sort of semiotic sociologist. But since Baudrillard rejects the category of the real, as consumer society has vitiated the real of all its former meaning, what is our epistemological point of reference? Is any text, any pronouncement, any literary effect permitted? Baudrillard's research strategy is based on redoubling, that is, investigating the more true than the true, the more beautiful than the beautiful. And the result is *hyper-real*, more real than the real. But is the hyper-real a condition of things and/or of symbols? If it is a condition of things, then it is possible to claim that Baudrillard is a materialistic sociologist who explores how social and historical changes in the production of material reality have determined human possibility. His analysis of consumer society can then be interpreted in terms of structures, economics and material reality. If one sees his whole *oeuvre* symbolically, then Baudrillard's description of the consumer society is, itself, a simulacrum – a textual strategy designed to allow free play to simulation and appearance. The answer is, I believe, somewhere in the middle. The analysis is materialist, but the textual strategy is symbolic. There is instability between Baudrillard's form and content. This occurs because his theory of the consumer society is not entirely consistent with his other fundamental realm of speculation, that of communication.

The debate as to whether Baudrillard is 'really' postmodernist results from this instability. His materialistic sociology is hyper-modernist. It takes the typical determinants of modernist sociological analysis and pushes them to their extremes. This produces the redoubling effect and his analysis of reversibility. To explain reversibility it is necessary to return to the analysis of Mauss and the gift. In pre-capitalist society, relations were mutual and reversible. The logic of cause and effect was not linear – that is, it did not run in one single direction. Any cause could be an effect and vice versa. Capitalism installs relationships of linearity: the owner determines what happens in the factory, nature gets (re)interpreted in a causal frame of reference (see also Burrell, 1997). But post-capitalist society abandons the assumption of the linearity of nature via ideas like the uncertainty principle and co-evolution. In capitalist linear constructions, reversibility creates a revolution; outside of it, reversibility is the most normal thing in the world. Baudrillard embraces the principle of reversibility in a way that leads to total immanence. In total reversibility, all flows are also counterflows; all action is reaction and the dialectic has ceased to exist. In reversibility, things don't go anywhere – they just *are*. For the intellectual who wants to 'draw conclusions' or 'make a point' reversibility is an intellectual catastrophe. Reversibility is the opposite of the dialectic; it is a product of redoubling. It deeply unsettles our way of thinking. Baudrillard demonstrated this with his three articles '*La guerre du Golfe n'aura pas lieu*', '*... a-t-elle lieu?*' and '*... n'as pas eu lieu*' in *Libèration* in 1991, collected and translated as *The Gulf War did not take place* (1995). In these articles he claimed that the Gulf War would not, could not and did not take place. He argued that the war would not take place because, in a logic of reversibility, nothing so modern as a causal struggle to the death was possible. After all the death of reality had already taken place! And he argued that since the news of the war was not news but simulacra, the war was not a war at all, but simulation.

> ... what is really happening on the ground there, in Iraq, it is so vile. It is enough to drive you either into depression or into a rage! It arouses feelings you can neither describe nor transpose. What can a writer say about this heap of cowardice and stupidity? While the situation presented itself in abstract terms of war or no war, it was an exciting problem. But now we are in the real. If I fall into the real, I experience the same anger as the others ... (Baudrillard in Gane, 1993: 181)

Baudrillard has justified his textual strategy by using a quote from Brecht: 'Where nothing is in its place, there's disorder. Where everything is in its place there's nothing there, and that's order' (Baudrillard in Gane, 1993: 180). By placing his own text in the non-real, Baudrillard tries to respond to the nature (reality?) of contemporary society. The strategy is based on a whole series of rejections: the rejection of Modern society and its logic of irreversibility as well as of post-modern society and its logic of total similitude.

Baudrillard has attempted to protest against the terror of capitalist control and the terror of post-capitalist emptiness. An empowered linear terror of Modernism appeals no more to him than the un-empowered (powerless) implosion of the postmodern. He no more wants to embrace the 'we conquer you' of Modernist competition, than the 'all action is senseless' of Postmodern spectacle. He remains in this sense a situationist – someone who is trying to describe events. Ultimately, his primary engagement is as a writer, as a person who describes. He is much more a writer than a sociologist, and indeed he explicitly turned his back on sociology in the 1970s if he is to be taken at his word. His primary commitment is not to analysing the depth structures of society, a much too Modernist project for him. After all, the idea of differentiating between depth and surface levels merely reproduces the split between the powerful and powerless, between the hands and the head, and ultimately between the means of production and the economic infrastructure. If sociologist means observer of society, then Baudrillard is one. But one can better call him a chronicler of his times.

Baudrillard: the form itself of what is written

> It is writing's fatal strategy to go to extremes. And that strategy is a happy one, a vital one. That is my vitality, and that is why I will always survive. I'm melancholic, but most certainly not depressive. You never see the form itself of what I write, so you search the content, an ideologized content. So really that produces a negative balance, and that's enough to depress anybody ... (Baudrillard in Gane, 1993: 181)

The second basic theme to Baudrillard's *oeuvre* centres on the ability to write. The theme includes issues such as: why write, what makes it (im)possible to write, and what *is* writing. In the second half of the eighties, Baudrillard published *Amèrique* (1986) and *Cool Memories* (1987) wherein his writing is less programmatic and more demonstrative than before. Between *Les Strategies fatales* (translated as *Fatal Strategies*) (1983) and *Amèrique* (1986), there is a considerable stylistic breach. *Les Strategies fatales* begins:

> Things have found a way of avoiding a dialectics of meaning that was beginning to bore them: by proliferating indefinitely, increasing their potential, outbidding themselves in an ascension to the limit, an obscenity that henceforth becomes their immanent finality and senseless reason.
>
> But nothing prevents us from assuming that we could obtain the same effects in reverse – another unreason, also triumphant. Unreason is victory in every sense, which is the very principle of Evil. ... This is ... the principle of Evil, as expressed in the *evil genie* of the object, in the ecstatic form of the pure object and in its strategy, victorious over that of the subject. (Baudrillard, 1983, trans. 1990: 7)

This text pretty much follows the line of argument I have already presented. It emphasizes the supremacy of the object, embraces the strategy of redoubling and takes distance from the theme of the consumer society. Later in this book, Baudrillard compares Baudelaire's theory of the absolute commodity to Benjamin's theory of reproduction, concluding that Baudelaire's call for commodities without an aura, or any anthropomorphic significance, was superior to Benjamin's theory that depends too much on alienation and, thereby, retains a concept of the subject (Baudrillard, 1983, trans. 1990: 118–19). In this fairly late stage of Baudrillard's thinking about the consumer society, the logic of consumerism is subordinated to the logic of the *absolute commodity*. The logic of objectality is, here, paramount. This is a book about fatal strategies – strategies of cognition that destroy the subject, the self and the existential quality of being alive. Fatal strategies are a sort of sadistic game with subjectivity. They taunt, sabotage and demean the subject. Canetti emerges as Baudrillard's inspiration:

> a painful thought: past a certain point in time, history has not been real. Without realizing it, the whole human race seems to have suddenly left reality behind. (Canetti quoted in Baudrillard, 1983, trans. 1990: 14)

Baudrillard plays (in the tradition of Descartes) with such 'evil genie' suggestions as: 'What if we can only see things which happened long ago but not those now occurring?'; or 'What if what two people saw at the same moment really occurred at different times?' The book examines ways of *being* that make rational, linear, orderly perception and experience impossible. Baudrillard sees all of us as hostages and terrorists. There is no clarity in who possesses whom or what is negotiable. The claim that the one makes of the other, the knowledge that the one has of the other, are all ways of *taking hostages*. For Baudrillard love is inferior to seduction. Love is a mere form of idealization without mutuality and interaction. Seduction is play that requires participation of the other and follows the logic of reversibility. *Love* you do alone in individual subjectivity – it is an act of self. *Seduction* is a withdrawal of self and an abandonment into interaction; it is a fatal strategy.

Poststructuralism may have been a theory of the 'end of the subject', but poststructuralists operated in a clean and rational way. Baudrillard enacts the fantastic martyrdom of the subject. Though his prose certainly has verve and his images are lively enough, the question arises 'What is this really all about?' The tropes are energetic and ecstatic but they confront us with the continual denial of the self. All interiority is disavowed – there is no self left to self-consciousness or to self-awareness. All consciousness is propelled outwards; inward looking sensitivity is denied, blocked, frustrated. Is this denial of self, ultimately a *hysterical* text, however clever some of the surface meanings may be?

Contrastingly, *Amèrique* begins:

> Caution: Objects in this mirror may be closer than they appear!
> Nostalgia born of the immensity of the Texan hills and the Sierras of New Mexico: gliding down the freeway, smash hits on the Chrysler stereo, heat wave, snapshots aren't enough. We'd need the whole film of the trip in real time, including the unbearable heat and the music. We'd have to replay it all end to end at home in a darkened room, rediscover the magic of the freeways and the distance and the ice-cold alcohol in the desert and the speed and live it all again on the video at home in real time, not simply for the pleasure of remembering but because the fascination of senseless repetition is already present in the abstraction of the journey. The unfolding of the desert is infinitely close to the timelessness of the film ... (Baudrillard, 1986, trans. 1988: 1)

Gone is the game of tautologies and the radical denial of self. The often-quoted aphorism of the mirror has at least three possible significances. The mirror could refer to the mirror phase of psychological development in Lacan. This connotation would be an enormous reversal for Baudrillard, because he had always embraced Lacan as the destroyer of psychoanalysis and not as a theoretician of the subject. Lacan's semiotic psychoanalysis, desubstantialized psychoanalysis, that is, it no longer dealt with drives – Id, (super-)ego, Thanatos for example. It redefined psychoanalysis as the language of self. Human identity, consciousness, being, is compared to a language – metaphorically spoken, how the language is constructed, manipulated and structured determines the psyche. There is little left, here, of the special object of study of psychoanalysis – Lacan transformed psychology into semiotic poststructuralism. But the mirror, in Lacan, refers to the well-known phenomenon of young children who see their reflection in the mirror and go to look behind the mirror, searching for the person they have seen in the mirror. The individual, obviously, has yet to appropriate their own mirror image, as an icon of themselves. What psychology is all about for Lacan, is how the person takes on their text of the self from what is reflected – how they internalize the mirror. What version of what is reflected back to them in interaction do they make their own, how and why? Thus if objects in the mirror are closer than we think they are, they say more about who or what we are than we might imagine. What we see in the mirror is more a reflection of ourselves than we had imagined. Thus the book may pretend to be about America, but it may really be more about us.

This mirror effect, of Europe and America, the far and near, the Other and the self forms a second possible meaning to the aphorism. Is it really a book about America, and if so in what sense? Many of the concepts that Baudrillard had developed theoretically as intellectual provocations from 1970–1985, reappear in the (anti-)real of America. The loss of reality, primacy of the image and passivity of the masses, were all, suddenly, right there before him. Baudrillard, an *ësociologistí* who never did any empirical work, finally found an ideal, concrete referent for his prose in the USA. What is interesting for Baudrillard in the Americans, is that their lives, in vast stretches of empty (cultural if not also physical) landscape and in an orgy of goods and services, are indifferent or even autistic to the gaze of the Other. The Americans have no use for his text. America is portrayed as a universe of cultural simulation dominated by the logic of survival. America is self-confident, self-satisfied, self-sufficient; it is Utopia-achieved. But it is also empty, narcissistic and lonely. Its hero is the

> ... man running straight ahead on a beach, swathed in the sounds of his walkman, cocooned in the solitary sacrifice of his energy, indifferent even to catastrophes since he expects destruction to come only as the fruit of his own efforts, from exhausting the energy of a body that has in his own eyes become useless. ... This entire society, including its active, productive part – everyone – is running straight ahead, because they have lost the formula for stopping. (Baudrillard, 1986, trans. 1988: 38–9)

Americans are, supposedly, more active than active, more determined than determined – they live in a culture of simulacra. But consciousness of the simulacrum, as a theme to be thought about, is entirely European; in the mirror (of America) we see our (European) consciousness.

The mirror (simulacrum) is a screen: the screen of the film, the screen of the computer and the screen of multimedia (ICT). Baudrillard stresses that America is meant to be experienced as *film*. European consciousness is that of *theatre* – it produces defined, carefully arranged and focused portrayals of circumstance. Baudrillard shifts the terms of his temporization: Europe becomes bourgeois and pre-modern, America modern. Europe is hierarchical, class-bounded and ordered, i.e. theatre. America is movement, surface and furtive, i.e. film. The American mentality is focused on communication, people and their constructs. It is a film: the camera pans vast stretches of landscape without focusing on any detail. America is not a story about intimate, personal or immediate experiences, but offers a panorama of enormous emptiness within which there is tremendous possibility. But if one gets too close to the screen of the simulacrum, one sees nothing. The screen works only if the audience keeps its distance, that is, remains an uninvolved, pure spectator. America is to be appreciated as a simulacrum, as an image examined at a distance. If one tries to get close to its reality, the reality disappears and there is nothing left.

The dominant metaphor for America is the desert – the book is Baudrillard's voyage into the desert. The book celebrates his appreciation of nothingness. The confrontation with the no-thing banishes the hysterical hyperbole (too often present in books such as *Fatal Strategies*) from his prose. Baudrillard is much better able to cope with his own (exaggerated) categories in terms of Las Vegas, Death Valley and America than in terms of purely conceptual (European) landscapes. Ironically, there is in this writing an (unacknowledged) return to Sartre, whose *Being and Nothingness* was based on the existential relationship between the self and the void. *Amèrique* is a much more balanced and stable text than that which preceded it; but does that make what it has to offer better than *Fatal Strategies*?

Cool Memories followed quickly in the footsteps of *Amèrique*. It makes it clear that Baudrillard's textual strategy has indeed changed. *Cool Memories* is an assembly of aphorisms and textual miniatures. Its title (written in English in the original French edition) is, in McLuhan's terms, very significant. The cool in McLuhan cannot be absorbed or studied. It is momentary and passing, but forms the basis of social contact and interaction. The cool works less via cognitive clarity and intellectual strategy; it is more an invitation to share debate and to participate. Throughout the eighties, Baudrillard maintained a very pessimistic vision of communication. He saw the sixties as a period of celebration, discussion and interaction; and the eighties as an epoch of impersonal contact, sterile professionalism and consumerist ambiance. Genuine debate, friendship and involvement had been replaced by shopping centre conviviality. Material success, and the soft ambiance of consumerism, characterized the epoch. The cool text would appeal to the shared universe of discourse and debate that Baudrillard found wanting in the current period. Thus, is the book as positive as my reading of the title would make one expect? It begins:

OCTOBER 1980

The first day of the rest of your life.

The initial stunning impact of the deserts and California is gone, and yet to be fair, is there anything more beautiful in the world? It seems unlikely. I have to assume, then, that I have come across – once in my life – the most beautiful place I shall ever see. It is just as reasonable to suppose I have also met the woman whose beauty stunned me most and whose loss wounded me most. A second eventuality of the same order is unlikely – in any case the freshness, the artlessness of the event would be lost. It is just as probable that I have also written the one – or two – best books I shall ever write. They are done with. That is how things go. And it is most unlikely that a second burst of inspiration will alter this irreversible fact.

This is where the rest of life begins.

But the rest is what is given to you as something extra, and there is a charm and a particular freedom about letting just anything come along, with the grace – or ennui – of a later destiny.

It is always possible to tell yourself that it is not tomorrow but the day after which is the first day of the rest of your life, and that it is not this face or this landscape, but the one after. (Baudrillard, 1987a, trans. 1990: 1–4)

Attias' annotated on-line bibliography of Baudrillard, mis-represents this beginning as follows: "This and America are the two best books I shall ever write. They are done with. That is how things go" (Attias, 1996: 15).

The original text is softly melancholic: it asks the reader to begin (reading) *after* the end (of the author's greatest achievements). In it, the writer is vulnerable and approachable; in Attias' (1996) version of Turner's translation, the writer is matter of fact and arrogant. A key factor in *Cool Memories'* success is that Baudrillard has made his authorial persona much more human or approachable. The text is characterized by a certain sort of subjectivity or self. It is a very special self, one utterly unself-conscious, with no self-doubt, self-questioning or self-analysis. The inward looking, self-tortured, introspective intellectual is nowhere to be seen. It is a self that freely observes: (1) theory (ideas, philosophy), (2) women and (3) society (politics and culture). The self is present as style – it is the force that reduces everything into short observations and makes extremely effective use of language. The self is an aesthetic force, able to organize all the passages, quotes and observations into a very successful collage. But this self is not an object of consciousness. The self is performative – it does things; but it is not self-referential – it does not examine itself.

The goal of *Cool Memories* was to be participative, to be read, to be talked about, to be a *cause célèbre* – and it succeeded. The book was a best seller in France. But did it generate intellectual community, in the sense that people would discuss, debate and talk to one another? Without having researched the reception aesthetics of the book (how readers responded to the text) I can only answer speculatively. I do not think that *Cool Memories* is an effective vehicle for provoking any such participative response, because it is constructed in a way that makes it almost impossible to talk about it. Normally, discussion of a text centres on what the writer (via their authorial voice) believes, claims and/or demands from the reader. But Baudrillard's authorial voice is exhibitionistic – it puts intellectual, political and sexual attitudes on display, but it is not participative. The authorial persona makes no demands on the reader other than that the reader should look at what is on display. One is called upon to witness a whole series of paradoxes, but what one is supposed to do with this experience is never filled in. The writer seems indifferent to the readers' responses and the lack of demand, the feigned indifference, works seductively. As Baudrillard has insisted that the essence of seduction is to be found in the seducer's indifference (which Baudrillard identifies as *feminine*), the literary seducer makes the textually seduced into a voyeur. A voyeur, because text is appreciated visually – it is seen, read and absorbed by the mind's eye. *Cool Memories* seduces, but it does not activate. People who are threatened by seduction will rant and rave against Baudrillard. The anger is prompted by Baudrillard's denial of reality – he seduces instead of imposing a truth. Some readers, whose expectations are rooted in the tradition of modernist authority, are horrified when they discover that they are being seduced. They react violently against the text that has dared to appeal to their (intellectual and sexual) imaginations instead of imposing linear and rational truth. They do not accept that text should do what Baudrillard has made it do. They want to stuff the evil genie of Baudrillard's fantasy, doubt and wonder back into the bottle. They accept more easily Descartes' agenda of defeating disbelief and speculation than Baudrillard's of embracing seduction. The many vivid denunciations of *Cool Memories* (and *Amèrique*) simply prove how effective Baudrillard's textual strategy really has been.

But to what degree has Baudrillard merely proved that he understands the consumer society so effectively that he is capable of creating one of its ultimate objects, a best seller? To pursue this question further – how does Baudrillard really treat the three themes from which he has constructed *Cool Memories*? Philosophy, for Baudrillard, has become a form of commentary, not an activity of rigorous thought. He treats philosophy as a cultural artifact and not as a process of reflection – as a modernist icon and never as investigation. Philosophy, for Derrida or Lyotard for instance, is an effort of thought, analysis and reflection; but for Baudrillard it has become an object of (past) claims to truth.

> Philosophy has never been anything but a disavowal of the reality principle. Up to now, it has been the business of philosophers. Today this unreality has entered into things. This then is the end of philosophy and the beginning of something else in which reality merges with its ironic refraction. (Baudrillard, 1987a, trans. 1990: 169)

> Philosophy and psychology died at the same moment as the *other*, and the desire for the other died. Only the empty sign of their concept shines out now, in a sky devoted to the mental simulacrum and the pataphysical comfort of our great cities. (Baudrillard, 1987a, trans. 1990: 8)

> And yet what are the writings of Barthes, Lacan, Foucault (and even Althusser) but a philosophy of disappearance? The obliteration of the human, of ideology. The absent structure, the death of the subject, lack, aphanisis. They have died of these things and their deaths bear the characteristics of this inhuman

configuration. They bear the mark of a Great Withdrawal, of a defection, of a calculated failure of will, of a calculated weakening of desire. They all became shrouded in silence towards the end, in their various ways, and words fell away one by one. One can see no rosy future for their philosophies. They are even in danger, to the great despair of their disciples, of having no consequences at all. Because theirs are subtle modes of thought and ones therefore which subtilize their own traces and which have never, when all is said and done, produced constructive effects ... Those thinkers whose minds were rooted in a humanist configuration whether liberal or libertine (Lévi-Strauss, Lefebvre, Aron – and Sartre too) survive better. Whether or not they are still alive, they have not *ëdisappearedí* in the same way; they have not been infected with the virus; their works perpetuate them and they bear the glory of those works without weakening ... (Baudrillard, 1987a, trans. 1990: 160–1)

These comments treat philosophy as some sort of achieved artifact – as belonging to the past. In them, Baudrillard plays the moralist; but he certainly does not invite the reader to think through any difficult issues. Baudrillard's reflections on society and politics follow a parallel path:

> We are becoming like cats, slyly parasitic, enjoying an indifferent domesticity. Nice and snug in 'the social', our historic passions have withdrawn into the glow of an artificial coziness, and our half-closed eyes now seek little other than the peaceful parade of television pictures. (Baudrillard, 1987a, trans. 1990: 24)

> It feels so good to disappear among the masses! Even better than getting high on transcendence (God) is to wallow in the nausea of immanence. The Masses. A dream opportunity for the individual to disappear and yet still be able to lament his alienation and his loss of subjectivity. Isn't this just what the masses were invented for? Because we did invent them, just as we invented the cold, blue light of television, so that, gazing deep into the screen, we could await the dazzling sign of a definitive event. (Baudrillard, 1987a, trans. 1990: 57)

> Executives are like joggers. If you stop a jogger he goes on running on the spot. If you drag an executive away from his business, he goes on running on the spot, pawing the ground, talking business. He never stops hurtling onwards, making decisions and executing them. (Baudrillard, 1987a, trans. 1990: 213)

Again, no shared project of reflection. In a psychoanalytic or (neo-)Marxist text, one of deconstruction (*différance*) or of the *différend*, the writer will ask the reader to think with them in order to achieve some sort of (joint) understanding. There is no attempt to open up any such process in Baudrillard – how he arrives at his conclusions is mystified. And, finally, his reflections on women:

> If you say 'I love you' then you have already fallen in love with language, which is already a form of breakup and infidelity. (Baudrillard, 1987a, trans. 1990: 153)

> No doubt it was better that this purely fornicatory and imaginary relationship, with her sexual voracity and her ankle bracelets, which we carried on all over the place – in the Badlands, in the Chelsea Hotel, in motels, in the sand, between the sheets – and which always meant immediate lovemaking in the minutes that followed, never satisfied, but just as sweet and flexible and blonde, her eyes raised like a slave-girl's and her hand outstretched towards her sex, she free and

servile, feminine and muscled, laughing and admiring, animal blood and metallic eyes – it was natural that this relationship should finish with a pathetic fellatio on a motel balcony, in the morning mist and a hypothetical child which no doubt was not mine and which I shall never see. I have even forgotten her name, but I have not forgotten the straw scent of her sex, nor the twenty-dollar bet on salt or snow, nor the sudden menstrual nosebleed I had one morning when I saw her arriving at my place in all her California splendor. (Baudrillard, 1987a, trans. 1990: 205–6)

Women are like historical events: they happen once in our lives as events and they are then entitled to a second existence as farce. The event of seduction, the farce of psychology. The event of passion, the farce of the work of mourning. Fortunately, it is the same the other way around. You very probably have the good fortune to enjoy a second existence in the minds of the women you have known, as melancholy farce. (Baudrillard, 1987a, trans. 1990: 7)

Throughout, women are depersonalized; they have no name or being for themselves – they represent the force of *seduction*. There is only one subject in the text of *Cool Memories* – that of the authorial *I*. Philosophy, society/politics and women (sex) all are epiphenomena in the service of one absolute: the aesthetic force of writing. The book propagates text (creation) as total narcissism. The ultimate consumer object – the object of simulation as well as simulacrum, for which one can live, is the book.

Organizational pataphysics

Baudrillard is the prototype of the postmodernist who attracts the ire of traditional Modernist (realistic) academics. His glorification of text, wherein he prioritizes the creativity of writing above concern for reality (verisimilitude), terrifies the (post-)positivists. The aggression that his strategy evokes, makes one suspect that he may be right in calling it *fatal* – perhaps it is fatal for the self-assuredness of (some) traditional researchers. He attacks the pretension that one could write for science, or to discover the real, or out of humanist commitment. Baudrillard luxuriates in the supposition that the only reason anyone writes is to save themselves from their own death, despair and confusion. Baudrillard's assertion – that in a melancholic society, where there are no causes to share, no debate to be engaged in and no social sphere to enthrall one, situationalist aesthetic activity is the only escape from depression or worse – is not easily dismissed.

Anyone studying the consumer society, and it is almost impossible not to do so in some form as it is so very omnipresent, can profit from studying Baudrillard. But his attempt to assert the primacy of the object makes his thought very special. Most critical reflection on the consumer society follows some sort of alienation theory and tries to reassert the primacy of the phenomenal subject. In contemporary organizational studies, so-called *process thinking* is characterized by this strategy. Most thought which claims to be postmodern in organizational studies, broadly following Lyotard or Foucault, stresses that the loss of the real objective or grand narrative leads to limited or local truths. The *process* of organizing (organizing as subject) is proposed as an alternative focus to organizational *structure* (organization as object) for research. But Baudrillard proposes the opposite strategy. He accepts, in essence, postmodern assumptions, but draws exactly opposite conclusions. If capitalist modernism has liquidated itself in a society of simulation (service industries, post-industrialism, a knowledge-based economy) then the sole operative pulsion (energy, dynamism) left has to be based on out-simulating simulation. This is to be achieved by positing the primacy of the object – that is, the organization. Organization studies need to stop trying, *de facto*, to save the modernist self or subject from extinction. For Baudrillard there are two possibilities: (1) follow the logic of the *more organized than the organized* into the absurdity of ecstatic control and into the insane overdetermination of all actions, or (2) follow the strategy of the author-alone, who saves his own subjectivity by hiding it behind his situationalist text. By going further in the direction of objectification than objectification would go one can, supposedly, tap its energy in order to create an absurd text that deconstructs, tears apart and renders totally paradoxical, the dominant logic.

But what is the value of such an opposition? It may be unsettling, or an attention attractor, but so what? Of course, one can argue that no purpose, or sense of the purposive, is possible in a postmodern consumer society. But where does that leave us? Baudrillard makes it clear in his interviews that he is not really able to function in any organization or regime of work (not even the university) – his choice for hyper-individualism is consistent with his own thought, but not very generalizable. As the total outsider, his situationalist critique may well gain in power, but an intellectual strategy which can only *see* the postmodern consumer society but cannot live or survive within it, is a very rarefied sort of thing. Thus Baudrillard can shock, distress, disconcert, appall and anger us. He can also enthrall, fascinate and seduce us. But he has abandoned his very idiosyncratic form of sociology and the study of the consumer society to become a purely aestheticized voice radically turned inwards towards a very personal strategy of survival. His ego documents form an outstanding ethnography of the postmodern self, but are not participative – his (literary) strategy is socially impenetrable. And since organization studies are inherently about something social, Baudrillard has, in effect, become their antithesis.

Notes

1 Baudrillard insists on *not* footnoting sources unless absolutely necessary. He stresses, thereby, the primacy of his text and the author's prerogatives, at the cost to intertextuality. I have followed his example in this chapter. See also the note at the beginning of the bibliography.

2 I followed this strategy in my chapter 'Postmodernism Goes Practical' (1996) wherein I centred my Baudrillard interpretation in *Simulacres et Simulation* and *Les Strategies fatales*, i.e. in his later theoretical work.

3 In my article 'Researching Organization by Implosion and Fatality' (1995) I develop this possibility further.

Bibliographical note

Readers who are interested in Baudrillard's more anthropological and anti-production critique of the consumer society are advised to refer to Baudrillard (1976) (1970) and (1968), in that order. Readers who want to pursue the later formulation, stressing simulation and simulacra/fatal strategies, are referred to (1981) and (1983). This is not a complete bibliography, just those works which informed this paper.

References

Attias, B. (1996) 'Welcome to the world of Jean Baudrillard' *S(t)imulacrum*(b) **http://www.csun.edu/~hfspc002/baud/** (accessed 23 July, 2000).

Baudrillard, J. (1962) *'Uwe Johnson'*, *'Les Romans d'Italo Calvino'* and *'La Proie des flammes'*, *Les Temps Modernes*, Vol. 3 (a, b and c): pp. 1094–107, 1728–34 and 1928–37.

Baudrillard, J. (1968) *Le Système des objects*. Paris: Denoel. [Trans. J. Benedict (1996) as *The System of Objects*. London: Verso].

Baudrillard, J. (1970) *La Société de consummation*. Paris: Gallimard. [Trans. C. Turner (1997) as *The Consumer Society*. London: Sage].

Baudrillard, J. (1972) *Pour une critique de l'économie de signe*. Paris: Gallimard. [Trans. C.D. Levin (1981) as *For a Critique of the Political Economy of the Sign*. St Louis: Telos].

Baudrillard, J. (1973) *Le Miroir de la production*. Tournail: Casterman. [Trans. M. Poster (1975) as *The Mirror of Production*. St Louis: Telos].

Baudrillard, J. (1976) *L'Échange symbolique et la mort*. Paris: Gallimard. [Trans. I. Grant (1993) as *Symbolic Exchange and Death*. London: Sage].

Baudrillard, J. (1977) *Oublier Foucault*. Paris: Galilée. [Trans. S. Lotringer (1987) as *Forget Foucault*. New York: Semiotext(e). This edition also includes an interview 'Forget Baudrillard'].

Baudrillard, J. (1978a) *Á l'ombre des majorités silencieuses ou de la fin du social*. Fontenay-sous-bois: Utopie. [Trans. P. Foss, J. Johnston and P. Patton (1983) as *In the Shadow of the Silent Majorities*. St Louis: Telos].

Baudrillard, J. (1978b) *Le P.C. ou les paradis artificiels du politique*. Fontenay-sous-bois: Utopie.

Baudrillard, J. (1979) *De la Séduction*. Paris: Denoel-Gonthier. [Trans. S.Glaser (1994) as *Seduction*. New York: St Martin's Press].

Baudrillard, J. (1981) *Simulacres et Simulation*. Paris: Galilée. [Trans. S.Glaser (1994) as *Simulacra and Simulation*. Michigan: University of Michigan Press].

Baudrillard, J. (1983) *Les Strategies fatales*. Paris: Grasset. [Trans. (1990) as Fatal Strategies. New York: Semiotext(e)].

Baudrillard, J. (1986) *Amérique*. Paris: Grasset. [Trans. C. Turner (1988) as *America*. London: Verso].

Baudrillard, J. (1987a) *Cool Memories*. Paris: Galilée. [Trans. C. Turner (1990) as *Cool Memories*. London: Verso].

Baudrillard, J. (1987b) *L'autre par lui-même*. Paris: Galilée. [Trans. S. Lotringer (1988) as *The Ecstasy of Communication*. New York: Semiotext(e)].

Baudrillard, J. (1990a) *Cool Memories II*. Paris: Galilée. [Trans. C. Turner (1995) as *Cool Memories II*. Cambridge: Polity Press].

Baudrillard, J. (1990b) *La Transparence du Mal*. Paris: Galilée. [Trans. J. Benedict (1993) as *The Transparency of Evil*. London: Verso].

Baudrillard, J. (1990c) *Revenge of the Crystal*, ed. and trans. P. Foss and J. Pefanis. London: Pluto Press.

Baudrillard, J. (1991) *La guerre du Golfe n'a pas eu lieu*. Paris: Galilée. [Trans. P. Patton (1995) as *The Gulf War did not Take Place*. Sydney: Power Publications].

Baudrillard, J. (1992*) L'illusion de la fin*. Paris: Galilée. [Trans. C. Turner (1994) as *The Illusion of the End*. Cambridge: Polity Press.

Baudrillard, J. (1995) *Le crime parfait*. Paris: Galilée. [Trans. C. Turner (1996) as *The Perfect Crime*. London: Verso].

Baudrillard, J. (1997a) *Écran total*. Paris: Galilée.

Baudrillard, J. (1997b) *Le paroxyste indifferent: Entreties avec Philippe Petit*. Paris: Grasset. [Trans. C. Turner (1998) as *Paroxysm: Interviews with Philippe Petit*. London: Verso].

Bayard, C. and Knight, G. (1995) 'Vivisection the 90s: an interview with Jean Baudrillard' *CTHEORY* (article 24, 3 May). **www.ctheory.com**. (accessed 23 July, 2000).

Burrell, G. (1997) *Pandemonium: Towards a Retro Organization Theory*. London: Sage.

Castells, M. (1996) *The Rise of the Network Society*. Oxford: Blackwell.

Gane, M. (1991) *Baudrillard's Bestiary*. London: Routledge.

Gane, M. (1993) *Baudrillard Live, Selected Interviews*. London: Routledge.

Kellner, D. (1989) *Jean Baudrillard from Marxism to Postmodernism and Beyond*. London: Polity Press.

Kellner, D. (1994) *Baudrillard: A Critical Reader*. London: Routledge.

Letiche, H. (1995) 'Researching organization by implosion and fatality', *Studies in Cultures Organizations & Societies*, 1 (1): 107–26.

Letiche, H. (1996) 'Postmodernism goes practical', in S. Linstead, R. Grafton Small and P. Jeffcutt (eds), *Understanding Management*. London: Sage. pp. 193–211.

Majastre, J.-O. and Peuchlestrade, G. (eds) (1996) *Sans oublier Baudrillard*. Bruxelles: La lettre volée.

Poster, M. (1988) *Jean Baudrillard: Selected Writings*. London: Polity Press.

Rattansi, A. (1995) 'The life and times of post-modernity', *Sociology*, 29 (2): 339–50.

Sartre, J.-P. (1977) *Being and Nothingness*. London: Methuen University Paperbacks.

Sinaiko, H. (1965) *Love Knowledge and Discourse in Plato* Chicago: University of Chicago Press.

Taylor, A. (1995) *Baudrillard on the Web*. **http://www.uta.edu/english/apt/collab/baudweb.html** (accessed 23 July, 2000).

Wernick, A. (c1994) 'Baudrillard's remainder', *CTHEORY* (review number 30, undated) **www.ctheory.com** (accessed 23 July, 2000).

8
Gianni Vattimo, Umberto Eco and Franco Rella

Assunta Viteritti

First premise: a trace to introduce the discourse

White Noise[1] (1985) tells, in an entertaining and surrealistic style, the story of Jack Gladney, Dean of the Department of Hitlerian Studies at the College-on-the-Hill (somewhere in North America). Jack has been successfully running the department since March 1968. At the beginning of the novel Jack introduces his colleagues:

> Department heads wear academic robes at the College-on-the-Hill. Not grand, sweeping, full-length affairs but sleeveless tunics puckered at the shoulders. I like the idea ... The robe is black, of course, and goes with almost anything ... There is no Hitler building as such. We are quartered in Centenary Hall, a dark brick structure we share with the popular culture department, known officially as American Environments. A curious group. ... The department head is Alfonse (Fast Food) Stompanato, a broad-chested, glowering man whose collection of pre-war soda pop bottles is on permanent display in an alcove. All the teachers are male, wear rumpled clothes, need haircuts, cough into their armpits.

A little later on in the text, Murray, one of Jack's colleagues, congratulates him on his singular success in promoting the Department.

> You've established a wonderful thing here with Hitler. You created it, you nurtured it, you made it your own. Nobody on the faculty of any college or university in this part of the country can so much as utter the word Hitler without a nod in your direction, literally or metaphorically. This is the center, the unquestioned source. He is now *your* Hitler. It must be deeply satisfying for you. The college is internationally known as a result of Hitler studies. It has an identity, a sense of achievement. You've evolved an entire system around this figure, a structure with countless substructures and interrelated fields of study, a history within history. I marvel at the effort. It was masterful, shrewd and stunningly pre-emptive. It's what I want to do with Elvis.

Further still, Jack recounts his decision to change his name and looks, instigated by the Chancellor's criticism of their suitability as befitting his particular position.

> ... the Chancellor had advised me, back in 1968, to do something about my name and appearance if I wanted to be taken seriously as a Hitler innovator. Jack Gladney would not do, he said, and finally agreed that I should invent an extra initial and call myself J.A.K. Gladney, a tag I wore like a borrowed suit. The Chancellor warned against what he called a tendency to make a feeble presentation of self. He strongly suggested I gain weight. He wanted me to 'grow out' into Hitler. He himself was tall, paunchy, ruddy, jowly, big-footed and dull. A formidable combination. If I could become more ugly, he seemed to be suggesting, it would help my career enormously. So Hitler gave me something to grow into and develop toward, tentative as I have sometimes been in the effort. ... I am the false character that follows the name around.

A shadow hangs over Jack's success however: Jack does not understand German, a problem for the three-day international conference for Hitlerologists planned for the coming Spring, with various workshops and group activities.

> My struggle with the German tongue began in mid-October and lasted nearly the full academic year. As the most prominent figure in Hitler studies in North America, I had long tried to conceal the fact that I did not know German. I could not speak or read it, could not understand the spoken word or put the simplest sentence on paper. The least of my Hitler colleagues knew some German; others were either fluent in the language or reasonably conversant. No one could major in Hitler studies at the College-on-the-Hill without a minimum of one year of German. I was living, in short, on the edge of a landscape of vast shame .... Because I'd achieved high professional standing, because my lectures were well attended and my articles printed in the major journals, because I wore an academic gown and dark glasses day and night whenever I was on campus, because I carried two hundred and thirty pounds on a six-foot three-inch frame and had big hands and feet, I knew my German lessons would have to be secret.

The story of Jack and his department is fictitious, but has verisimilitude, as we shall see.[2]

Second premise: orientation

Jack finds himself in an organizational world that is *perceived and interpreted*, a world which is continuously re-invented, re-constructed and re-interpreted, especially on the aesthetic and relational planes. The characters in *White Noise* occupy an organizational space, one *ironic* and *conversational* (Rorty, 1979), seemingly lacking a clearly defined and aware orientation. They continuously interact within a *texture* (Cooper and Fox, 1990; Gherardi and Strati, 1990) of meanings that is ambiguous and implicit. Jack's world is an organizational one, in which the sedimented traits of traditional bureaucracy – structures, rituals of belonging, rules, conventions, procedures, norms and competencies – transform themselves into *simulacra* (Baudrillard, 1983), semblance and pretence. Jack's world is plural and polysemic, a world in which fragments of meanings and practices – which remain most of the time unrecognized – are continuously at stake. It is a surrealistic scenario, inhabited by improbable characters, and yet it remains plausible: an organizational world, animated and inspired by grand *rational* discourses, but continuously interspersed with *fluxes* of interpretation, discourse and behaviour, that infringe on and divert them. Organizations risk continuous *drift*, such that counteractive planning strategies are unable to hold them in check. The subjects are immersed in a relational field, where interpretations and languages face each other. The latter are, however, able to produce – *albeit weakly* (Vattimo and Rovatti, 1983) – *paths of sense*, which are embedded in a flux that occurs between destructuration and stabilization, both individual and collective.

Organizations are nothing more than people's actions and are constructed with reference to the meanings which are produced within this flux. They are communicative *fields* whose very weak borders are continuously shifting, and within which traces of an always unfinished and unresolved rationalization can be found. Organizations are relational fields not only informed by instrumental idealizations – which tend to encompass, through the managerial *rhetorics* (Höpfl, 1995; Linstead, 1995) of rationalization, both individual and collective action – but also by forms of resistance and reaction. The mobile fields of organizations are fed by the images of the real and personal life. They are a space in which the everyday experience engenders continuous processes of redefinition. In organizations as relational fields, rationality 'is a product of collective action' (Hassard, 1994) rather than externally dictated. The paradigm of modernization, oriented as it is towards a strong *ontology of being*, has to cope with a weak *ontology of becoming* (Chia, 1995) which plunges organizational life into a tension over a never-resolved becoming. Organizational life is, then, embedded in a *hermeneutical ontology*, where decisive or enlightening interpretations (Vattimo, 1988) external to the interpretative process itself, are not available. There are, rather, tensions between different hermeneutics which flow within the organizational stream. Organizations are spaces where continuous displacement and cross-reference of meaning is produced, encompassing all organizational actors (Eco, 1990).

But let's leave Jack. He will continue his story elsewhere whilst we will attempt, from hereon in, to tell our own.

Third premise: the proposal

The remainder of this chapter consists of two parts: firstly, a tracing of the postmodern found in the philosophical, linguistic and literary work of three Italian authors – Vattimo, Eco and Rella – with their implications for the organization studies field; and secondly, some reflections proposing a way of understanding the place of the postmodern in organization studies.

In the first section, I offer a reflective journey with the three authors: Gianni Vattimo, Umberto Eco and Franco Rella. These Italian interpreters make reference, though in very different ways, to the postmodern debate. Vattimo, the official representative of the philosophical strand of Italian postmodern thought, grounds his work in Heidegger's hermeneutical philosophy and in Nietzsche's nihilism. He argues for the possibility of thinking in terms of a *weak* rationality, where any ontological and unifying claim is abandoned in favour of a *viable* reason which accepts its immersion, its *being-thrown in the world*. Reason, then, renounces the ambition of exhaustive explanation and knowledge, becoming an immanent component of human experience. However, such weak thinking entails neither giving up, nor abrogating, meaningfulness for human agency. It is rather an attempt to re-instigate a possibility for a new, weak beginning.

Eco travels within the transformation of contemporary linguistics in its post-structuralist phase, where the traditional, privileged domains of linguistic enquiry have undergone a dramatic change. Eco enters the transformation of semiology, as it moves away from the logic of correspondence, conveyed by the idea of the dictionary, to embrace the images of the encyclopaedia and the labyrinth, where the direction and construction of discourse are provided through subjects' interaction. Language then resembles, more and more, what Deleuze and Guattari define as a rhizome, a *locus* for production of interpretation, which, according to Eco, is not unrestricted (as perhaps it is in Derrida's and Culler's versions of deconstruction), but can be constrained by the sense attributed to it, differently, by agents.

Rella's theoretical work, developed within the domain of literary criticism, *traverses* modernity: a modernity living on its frontier. Rella investigates those *figures* capable of evoking, thinking and living the transformation of modernity. In his view many declensions of modernity are possible and the postmodern option is the search for possibilities, an exploration for still other paths within the same modernity. Rella, a scholar of Benjamin, Balzac, Novalis, Schlegel and others, looks for the routes that lead to revivifying some of the figures of the modern – whose vigour is far from exhausted – offering possible guidance for contemporary subjects.

In the final section, an interpretation of the postmodern in organizations is proffered, starting from the insights generated by the three Italian authors. Distancing oneself from the ontological perspective firmly grounded in rationality – understood as a unifying and rationalizing project – allows room for searching for *weak and vital*, but not irrational, conceptions of organization. These may be capable of highlighting previously neglected features of organizational life: the signs; the plurality of interpretations and ways of knowing; the presence of disseminated practices that can be re-assigned to subjectivities who resist the strong idea of rationalization; the polysemy and tension generated by the discourses and practices of managers and managed, who continuously interrelate over the meanings produced. Such constant flows within organizations are differently interpreted by subjects who are able to attribute meanings, to produce sense within flux, to share convictions and also, to transform interpretations and conceptions during action. In this new view of organization, the contribution of the three Italian authors – Eco, Rella and Vattimo – is significant.

Eventually, a synthesis is outlined, incorporating some insights stemming from the wider debate on the postmodern in organizations, combined with the insights of the Italian debate, to produce the approach which is here suggested.

Directions in the Italian debate: Vattimo, Eco and Rella

Postmodern 'weakness': Gianni Vattimo

Gianni Vattimo was born in Turin in 1936. He was a student of Pareyson, Gadamer and Loewith. He taught Aesthetics at the University of Turin where he is now teaching Theoretical Philosophy. He has taught in many American universities, and has been the editor of both Italian and international journals of philosophy. He is acknowledged as one the major interpreters of contemporary hermeneutics and as an international figure in postmodern philosophy. The majority of his work has been devoted to the study of Heidegger and Nietzsche, who still inform his theoretical endeavour.

In 1983 he edited *Il pensiero debole*, a collection of essays by Italian scholars from various disciplines – art, philosophy, linguistics and sociology. It is this book that inaugurated Vattimo's original thinking on the postmodern.[3] Here, he argues *il pensiero debole* (weak thinking) as a metaphor, but also, in a certain way, a paradox. It is neither about defeat, nor giving up; but rather concerns an attitude, based on lightening-up the idea of the modern and of rationality (Vattimo and Rovatti, 1983: 10). His starting point is the assumption that contemporary philosophical debate displays a convergence: the grounding for a unique, ultimate and conclusive knowledge no longer exists. The question addressed is whether, after the crisis of foundational principles, any claim to truth has to be given up, or whether there might not yet be an appeal to less ambitious reasons.

He then follows two paths in constructing his conception of the postmodern. The first is concerned with disempowering the idea of reason; the second with critiquing the idea of modernity as the progressive enlightenment of human history (Vattimo, 1988). In the first instance, his aim is to disempower the Cartesian grounding of rational thinking, in order to develop a hermeneutical conception of reason, based on his reading of Heidegger and Nietzsche. Vattimo raises the question of whether rationality has to be abandoned or, rather, to accept its own disempowerment and thereby lose ground; no longer fearing withdrawal to the shadows, but at the same time resisting the process of becoming paralysed due to the loss of a bright, unique and Cartesian reference point (Vattimo, 1988).

What is thereby transcended is predominantly strong thinking, with its deductive grounding, while any discourse can only have a hermeneutical grounding. The reference here is to Heidegger and his notion of *Being-thrown-in-time*, where time is not the linear, progressive time of the powerful, but rather, is dialectical and cyclical; a time of difference, of unveiling, where Vattimo *relocates* Nietzsche's cry 'God is dead'. Being is not; it is thrown in a world: it shapes our experience of this world within horizons which are constructed by a series of echoes and resonances – of languages and messages. Such being is immersed in time, it has been weakened and has undergone processes of overcoming, distortion (the reference here is to Heidegger's notion of *Verwindung*) and transience.

Vattimo's Heidegger and Nietzsche are closer to the experience of contemporaneity. Such experience means a weakening of metaphysical Being (Vattimo, 1988) and thus twilight for the hegemonic ideas of consciousness and the Christian-bourgeois Subject, in favour of a notion of the witness who is immersed in history (Vattimo, 1993). Does not the weakness of thinking, however, imply the disempowering of thinking itself, its ability to make plans? Indubitably, planning has such a weakness, but this does not betoken a complete dismissal of the endeavour. Rather, Vattimo rethinks planning: he deconstructs it via a critique of modernity. The time for modernity as illumination and progress is over as we live the experience of the end of history, of immanence. Restating Gehlen's thought, Vattimo argues that the continuous renewal of consumption and technology is no longer the vital drive behind the system, as it was for the birth of modern societies, when the emphasis was on the futuristic tension: progress is, rather, routinized and secularized (Vattimo, 1988). The dissolution of history as a narrative-to-be-accomplished, is, according to Vattimo, the distinguishing feature of contemporary history, compared to the modern (ibid.). The postmodern arises as the extremity of the secularization process: it is its limit. Human experience appears to be de-centred, participant in multiple centres, which are mediated by communication and the interpretations that subjects produce. Weak thinking is a hermeneutic totality, which is immersed in temporality. This process is based on Heidegger's thought, which for Vattimo approaches the forms of Nietzsche's accomplished nihilism, where we view the post-historical and post-modern individual who has learnt how to live with herself and her own groundlessness, following the demise of grand unifying systems.

However, groundlessness is not, for Vattimo, the decline of human. Rather, it is only from such groundlessness that an individual, able to accept their own unstable, plural condition – where the main task is interpretive actions *immersed* in events – can be generated. Vattimo elucidates the main points of postmodern thinking, which result in the overcoming of the metaphysical idea of existence:

- a thinking of *fruition*, which for subjects immersed in time, entails a continuous *remembering*, a re-living, not only of the present time, but also of forms of the past that need to be brought back into the present and thereby re-utilized for the development of a postmodern ethics;
- a *synthesizing* thinking (*pensiero della contaminazione*), of epistemic models in which the contemporary subject is immersed;
- a thinking of *Ge-stell*,[4] able to enter a relationship with the technical, the latter permeating the world and imposing itself on it.

The only possibility for subjectivity here is to accept immersion in the component parts of a modernity which has given up any reference to metaphysics. Nonetheless, the subject enters a non-passive relation to contemporaneity. This is not the Cartesian subject able to think being, but a *weak* subject who can dynamically avail themselves of a world they do not control. They can synthesize all the signs that the world shows them, without recoiling from the technically imposed world, which is plunged into and experienced. Such experience in any case, is active and historical, as the subject is one able to enter a dynamic relationship with existence.

Between the end of the 1980s and the beginning of the 1990s, Vattimo developed his thinking on the postmodern, although with different emphases. In his recent work, a greater engagement with the ethical and political is apparent (cf. Vattimo, 1992). In a climate in which recourse to the category of postmodernity is dominant, to the point of becoming mere fashion, the author asks himself whether it is still worthwhile adopting the term, or whether it should be dismissed. Vattimo argues the former, that the term postmodern still makes sense, representing a chance, albeit a weak one, for promoting the contemporary individual; one immersed in a world in which the concepts of reality and unity have been eroded.

Media domination fulfils Nietzsche's prophecy of a world-become-fable, whereby media- and scientific-inspired images constitute the objective reality (Vattimo, 1992). The latter now depicts the encroachment and synthesizing of various images, interpretations and reconstructions. It is a reality which engenders a sense of *disorientation* and a multiplication of local rationalities (ibid.). Out of confusion, an emancipatory effect can nevertheless be generated. The world of *generalized communication* and of plural cultures permits the encounter with other worlds and forms of life, thereby opening opportunities for the freedom of the individual (ibid.). The individual is able to move in this media-inspired world that they themselves have helped to produce, finding their own way and sense – thanks to weak thinking – amongst the proliferation of interpretations and meanings (Vattimo, 1990).

Vattimo's development of weak thinking in his more recent work approaches a notion of hermeneutical rationality 'as the metatheory of the play of interpretations' (Vattimo, 1997: 9). Though moving within a Heideggerian/ Gadamerian axis, Vattimo, as he himself argues, wants to promote the idea of weak rationality, where hermeneutics is neither driven by being (as in Heidegger), nor merely linguistic (as in Gadamer). This rationality, furthermore, resembles neither the argumentative construction of Habermas's communicative reason – which according to Vattimo retains metaphysical elements – nor Rorty's *conversational* model. Vattimo's rationality is interpretive, one which enters into relation with modernity as it has become. It is consequential, a rationality which takes into account historical becoming, a history that the subject, through the three above-mentioned elements – fruition, synthesizing and *Ge-stell* – remembers and recreates as their own experience. In his recent work, Vattimo ponders the problem of how a hermeneutic rationality, which is weak if compared with the idea of a grounding reason, might still be capable of engendering sense.

In *Beyond Interpretation: The Meaning of Hermeneutics for Philosophy*, Vattimo explores the possibility of reconstructing rationality, starting from a hermeneutic viewpoint. He examines the charge, levied by proponents of historical rationalism and neopositivist scientism, of hermeneutics as a manifestation of irrationalism. He also takes due note of the hermeneutical foundation of Heidegger's thought, which is strongly opposed to a rationalistic ontology, that has lost its hegemonic position. Vattimo's problem is how to counter the charge of irrationalism levelled against hermeneutics, itself not without some justification. It must be overcome through elaborating a specific notion of a non-metaphysical rationality. How is a hermeneutical rationality possible? In order to attempt to construct a new kind of rationality, Vattimo critically utilizes those theoretical positions which treat hermeneutics as being a weak form of rationality. In particular, he takes on board Rorty's distinction between hermeneutics and epistemology, where philosophy as the construction of publicly recognizable arguments would be part of epistemology, in contrast to hermeneutics which would only refer to the encounter between systems of metaphors, the understanding of which cannot be demonstrated or proceduralized and therefore evades rational criteria. Vattimo then reflexively examines whether Rorty's distinction itself moves within the field of epistemology or hermeneutics: is it a publicly recognizable argument or is it hermeneutics – which to Rorty's mind equates to poetics?

Starting from Rorty's argument, Vattimo wants to dissociate his position from the limitations he perceives in hermeneutical thinking as displayed by Rorty, Derrida and Gadamer. Rorty's aesthetic hermeneutics – the encounter of metaphors, poetic intuition – is too weak a hermeneutic, unable to put forward publicly acknowledgeable arguments, as epistemology can. Secondly, he dissociates himself from Derrida's hermeneutic perspective, which is deconstructivist. Here, 'to write' takes the place of language, turning the deconstructionist experience, as Vattimo perceives it, rather into an artistic performance than a path of interpretative methodology. The fruitfulness of Derrida's work resides in imitation – as in an artist's work – and discourages development. Derrida's unveiling of writing – the searching for margins, borders and frames – for Vattimo instantiates Derrida's aesthetic irrationalism, his looking for a new form of symbolic essentiality, a new metaphysical background. The aesthetic and irrational drive that Vattimo finds in Derrida is a problem for hermeneutics – which is not amenable to argumentation, in Rorty's sense. Such deconstructionist discourse betrays its own metaphysical background which re-emerges out of the work of deconstruction on writing. Gadamer's hermeneutics takes language as the unique form of being with which it is possible to enter into relation. As such, according to Vattimo, it does not supply a form of validation for theory. What is thus referred to as the irrationalism of hermeneutics is the aestheticism that one finds in authors such as Rorty, Derrida and Gadamer. At this point Vattimo proffers his alternative, rationally grounded, hermeneutics.

> A clarification of this kind calls for hermeneutics to cease thinking of itself, more or less consciously or explicitly, as a theory founded on phenomenological analysis that is 'adequate' to experience. Hermeneutics is itself 'only interpretation'. Its own claims to validity are not founded on a presumption of access to the things themselves; to be consistent with the Heideggerian critique

of the idea of truth as correspondence from which it professes to draw its inspiration, it can only conceive of itself as the response to a message, or as the interpretative articulation of its own belonging to a tradition (*tra-dizione*), *Über-lieferung*. This tradition is not simply a succession of 'conceptual schemes' – for thought in this way, it would leave an *ontos* outside itself, a thing in itself thought in metaphysical terms ... The destiny of Being, naturally, is given only in an interpretation, and does not have objectivistic–deterministic cogency ... the rationality we have reached consists in the fact that, essentially involved in a process (into which we are always-already 'thrown') we always-already know, at least to a certain extent, where we are going and how we must go there. But to orient ourselves, we need to reconstruct and interpret the process in as complete and persuasive a manner as possible. It would be an error to believe that we can jump outside the process, somehow grasping the *arche*, the principle, the essence or the ultimate structure. Rationality is simply the guiding thread that can be comprehended by listening attentively to the messages of the *Schickung*. (Vattimo, 1997: 108–9)

This hermeneutics allows us the possibility of following the thread of rationality within human experience, which is its only location. Vattimo is looking for a stronger hermeneutics, one based on our immersion in experience. We live the accomplishment and overcoming of metaphysical thinking, in the disenchanted and nihilistic world of proliferating technique (*Ge-stell*). We are thrown into this hermeneutical totality, whilst attempting to grasp the meaning of its transformation:

> Hermeneutics is not a theory that opposes an authenticity of existence founded on the privilege of the human sciences to the alienation of the rationalized society; it is rather a theory that tries to grasp the meaning of the transformation (of the idea) of Being that has been produced as a consequence of the techno-scientific rationalization of our world. It is not hard to see that this way of developing the hermeneutic discourse is different to that which, with aesthetical implications, characterizes writers such as Rorty and Derrida. It may perhaps be closer to Foucault and to what he once called the 'ontology of the actuality'. (Vattimo, 1997: 110)

An argumentative kind of hermeneutics, for Vattimo, thus becomes possible. This enters into relation with the rationalization of technique and with modern scientism, but not as polemical refusal (as deconstructionist aestheticism does, when it opposes the outcome of the end of metaphysics with the search for the truer and more authentic). Hermeneutics does not attempt to confute modernity, through discourses and metaphors opposing an authenticity behind-the-things, which thereby engenders the risk of a new metaphysics. Hermeneutics is rather a consequence of modernity, a way-of-being within contemporaneity, which takes the past into account. An interpretive distance, based on a process of historical re-construction, is produced, one that is rationally grounded. This process defines us and permits the relating of ourselves with the world as the outcome of the end of metaphysics, or, in Heidegger's words, the world of *scientific objectification*. Irrational escape, which can only create a new kind of metaphysics, is impossible. What then is possible, is an entering into relation with the *Ge-stell*. It is only the establishment of this relation with the rationalization of the contemporary world that is capable of holding-in-check both the self-nullifying multiplication of signs and the passive acceptance of the dictates of rationalized technique.

Vattimo's world is *dis*-enchanted; one where hermeneutical action provides the only defence that is rationally, albeit non-positivistically, grounded. The hermeneutical subject accepts nihilism as their only possibility, a subject immersed in the multi-faceted world of technique, with ethics uninspired by grand narratives and ideals. They have rather a weak, minimal ethics, as a subject who, *sottovoce*, is witnessing the disenchantment of the world.

Vattimo's hermeneutics is weak, in the sense that it acknowledges the outcome of a world which renounces metaphysics. It has no melancholy over this loss, being based on a hermeneutical ontology whereby hermeneutics is immersed in history and history is given only through the dialogue of interpretations. What kind of subject lives this hermeneutical ontology?[5] One who withdraws from a stable and defined identity, in an attempt to reduce the space for the intervention of power, who resists processes of identification. It is a subject who steps off the pedestal of philosophical modernity, whose defence is a matter of 'shrinking': they reduce themselves to games of multiple identities, a 'slipping away'. It is a subject that avoids pre-established hierarchies through recognizing their own 'passivity' and the possibility of *withdrawing to the shadows* in relation to unifying models. The subject not only concentrates on their bright side, on the certainty of *cogito*, but also opens the field of weakness, plurality, so that they can contribute to renewing the thinking of the subject.

Wandering in the text with the reader: Umberto Eco

Umberto Eco was born in 1932. He is both a philosopher and novelist, displaying a strong interest in the problems of language and, like Vattimo, he studied with Pareyson. He has taught at many universities, both in Italy and elsewhere. Presently, he teaches Semiotics at the University of Bologna. His work is wide-ranging, encompassing medieval aesthetics, the artistic *avant-gardes*, communication in mass societies, semiotics and the literary production of novels (including *The Name of the Rose*, published in Italy in 1980 and *Foucault's Pendulum* in 1988). He is a prolific commentator, both for professional journals and magazines.

Eco's proposal consists of a methodology of enquiry which integrates a critique of the structuralist perspective with Peirce's semiology. He outlines the project of a semiotics that is interested in any communicative domain of human activity, a project that accepts the critiques of French linguistic structuralism (with regard to Ferdinand de Saussure), but which does not reach as far as the drift of Derrida's deconstruction. In this section, three themes will be examined in the broader context of Eco's work, as they bear most relevance for this essay:

- a brief reconstruction of the author's intellectual journey, from post-structuralism to the problems of interpretation;

- the development of his notion of Meaning as the transition from the closed structures of the dictionary, to the open structure of the encyclopaedia;
- the reconstruction of the issue concerning the relation between text, author and reader, whereby the text becomes the terrain for the co-construction of meaning, avoiding both signifying structures, as structuralism, and the drift of the absence of meaning, as deconstructionism.

Eco's starting point, following Pareyson, is that a literary work is not closed and endowed with meaning in itself, but is open and indeterminate, a space in which the views of critics, authors and readers intertwine. Eco's major critique of French structuralism in the 1960s – *The Open Work* (1989 [or. edn 1962]) and *La struttura assente* (1968) – leads, from the 1970s on, into his work on semiotics and the philosophy of language. Eco views semiotics as a path of philosophical thinking on the construction of meanings and meaning-systems; as a study of all forms of human communication which socially produce meanings that find their own historicity in the concrete and analysable forms of communication. Eco's argument lies outside the structuralist logic of the signifying-constraint, understood as the search for correspondence and for mimesis between sign and meaning.

Eco critically looks at the problems of interpretation and of semantics, through a hermeneutically oriented analysis. According to Eco, interpretation amounts to establishing a relation between author, reader and text. The text, as will be argued at greater length later, is not a dictionary, but gives rise to a network of cross-references that invoke, rather, the metaphor of the encyclopaedia. The text as encyclopaedia allows us to range amongst these meanings, rather in the manner suggested by Barthes, avoiding both the restrictive tendencies of code-based models of signifying structures (dominated by the search for correspondences), and the potential limitlessness of deconstructionism (which, for Eco, risks the production of an uncontrollable interpretive drift).[6] Eco starts from the idea that there is an interpretive co-operation between reader and text and to this aim he utilizes the metaphor of the narrative as walks in a wood. In the wood, the author lingers and keeps the reader company in a common activity of thinking upon and interpreting the text. In his intellectual trajectory, Eco faces the limits of structuralism and highlights its contradiction, which consists in the conflation of *method* – the investigation of the deep structures that regulate the relations between signs, language and social structure – with the *essence* of that structure said to determine those relations.

For Eco, the analysis of signifying structures – insofar as it is transformed from a method to the search for the origin – descends into ideology. Eco develops a convincing critique of structuralism, drawing on Heidegger's hermeneutics, Lacan's psychoanalysis and the critical interventions of Derrida and Foucault. A code-of-codes, able to unveil the structure of the real, does not exist. In the real, we are immersed, in a hermeneutical sense. All that we are able to know are the ways of knowing, the methods and models of knowledge that are themselves hermeneutically constructed. The language in which we are immersed is not a signifying wrapping that can be made the object of a *positive* kind of enquiry and removed to reveal its underlying truth; it is, rather, that which speaks us.

Eco draws upon Heidegger's concept of language, which is not spoken *by* the subject, but speaks the subject. It is impossible to grasp the essence of language, as its origin moves uninterruptedly, denoting the impossibility of revelation, at least in a fundamental sense. Although its origin cannot be grasped, language itself can be known through performing acts of switching sense. In order to liquidate structuralism, Eco draws on the work of Derrida and Foucault. The former has set out the inexhaustible engendering of discourses, the latter the description of plot and of events based, not on the search for the origin, but on drawing maps for an archaeology of the human sciences. Eco unmasks the search for an originating structure within the semiotic task as fruitless as such a structure is non-existent. The semiotic task is predominantly a work of research and thinking able to *confer sense* to the interpretation.

In *A Theory of Semiotics* (1976), Eco sets out his theory of systems of signification and processes of communication. Here, his work on signs and codes is intended as social critique, where the actor of semiotic practice is firstly the human subject, whilst also being the outcome of historical and social segmentation. Nothing is prior to the semiotic, understood as the continuous and never-finished system of systems, of significations, that are reflected one upon the other. Any attempt at setting one of the semiotic modalities as originary of the others is an ideological fallacy. If semiotics accepts itself as methodology only, it is able to avoid the risk of becoming ideology and recognize, as the unique field of its own discourse, the social universe of signification and of meaning-attribution.

The sign is at the centre of any semiosis; not the sign that creates mimesis, or stable correlation, but the one that is based on inference, signification and interpretation. Following in the wake of Peirce, Eco links the concept of sign to its production of an *unlimited semiosis*, which is the inference generated between sign-expression and content. The sign does not create synonyms, but only interpretations, which, according to Eco, need to face up to the excess of uncontrolled interpretability.

For organization studies, Eco's reformulation of the idea of meaning as dictionary to one of meaning as encyclopaedia is particularly significant. A dictionary semantics presupposes a linear correspondence between sign and meaning, a hierarchical dependency which creates an exclusive and limited correspondence, and which oversimplifies the conditions in which meaning occurs in the real world. This modality is opposed by Eco's view of meaning as encyclopaedic. There is no place to which the origin of the signifying chain might be traced; rather, we have to deal with a constant and signifying *process*. Any sign can be interpreted, not within a linear correspondence, but only in connection with another sign. Each is translated in a chain of interpretants which is potentially infinite or, as Eco suggests, indefinite. The metaphor of the encyclopaedia allows for a circular view of signification and of communication processes. The encyclopaedia is the site for cross-references where the subject finds their orientation on the basis of their own semantics. It is a *locus* for orientation; a labyrinth, from which it is possible to find more than one way out. The sciences themselves are a semantic labyrinth where the philosopher, the one who knows, orientates his direction, looks for provisional backstreets and takes the paths which select parts of the encyclopaedia (or what Eco defines as partial encyclopaedias). This encyclopaedia of signs resembles Deleuze and Guattari's rhizome:

> ... every point of the rhizome can and must be connected with every other point. ... There are no points or positions in a rhizome; there are only lines. ... it is dismountable, reversible ... A network of trees which open in every direction can create a rhizome (which seems to us equivalent to say that a network of partial trees can be cut out artificially in every rhizome). (Eco, 1984: 81)

Subjects orientate themselves within the encyclopaedia, connect points and create interpretations. Every text is an encyclopaedia, where the reader is involved in creating paths of interpretation. This is crucial for Eco, because the concept of the reader, and the role of the interpreter, have now changed.

> On the one side, it is assumed that to interpret a text means to find out the meaning intended by its original author or – in any case – its objective nature or essence, an essence which, as such, is independent of our interpretation. On the other side, it is assumed that texts can be interpreted in infinite ways. (Eco, 1990: 24)

These attitudes reflect different relations with the text, but both are guilty, according to Eco, of epistemological fanaticism. Eco dubs the first account a *fundamentalism* or *magical realism*, a knowledge which befits the thing, the possibility of grasping the objectivity and essence of text. Here, interpretation is constrained by an adherence to the text which objectively *speaks the world*: the interpreter *speaks* the text and repeats it, as the text is objectively intentioned. On the second account, Eco critically regards its production of a – typically deconstructionist – semiotic drift, where the text is a space that can be infinitely deconstructed, the interpreter generating discourses that produce an unlimited and unlimitable drift. Eco, by drawing on Peirce's notion of unlimited semiosis, opposes both these views of interpreter and interpretation. Interpretation – the relation to a text that for Eco is equivalent to our relation with the world – takes as its starting point the idea that semiosis is virtually limitless, although this indeterminate series of possibilities is organized, framed and reduced by our cognitive aims. In Eco's words: 'In the course of a semiosic process we want to know only what is relevant according to a given universe of discourse' (1990: 28).

The text suggests interpretations, being a pre-formed area which outlines the author's intentions, a pre-formed plane with which the reader enters into relation. A continuous oscillation is created between text and interpreter. The text is thus a frame for a wide range of possible interpretations. Eco accords legitimacy to the variety of meanings that can be generated around the text, but criticizes the deconstructionist drift which, he argues, produces overinterpretation (Eco, 1992). The latter loses sight of the fact that we are, with text, at a crossroad of intentions: the author's, the text's and the reader's. Eco argues that interpretation swings between these three elements: the intentions of the author and the text create an imprinting that cannot be ignored and the reader moves from this premise, which is the text, to produce interpretation and sense, which are nevertheless textually anchored. The text is a space in which interpreters move, a wood which invites and is amenable to more than one way of walking through it (Eco, 1994). One or more trails can be explored, a general outline of the wood can be delineated, which paths are accessible and which ones are not can be verified. The reader enters the wood, goes through it, tries his or her own way, comes back, re-tries and, all the while, is exploring.

On the 'threshold' of modernity: Franco Rella

Franco Rella was born in Rovereto in 1944. His work is at the intersection between philosophy and literature, moving through the 'figures' of modernity. Rella teaches art literature at the University of Venice. His many works trace a variegated journey exploring the tensions of modernity at its boundaries.

Rella aims to traverse the ambivalences of the modern, through the work of Lacan, Deleuze, Foucault (Rella, 1994a), Schlegel and Novalis (Rella, 1987), Baudelaire, Proust, Kafka, Nietzsche, Benjamin (Rella, 1984b) and many others. He recounts and reassesses the history of Western thought, from Greek myth to the negative thought of the twentieth century. He wants to recover a more complex idea of modernity, using figures contained in literature, poetry and philosophy. Modernity, on the one hand has progressively severed – through the affirmation of science – myth from reason, whilst on the other, the above-mentioned authors have attested to the problematic character of the separation. Rella introduces us to the dark side of modernity, which does not allow itself the luxury of illumination by the illusion of a reconciling and decisive reason.

One of Rella's first works – *The Myth of the Other: Lacan, Deleuze, Foucault*, published in Italian in 1978 – explores modernity's illusion of being able to grasp the *Other's substantiality* as an autonomous territory. The territory of the Other, as the author argues, is not somewhere else, but continuously insinuates itself as a shadow into our life. The central theme, which is developed in his later work, concerns an impossibility – typical of modernity – of recomposing the multiplicity of languages as a single over-arching and ordering language – i.e. the Language of Other, or the Other as Language.

Rella discusses the clash and irreducibility of languages by drawing on Freud's later work and his idea of the unconscious as a plurality of irreconcilable dialects, which cannot be integrated through what is – rather – a never-ending journey of analysis. Taking up this notion, Lacan does not consider the process of analysis as the recovery of a lost truth, as the reintegration of foreign territory. His premise is that we live, immersed, in signifying formations that we ourselves produce and that there is no outside: we are our own signifying linguistic formations. Lacan radicalizes Freud's work, assuming as a central theme the precariousness of languages and the impossibility of their telling the truth. The Other as a final ordering principle (such as Truth, Substantiality) which would be able to integrate and resolve interpretations, does not exist. Arguing in this vein, according to Rella, are to be found Deleuze and Guattari, who propound the concept of a non-thick reality as a rhizomatic plateau, unknowable and directionless; and Foucault, for whom there is nothing outside interpretations, which are shot through by power. The constraints on interpretations are institutions, architectural systematizations, regulatory decisions, laws, administrative measures, the enunciations of science and philosophical propositions. Amongst them, connections are created which produce dominant structures. In these reified interpretations there is no trace of the Other, no final Authority of meaning: there are only discursive and interpretive orders. The modern then, does not integrate the subject towards a substantiality, towards a homogeneity of languages, but rather, constantly reveals the ambivalences and shadows of the Promethean promise.

From this point on, Rella's journey has consisted of exploring the work of those authors who, in differing ways, have thematized the *obscurities*, the ambivalences and the dark side of modernity. In subsequent work (Rella 1984a, 1987, 1993, 1994b), he examines some of the recurring and counterposed themes in the history of Western thought. In *Metamorfosi: immagini del pensiero* (1984a), he traverses the cultural images produced by our philosophical and literary tradition, and which remain fragments in our history. Rella starts by counterposing two of the most durable myths of human thought: Narcissus and Oedipus. The former operates a sort of self-exclusion from the real, fixating himself in his own image, one that he ultimately discovers to be mortal. The aura of death renders Narcissus' beauty ephemeral and his body a foreign, disturbing and fleeting landscape. Oedipus, until his blindness, does not revoke the real, but faces it and engages with it. This attitude leads Oedipus into the most profound obscurities of his soul, into the horror of incest, where reality no longer has a name: the will to know crushes Oedipus (Rella, 1984a: 14).

For Rella, the power of myth – obscure and tragic – is supplanted by the beginning of the process of rationalization (early geometry and later Cartesian method). Science opposes myth, and method, chance. This is the new natural order, where the separation which percolates through Occidental thought severs reason from the tragic. Separation, although theorized and practised by scientists and philosophers, is never fully accomplished: the tension between reason and myth, between the search for transparency and regions of the obscure and tragic, always resurfaces. The metropolises of the nineteenth and twentieth centuries are sites for the resurgence of this tension. The metropolis is the location where the tragic and rationalization mix, oppose and live together. Reason – as the power of science – for men of letters and philosophers, such as Thomas Mann, Heidegger and Benjamin, becomes *loss*. Myths then return as part of the landscape of modernity (Rella, 1984a: 28). Myth becomes memory, melancholy, the remembering which occurs in the Proustian work, or Kafka's forgetting (Rella, 1984a: 39). What journey can be made in this landscape of the soul? It is not possible merely to restore tragic thought, without the practice of reason and science always leaving a disturbing residue. Lost in this ambivalence, we are pilgrims, moving through worlds that oppose one other and live together within us. New Odysseuses of the twentieth century, we go through frontiers, limits, borders and thresholds, which are not moments of exclusion and distinction, but rather of mixture and opening (Rella, 1984a: 70). In his subsequent work *Limina. Il pensiero e le cose* (1987), Rella encounters the thought of Schlegel and Novalis, of Balzac, Van Gogh, Cezanne and others. For them – and for Rella – the modern condition is characterized by being estranged, rooted in an absence of place: *atopia*. This estrangement, which Heidegger discusses, is the condition of the modern subject for whom things appear to be a paradoxical swinging between extremes. This is the postmodern condition, a rootedness in the absence of place, a dissonating contemporaneity, where a different horizon of sense becomes necessary. The postmodern is this anterior-future, remembering past figures in order to find again the complexity of the modern and its own limits. Trawling the modern, its figures and images, leads us to and across these limits, the internal boundaries of modernity: we are contemporaneous as thinkers of the limit (Rella, 1987: 15). How is it possible to live this thinking at the border (*pensiero liminare*), which oscillates between the idea of reason as a source of the *strong, true* knowledge – which becomes power – and a 'weaker' knowledge which is interpretation on the margins of meaning? Rella takes Ricoeur's idea of narrative as the way in which it becomes possible to explore the complexity of modernity; one which does not surrender to the rationalization of knowledge-becoming-power, but which stays in the world, making reconstructions within time, narrative interpretations (Rella, 1987: 152). From the identity of rationalization we pass to narrative identity, which passes through the modern and renames it.

All of these themes appear in Rella's later work, *Miti e figure del moderno* (1993), where he crosses, narratively, the borders of modernity, its figures and myths. The subject, divided by the certainty of the Cartesian ego and the mystical ego of sentiment, is recomposed in a complex, plural and conflictual unity, the site of a battlefield. Within the subject, both myth and logos pass (Rella, 1993: 27). The subject is suspended between two worlds; one the world of the Cartesian power of reason and the other the world of the experience of being lost. In the intermediate space there are no lights, only shadows, a place where the obscurities of human transience, the vertigo of the modern and the multiplication of horizons cannot be avoided (Rella, 1993: 95). Rella, in linking philosophical thinking to literature, is attempting to enrich the vision of a modern which, in order to be thought today, at its own limit, *needs* ambivalent reflections: these are full of ambiguities, obscurities and uncertainties, but contain the possibility for generating new mixtures and horizons.

Rella's most recent work – *Le soglie dell'ombra. Riflessioni sul mistero* (1994b) – distances him more and more from systematic reflection, pursuing, rather, a tale of the human experience of modernity at its limit. The last chapter is entitled *On the threshold*. After having re-ascended the counterposed routes that traverse Occidental thought and having encountered shadows and mysteries, we reach a threshold that may be a new beginning (Rella, 1994b: 147), one in which the subject accepts the ambiguity and sorrow of the world; one which speaks not only of brightness, but also of the tragic and of power. To dissociate ourselves from the Word which is power, we have to make ourselves polyglots, nomads who traverse dialects and different experiences.

The Italian contribution to the postmodern and organizational studies: a vital weakness

Gianni Vattimo: hermeneutical ontology

How can the postmodern idea of weakness, as expressed in Vattimo's thought, be incorporated into organizational studies? Isn't such weakness antithetical to the modern conception of organization? To my mind, *Ge-stell* consists of the rationalized world, which expresses itself in the efficiency-led and rationalist thinking of Taylorism-Fordism; the representatives, *par excellence*, of the metaphysical in organizational thought. With subsequent critical developments, organizational studies detached itself somewhat from the metaphysical idea of the objective becoming of organizational things. There are no unifying trajectories, but organizational action is immersed in a hermeneutical ontology, which produces arguments confronting each other in interpretive flux. The renunciation of a unifying idea of rationality – such as that of industrial modernization – views organizations as a space, in which the rationalizing and unifying components of Taylorism-Fordism, and rationality itself, are *non-identical*. The search for sense in the hermeneutical transformation of the world changes: there is no longer a correspondence between the ontology of being and sense. Meaning detaches itself and becomes autonomous with respect to the sole component of rationalization: it enters into relation with the disenchanted world of technique. Rationalization becomes one of the components of the hermeneutical ontology, one with which the subjects enter-in-relation, itself a tool of interpretation, not its master. The organizational world is defined according to *how* subjects, all immersed in a *hermeneutical* totality, enter in relation with the *Ge-stell*. To my mind, various possibilities are given in this relation: one is the subject's full recognition and identification with the world of proliferating technique and rationalization; another is to interpret the *Ge-stell* as a space of opportunity, in which subjects can resist and – by availing themselves of the combined outcomes of past and present interpretations – generate the possibility of change able to transform the *Ge-stell* itself.

Vattimo's weak thinking deconstructs the idea of an absolute rationality, attributable in a pre-determined way to organizational situations. Organizations are spaces where interpretations act, confronting each other. Interpretations are immersed in a flux of action and relationships, which are not detached from subjects' modalities of interpretation, and where none of them is able to bear witness, definitively, to an absolute rationality. The continuous innovations wrought by management form a part of the field of *hermeneutical* production, but are unable to control it totally. Other *hermeneutical* components intersect, coming from subjects, both internal and external to the organization. The idea that there is a leading and dominant rationality within the organization is weakened; there are rather a multiplicity of rationalities which confront each other and live a continuous oscillation and tension as far as the production of meanings is concerned. Organizations are part of what Vattimo calls a *transparent society*: they are components of the confusion created by technique, in a world where messages multiply and strong ontologies are no longer possible. Organizations produce themselves in a co-construction of interpretations, which in different ways confront the *Ge-stell*. In this organization, de-centred from the unificatory model of the rationalization of technique, there moves a weak subject, who *explores* ways, experiments with interpretations and contrasts unifying visions. We are dealing with a subject who avoids pre-constituted identifications, abandoning himself to paths of identity more fragile and oriented to discovery. An identity which faces the *Ge-stell*, but which avails itself of all the signals provided by a world which no longer has unique declensions. Of course, it is not a 'bright' subject: we are rather dealing with a subject who whispers, who is immersed in a disenchanted world but does not despair. The organization as a component of the world, outcome of the abandonment of metaphysics, is a space in which interpretations of a greater number of subjects engage in dialogue. These subjects bear testimony to different hermeneutical traditions and, on the basis of their interpretations, enter into relation, in order also to explore the possibility of new beginnings.

Umberto Eco: cross-references of meaning ...

What is a *dictionary* in the organizational field? Organizational charts and job descriptions are all dictionary-texts, are systems of signs which speak of linear and sequential meaning-correspondences, forms of sign that speak the organization. But of what conception of organization do they talk? They talk and speak of a prescriptive organizational-world, directed by signs full of planning and purpose. This is the strong conception of the ontology of organizational being, of the rationalization which produces itself outside the flux of action. Structuralism, with the idea that all signs can be interpreted as signifier and signified, proposes the notion of dictionary-like structure: each sign refers to only one idea, to a concept which defines and *completes* it. Signifying structures constrain the possibility of innovating and modifying the sign, which has its own stasis. Faced with the sign, the interpreter is only a de-codifier, a relay.

To the structuralist dictionary-model, Eco opposes the models of the *encyclopaedia*, of the labyrinth, of the wood. To the organizational rationality of dictionary-logic, which prefigures patterns of organizational action, he opposes an idea of signification, of interpretation, which is generated through the relation between text and interpreter, between organization and organizational actor. The organization as an encyclopaedia-like text becomes a space for exploration, in which cognitive and emotive actors *wander*. Things organizational – roles, charts and managerial discourses – enter the interpretive game and define themselves in relation to the cognitive aims which *organize, frame and reduce the indefinite and infinite possibility of interpretations*. There are no objective, sequential, pre-defined, necessary, structured paths, but paths are delineated, founded on the stratification of meanings which organizational actors are able to activate. In the organization, as encyclopaedic space, paths of meanings are produced, linguistic cross-references, routes which relate interpretations and actions. Nothing is generated outside these meaning-references. Organizations, from being the site for translation of meanings into practice – in which rational, pre-formed plans are enacted – transform themselves into sites of signification, argumentation and action: a pragmatics where sense is an intertwining of meaning and action.

The other metaphorical figures, of the labyrinth and the wood, accentuate the vision of organizational space as a place of transit where interpretations and action meet. But which forms of rationality underpin these different metaphorical representations of the organization as text? And which ideas of subjectivity and intersubjectivity inform such figures? The image of the dictionary conveys a notion of objective rationality, both necessary and progressive. Such a rationalization commands meaning and interpretation, wherein action becomes adherence to the only meaning admitted by reason. Organizational action amounts to the adherence to the pre-formed plans for action, in which signs and meaning are pre-defined, in a structuralist sense.

Rationality is non-negotiable, non-transformable through interpretations. In this case, subjectivity and organizational intersubjectivity are constrained by fixed meanings. What is created is, on the one hand, adherence to the organizational text and at the same time, a counterposition to it. The sense of the text is defined in advance, is pre-established, unmodifiable, and is therefore only utilizable and adaptable rather than negotiable. In the idea of organization as encyclopaedic space, rationality is not pre-defined, but enters into a game and is defined according to interpretations generated by actors. Rationality is the continuous outcome of the relation between actors, who interpret the organizational text and decide what is reasonable or rational as the context shifts. It is an inexhaustible outcome, never concluded, always becoming and even *ir*rational. The sense of the 'text' here is emergent and negotiated, and can be analysed only in relation to the sense attributed it by the subjects, not against some absolute or *a priori* standards of rationality. Whilst the dictionary-text has pre-determined confines, the encyclopaedic text is mobile. It is delineated only by the conditions set by subjects who, never being in command of the whole picture (the whole text) in relation to these generated and combined interpretations, animate what Eco defines as partial encyclopaedias.

Franco Rella: the impossible rationalization

If Franco Rella was asked what an organization is, he would perhaps define it as *the site of rationalization*. But organization is also the site where rationalization becomes *myth*, an ideology. In organizations, from Taylorism to Weber's limits of bureaucratic rationalization, the separation between reason and myth materializes. During the twentieth century, the organization was regarded as the most important space for the affirmation of the possibility of the *scientific* functioning of human life: the organization as the site for the production of constraining significations, norms and rules for action which become vehicles for the global expansion of Western rationalization, power and domination of the other. The organization is the site where knowledge becomes institutionalized as power, and substantiates itself in the idea of companies' and institutions' efficiency. The rhetorics of the global market use the idea of a reason able to regulate human activity externally more and more as leverage for the legitimation of Western expansion. But even within orthodox organization theory, the Human Relations movement made apparent more than sixty years ago the re-emergence, as informal organization, of what Taylorism's rationalization aimed to obliterate. Informal organization itself pressurises, and the informal, uncontrollable life of those who act in organizations, becomes a problem for the ideology of managerial rationalization.

The informal, from being a residue of inefficiency in Taylorism, over the last decade has become – especially with James G. March's work – an object of analysis, acquiring a special and autonomous status and legitimation. The organization is not only the space where the strong idea of a substantial reason operates, but is also the space for discretionality, for uncertainty, for struggle and for power and resistance – as Crozier and Friedberg argue (Crozier and Friedberg, 1977). It is the space where subjects build courses of action, or subjective and collective projects, as Knights notes in Chapter 2, which cannot be assimilated solely into rationalization. What had been separated out re-combines with the emergence of the subject. In order to re-affirm a strong idea of reason, the organization has to be able to produce new myths – such as that of market globalization: it has to find new engulfing frameworks of meaning. To globalization, as a new ideology informing the organization, is counterposed – as Touraine tells us – the specificity of subjects who, also within organizational life, resist the unifying and globalizing pressures. The rationalization from engulfing and substantial myth, transforms itself into the empty figure of modernity at its limit. The organization, as space for a strong and substantial reason, transforms itself into vital flux; where different forces, being in continuous tension, act; where the achievement of a definitive rationalization is impossible.

On the postmodern organization: from rationalization as a
unifying model to rationality as an unresolvable relational field

What idea of organization can therefore be derived from the work of our three Italian authors? How would this idea relate to those which emerge from the debate concerning the relation between postmodernism and organization? A rapid and synthetic review of the ideas proposed by Vattimo, Eco and Rella, leads us to consider the organization as a space, neither pre-definable nor predictable by models of *strong* rationality. Organizational processes are inspired by a *weak rationality* and organizational actors – who are firstly social actors – find themselves immersed in processes of availing themselves of, and synthesizing, meanings traceable to each participant's hermeneutical tradition, or history of interpretive experience (Vattimo).

Organizations present themselves as *partial encyclopaedias*, as location of *unlimited semiosis*, contextually organized through the practices of actors who reduce the indeterminate and infinite series of possibilities. The organization is a field where actors continuously make meaning-references, meaning in reference to other meanings, where rationality is only a temporary, mobile and unaccomplished outcome: an open text in which interpretations co-operate to produce, contextually, non-definite and non-predictable models of rationality (Eco).

The organization then is the space where rationalization is *de facto* impossible and anyway impracticable, because the strong light of rationalization always produces its own shadows – that can be, for example, the outcomes in terms of power imbalances induced by the strong rationalization of planning. We therefore have to consider the complexity of social life, and thus organizational life also, as a *threshold* where the actors who are carriers both of myths and reason move, polyglot and nomadic actors who speak more than one language (Rella).

The organization is, therefore, a process whereby epistemologies and ontologies which are diversely inspired, act. It is not the *locus* for the ontology of definitive organizational being (Chia, 1995), or even of organizational ought-to-be. Organizations are sites of becoming, but these becomings are multiple. It is rather a space where *weak* hermeneutics *circulate*. The organization, which for the best part of the twentieth century, had the processes of rationalization as a unifying model to pursue (for example planning and prediction of optimized behaviour), today has to deal with an idea of rationality which is not completely pre-definable but is, rather, an unresolvable relational field (Hassard, 1994). Here, organizational actors-in-tension produce, in unstoppable flux, the emergence of organizational processes. These, in their own heterogeneity, are not outcomes of strong models, but rather of *details* (Cooper and Law, 1995) and *intensities* (see Carter and Jackson, Chapter 6 in this volume). An uninterrupted network of meanings can be observed, emanating from organizational *micro-practices* and *micro-decisions* (Gherardi, 1990; Chia, 1994). They are contexts of action, social processes in which signifying representations act, the outcome of selective interpretations which are cognitively and socially oriented.

The organization therefore is a social space that has to be considered through a *proximal view* (Cooper and Law, 1995), which is able to encompass all the heterogeneity of organizational life (knowledge-translated-into-practices, technological parts, habits, the representations of reality for which the actors are bearers, their ethical orientation). Here, languages, discourses, practices and the epistemological orientations of the actors, generate a *texture* (Cooper and Fox, 1990; Gherardi and Strati, 1990) and a *flux* of interdependencies which stratify organizational life. We might say that we shift from *sense-making* to *sense-giving*, from sense constructed on the basis of pre-defined designs, to one generated in the immanence of the action.

In the organization a continual tension is created between pre-formed planes oriented by an ontology of organizational being, and the discretional practices of the organizational actors, which are mainly synchronic, *resisting* the pre-constituted plans of formal rationality, oriented instead to a *weak ontology of becoming* (Chia, 1995). In the tension between pre-formed plans and organizational action, zones of uncertainty are created (Crozier and Friedberg, 1977), a distance between managerial discourse – itself still partly oriented to a pre-definition of scenarios of action typical of the logic of organizational rationalization – and the practices of the actors, who continuously infringe rationalization as a unifying and shared outcome. The heterogeneity of practices and meanings produced by actors in the flux of organizational life, finds attempts at its rationalization in managerial discourses. These, nonetheless undergo continual transformations, generating what could be defined as the *supplanting of managerial discourses, which undergo continual modification arising from the multiplicity of the organizational hermeneutics-in-game.*

The organization is an encyclopaedic space (Eco) or even a hyper-textual space (Strati, 1996), a rhizomatic network, in which meanings are not the outcome of an external rationality able to give direction. They are, rather, the outcome of the *pragmatics* of actors, who simultaneously and synchronically act in a non-predefinable way. The organization is a territory continuously in-construction by the *becoming* of the heterogeneity of components in action. It is the space for Italo Calvino's *Multiplicity* (1988), an uninterrupted tale crossed by multiple narrative lines.

Notes

1. The novel was written by Don Delillo, a US author, born in the Bronx, of Italian parentage.
2. I was introduced to this novel through a university lecture, *Scenes of Ordinary Postmodernity: Reflections on White Noise*, given by Professor Alessandro Ferrara of the Department of Sociology, Rome University 'La Sapienza', in 1995.
3. The collection, which was co-edited by Rovatti, includes essays by Eco, Carchia, dal Lago, Ferraris, Amoroso, Comolli, Costa and Crespi.
4. A Heideggerian concept, which indicates the centrality of the world of technique, with which the subject enters-into-relation.
5. This theme occupies one of the chapters of his *Filosofia al presente*. The book, unavailable in English, consists of dialogues with Italian philosophers and scholars. See especially the dialogue on the subject with Pier Aldo Rovatti, entitled *Farewell to the Subject* (1990: 108–21).
6. Works that share this concern are: *The Role of the Reader* (1979), *The Limits of Interpretation* (1990) and the presentations at the universities of Cambridge and Harvard, published respectively as *Interpretation and Overinterpretation* (1992) and *Six Walks in the Fictional Wood* (1994).

References

Alvesson, M. and Deetz, S. (1996) 'Critical theory and postmodernism: approaches to organization studies', in S.R. Clegg, C. Hardy and W.R. Nord (eds), *Handbook of Organization Studies*. London: Sage. pp. 191–217.

Baudrillard, J. (1983) *Simulacra and Simulation*. New York: Semiotext(e). [Trans. P.Foss, P.Patton and P.Beitchamn].

Burrell, G. (1988) 'Modernism, postmodernism and organizational analysis 2: the contribution of Michel Foucault', *Organization Studies*, 9 (2): 221–35.

Burrell, G. (1994) 'Modernism, postmodernism and organizational analysis 4: the contribution of Jürgen Habermas', *Organization Studies*, 15 (1): 1–45.

Calvino, I. (1988) *Six Memos for the Next Millennium*. Cambridge, MA: Harvard University Press.

Chia, R. (1994) 'The concept of decision: a deconstructive analysis', *Journal of Management Studies*, 31 (6): 781–806.

Chia, R. (1995) 'From modern to postmodern organizational analysis', *Organization Studies*, 16 (4): 579–604.

Cooper, R. and Fox, S. (1990) 'The "texture" of organizing', *Journal of Management Studies*, 27 (6): 572–82.

Cooper, R. and Law, J. (1995) 'Organization: distal and proximal views', in S. Bacharach, P. Gagliardi and B. Mundel (eds), *Studies of Organizations. The European Tradition*. Greenwich, CT: JAI Press. [Trans. Italian (1995) as *Il Pensiero Organizzativo Europeo*. Milano: Guerini e Associati. pp. 285–323].

Crozier, M. and Friedberg, E. (1977) *L'acteur et le systéme. Le contraintes de l'action collective*. Paris: Seuil.

Delillo, D. (1985) *White Noise*. New York: Viking Penguin Inc.

Eco, U. (1968) *La struttura assente. La ricerca semiotica e il metodo strutturale*. Milano: Bompiani.

Eco, U. (1976) *A Theory of Semiotics*. Bloomington: Indiana University Press.

Eco, U. (1979) *The Role of the Reader. Explorations in the Semiotics of Texts*. Bloomington: Indiana University Press.

Eco, U. (1984) *Semiotics and Philosophy of Language*. London: Macmillan.

Eco, U. (1989) *The Open Work*. Cambridge, MA: Harvard University Press. [Original edition 1962].

Eco, U. (1990) *The Limits of Interpretation*. Bloomington: Indiana University Press.

Eco, U. (1992) *Interpretation and Overinterpretation*. Cambridge: Cambridge University Press.

Eco, U. (1994) *Six Walks in the Fictional Wood*. Cambridge, MA: Harvard University Press.

Ferrara, A. (1992) *L'eudaimonia postmoderna*. Napoli: Liguori.

Gadamer, H.G. (1963) *Die phaenomenologische Bewegung*. Tuibingen: J.C.B. Mohr.

Gherardi, S. (1990) *Le micro-decisioni nelle organizzazioni*. Bologna: Il Mulino.

Gherardi, S. and Strati, A. (1990) 'The "texture" of organizing in an Italian Department', *Journal of Management Studies*, 27 (6): 605–18.

Habermas, J. (1987) *The Philosophical Discourse of Modernity. Twelve Lectures*. Cambridge, MA: M.I.T Press.

Hassard, J. (1994) 'Postmodernist organizational analysis: toward a conceptual framework', *Journal of Management Studies*, 31: 303–24.

Höpfl, H. (1995) 'Organizational rhetoric and the threat of ambivalence', *Studies in Cultures, Organizations and Societies*, 1 (2): 175–87.

Linstead, S. (1993) 'Deconstruction in the study of organizations', in J. Hassard and D. Pym (eds), *Postmodernism and Organization*. London: Sage. pp. 49–70.

Linstead, S. (1995) 'After the autumn harvest: rhetoric and representation in an Asian industrial dispute', *Studies in Cultures, Organizations and Societies*, 1 (2): 231–51.

Rella, F. (1984a) *Metamorfosi. Immagini del pensiero*. Milano: Feltrinelli.

Rella, F. (1984b) *Il silenzio e le parole. Il pensiero nel tempo della sua crisi*. Milano: Feltrinelli.

Rella, F. (1986) *La battaglia della verita*. Milano: Feltrinelli.

Rella, F. (1987) *Limina. Il pensiero e le cose*. Milano: Feltrinelli.

Rella, F. (1993) *Miti e figure del moderno*. Milano: Feltrinelli.

Rella, F. (1994a) *The Myth of the Other. Lacan, Deleuze, Foucault*. Washington, DC: Maissoneuve Press. [Original edition: 1978].

Rella, F. (1994b) *Le soglie dell'ombra*. Milano: Feltrinelli.

Rella, F. (1996) *L'ultimo uomo*. Milano: Feltrinelli.

Rorty, R. (1979) *Philosophy and the Mirror of Nature*. Princeton, NJ: Princeton University Press.

Strati, A. (1996) *Sociologia dell'organizzazione. Paradigmi teorici e metodi di ricerca*. Roma: Nuova Italia Scientifica (NIS).

Touraine, A. (1974) *The Post-Industrial Society. Classes, Conflict and Culture in the Programmed Society*. London: Wildwood House.

Touraine, A. (1991) 'Post', *For*, 12: 35–7.

Touraine, A. (1995) *Critique of Modernity*. Oxford: Basil Blackwell.

Vattimo, G. (1988) *The End of Modernity. Nihilism and Hermeneutics in Postmodern Culture*. Cambridge: Polity Press.

Vattimo, G. (1990) *Filosofia al presente*. Milano: Garzanti.

Vattimo, G. (1992) *The Transparent Society*. Cambridge: Polity Press.

Vattimo, G. (1993) *The Adventures of Difference. Philosophy after Nietzsche and Heidegger*. Cambridge: Polity Press.

Vattimo, G. (1997) *Beyond Interpretation. The Meaning of Hermeneutics for Philosophy*. Cambridge: Polity Press.

Vattimo, G. and Rovatti, P.A. (eds) (1983) *Il pensiero debole*. Milano: Feltrinelli.

9

Getting Past the Post? Recalling Ismism

Stephen Linstead

We didn't start the fire
But when we are gone
Will it still burn on
And on, and on, and on ...

We know that the more wealth we produce the more iniquity there is in its sharing; that the more sophisticated our technological system the more people arc excluded through ignorance; that the more our wealth grows the more the ecosystem is destroyed; that the more diverse our culture, the more incapable of communication are our identities; that the more democracy spreads the more we are manipulated; and that when we stop one form of war we discover another one more insidious ... We still live amid violence without remorse, in competition without cooperation, in solidarity without communication.
(Manuel Castells, *El Pais*, 26th December 2001 (courtesy of Pat Kane www.theplayethic.com))

I began this book with the idea of concluding it with a summary of critiques of postmodernism, responses to those critiques, and some sketches of possible approaches that come after or beyond postmodernism. Not necessarily solving all its problems, but putting things in perspective and widening the context. Summarizing the complexities and subtleties, lining them up along divides of difference and similarity, weighing them in the balance and perhaps finding some wanting, then demonstrating that I can see further or deeper, have read a bit more and can present new options in the sort of gift-wrapping that comes in handy for lecture handouts, publishers can use as a marketing tool, underlines the authority of the author (ironically even more so with a bit of self-reflexivity thrown in), could undoubtedly be tweaked to make a journal article as well and probably comes with fries. It wouldn't be terribly consistent with the arguments that I made at the beginning, that the postmodern is significantly *para*modern – but whenever did postmodernism require consistency? Martin Parker (1993) starts out in a similar way, disavowing the project but finding it unavoidable and in the process pretty much parting company with much of the content of his own edited book. I don't want to do your thinking for you, or even *my* thinking for you, as the purpose of this book was not to equip the reader with the means to adjudicate, but the means to explore further, even if the temptation to say more is almost irresistible. The contributors to this book want to induce its readers to read more, rather than less, to think more and *perhaps* argue less, and become more lavishly familiar with the work of postmodern writers rather than move hurriedly on to something else. Goodbye pomo.com ... next?

The death, of sorts, of postmodernism has been proclaimed for some time – indeed the powerful awareness of death which emerges from Hegel and is transformed through Nietzsche, Heidegger and Bataille is, in much postmodern thought, one of the most singular features of the human condition. That we live in futility only to be ultimately wasted does not absolve us from any responsibility for the character of that waste – on the contrary, and especially in a writer like Lyotard, this is a responsibility we *cannot* shirk and remain human. But Parker concludes his jointly edited book with the title 'Life *after* Jean-François', in a Hegelian implication that we already know all that it is significant to know about postmodernism and its arguments – and that such knowledge is already dead. Ironically the chapter's title does reflect the book's contents – much of the discussion of postmodernism is refracted and second-hand, a characteristic indicated by the fact that the excellent Gibson Burrell and Robert Cooper receive 29 and 27 citations respectively, but the best any *actual* postmodern or post-structuralist theorists manage are Derrida's 21 and Lyotard's 20. Gilles Deleuze – who might be argued to be coming into his own as *the* post-modern thinker and whose work with Guattari is having a massive contemporary influence on critics of globalization, as seen in the best-selling popularity of Michael Hardt and Antonio Negri's *Empire* – gets a measly 3, which is 9 less than Martin Parker. Having effectively mounted its arguments on a *simulacrum* of postmodernism, this *Matrix* of a book ends by dismissing the arguments of simulation, thereby warranting its own reality. Which just goes to show that if you think that everything that happens is real, and everything that is real happens, what can you expect?

Going further than Parker, Gary Potter and José López (2001) are in no doubt that postmodernism has had its demise. Apart from the appearance of a single question mark at the beginning of their introduction to their edited book *After Postmodernism*, they do not hesitate to pronounce that postmodernism '*was* one of, if not *the* most significant of the intellectual currents which swept the academic world in the last third of the twentieth century' which 'present*ed* an ultimately intellectually incoherent challenge' but nevertheless 'serv*ed* to capture the spirit of the contemporary age' (2001: 3). Indeed, this is no simple matter of stylistics – in case we missed the point, they emphasize 'the single most significant fact about postmodernism as an intellectual phenomenon in the year two thousand is this: it is in a state of decline! It lingers on, its influence for good or ill continues, but postmodernism has "gone out of fashion"' (2001: 4). What they go on to render as postmodernism would appear strange, or at best very superficial, to the contributors to this book, and whilst complaining that postmodernism 'demanded little in terms of evidence', provide none in support of their own polemic. They appear to *need* something to come *after* postmodernism so that their favoured candidate, critical realism, can stake its claim. But as should be clear from the contributions to this book, the 'ism' in postmodernism was as contested as the 'post', and on seeing what use was made of their intricate and elusive thinking, most of the major figures either rejected or avoided identification with the term, and often also with the terms most associated with their work. But we can't take postmodernism back, either as a discursive retraction or in time to a golden age prior to all misunderstanding. Bruno Latour (1999), in suggesting that the three terms of Actor-Network Theory are all unhelpful – actors are actants as agency is ascribed to objects, networks are rhizomes of transformation rather than conduits of transmission, and the theory is more of an ontology – argues that in looking back on, or *recalling*, the theory, perhaps the best thing to do would be to *re-call* it (or its terms) in the manner that automobile manufacturers recall faulty goods. But that would be no good either – we can't recall either ANT or postmodernism because the problem is not with the product and the product in any case is not ours to recall. So we go on, because there is nothing else we can do. We can't even stay where we are.

Marta Calás and Linda Smircich (1999) are both more sensitive and more tentative in their reflections on whether we are 'past' postmodernism. They emphasize 'the importance of the postmodern turn for transforming contemporary theorizing in the social sciences in general and organization studies in particular ... the importance for contemporary theorizing of having *gone through* these intellectual currents'. They call for a writing in friendship, rather than opposition and debate – compare the tone of their paper with that of Potter and López or even Parker. They consider that three areas of theory are useful places for organization studies to go after it has 'gone through' what they call the deconstructive (text-based interpretative) and genealogical (power/knowledge-based discursive) versions of postmodernism – poststructuralist feminism, postcolonialism, and ANT. They add a fourth but more general consideration, of adopting narrative approaches to knowledge and taking them seriously in our writing. I don't want to take issue too much with what they say here, except that the understanding of postmodernism upon which they base their assumptions is drawn from approaches in the literature which have utilized only part of the range of ideas available. The two approaches they identify – deconstruction and genealogy – are based on part of the work of Derrida and Foucault, mostly, as Jones notes in this volume, what might be regarded as a particular language-oriented reading of first and second phase Derrida, and the Foucault, primarily, of *Discipline and Punish* (but with a good few exceptions). Approaches to analysis which might be drawn from Baudrillard or Deleuze or Lyotard (except for the approach to narrative which was part of *The Postmodern Condition*) do not figure. The discussion of postfeminism does not draw on Julia Kristeva, Judith Butler is mentioned only for *Gender Trouble* and not her immensely important work on desire which extends far beyond sexual desire (O'Shea, 2002) and the Deleuzian approach of Elizabeth Grosz is unremarked; the postcolonial literature concentrates on the post-Derridean work of Spivak and Trinh without connecting to the work on globalization which draws increasingly on Deleuze and Guattari, and Deleuze alone (see Hardt and Negri, 2000). In short, despite the admirable qualities of their argument, it is difficult to accept that the condition of *going through* postmodernism can have been attained, as much incredibly important work has simply not been dealt with. Deleuze and Baudrillard remain to be integrated more fully into organization theorizing – and when one considers that Deleuze spends an enormous amount of time discussing change and Baudrillard consumption, one can only wonder why this hasn't happened earlier. To argue that postmodernism is past, or dead, or gone through is somewhat akin to Steve Martin roller-skating through art galleries in the film *LA Story*, itself a work very aware of the postmodern, and calling it research. Not been there, not done that and no, you can't have the T-shirt.

But isn't it arrogant to think that we *can't* get 'past' postmodernism? Isn't that just another version of the end of history debate, to suggest that the last chapter of the shaggy dog story that is modern knowledge is just a continuing circulation of anecdotes that don't connect and don't have a punch-line, to which we can add but not move on? Well, I'm not really arguing that – although it could possibly be argued the debate would have to take place by addressing the nature of time which is something we don't have right now. I'm just saying that we are nowhere near exhausting the possibilities of the ideas of so-called postmodern thinkers. Not only have we not integrated properly the better-known ones, there are several other more recent ones on the left or right – Badiou, Hardt and Negri, de Landa, Serres or Virilio for example – who are working on understanding all of those issues which many critics say postmodernism fails to address. Moving in the other direction, there are thinkers who shaped postmodern thought – Bergson on time, intuition, creativity and virtuality and Bataille on desire and transgression for just two examples – whose work is now being read and reinterpreted with new vigour in the field of organization studies as a result of the work of postmodern thinkers who brought it to our attention (for introductions to Bataille see *inter alia* Brewis and Linstead, 2000; Nodoushani, 1999: for introductions to Bergson see Chia and King, 1998, and the contributions to a special section and a special issue on Bergson of two journals edited by Linstead, 2002; Linstead and Mullarkey, 2003). More specific issues raised by a consideration of what postmodernity means for concepts such as metaphor, text and interpretation; ethics and the other; system and communication have brought the work of Ricoeur, Lévinas and Luhmann into greater focus on the margins of the postmodern. We have scratched the surface, and we found something – but there is so much more to discover.

This book promised an introduction to a more passionate postmodernism. This passion, I hope it has become clear, is not a passion *for* postmodernism, nor a passion for what postmodernism promises or actually *does* for organizations or organization studies. The first may emerge as a result of engagement with the ideas, the second may arise from putting them to work. But without a passion *for the ideas themselves* we are not likely to have either the patience, the discipline, the respect or the simple love to discover the potential they hold for us. We know the distance between ideas and action is fractal – it is a terrain which needs to be carefully ranged over rather than closed down or slipped through by the nearest shortcut. And just because the terrain of ideas may be problematic doesn't mean we can't act – that old modernist *non sequitur* which seems to be based on a misreading of the fable of Buridan's Ass. When we get closer to having mapped that terrain, we may be able to consider whether it is possible to think of postmodernism as 'past'. But hopefully, on the way, we will stop thinking in frameworks of 'ismism' altogether and deal with the ideas on their own terms.

References

Brewis, J. and Linstead, S. (2000) *Sex, Work and Sex Work*. London: Routledge.

Calás, M.B. and Smircich, L. (1999) 'Past postmodernism? Reflections and tentative directions', *Academy of Management Review*, 24 (4): 649–71.

Chia, R. and King, I. (1998) 'The organizational structuring of novelty', *Organization*, 5 (4): 461–78.

Hardt, M. and Negri, A. (2000) *Empire*. Cambridge, MA: Harvard University Press.

Latour, B. (1999) 'On recalling ANT', in J.Law and J.Hassard (eds), *Actor Network Theory and After*. Oxford: Basil Blackwell.

Linstead, S. (2002) 'Organization as reply: Henri Bergson and Casual Organization Theory', *Organization*, 9 (1): 95–111. Introduction to a special section on Henri Bergson.

Linstead, S. and Mullarkey, J. (2003) 'Time, creativity and culture: introducing Bergson' *Culture and Organization*, 9 (1). Introduction to an edited special edition *En-during Culture: Henri Bergson and Creative Social Science*.

Nodoushani, O. (1999) 'A postmodern theory of general economy: the contribution of Georges Bataille', *Studies in Cultures, Organizations and Societies*, 5 (2): 331–45.

O'Shea, A. (2002) 'Desiring desire: how desire makes us human, all too human', *Sociology*, 36 (4): 925–40.

Parker, M. (1993) 'Life after Jean-François', in J.Hassard and M.Parker (eds), *Postmodernism and Organizations*. London: Sage. pp. 204–12.

Potter, G. and López, J. (2001) 'After postmodernism: the new millennium', in J.López and G.Potter (eds), *After Postmodernism: An Introduction to Critical Realism*. London: Athlone. pp. 3–21.

Author Index

Subject Index